With One Heart Bowing To The City of Ten Thousand Buddhas

Dharma Masters Heng Sure and Heng Chau

Dharma Realm Buddhist University
Buddhist Text Translation Society
Talmage, Ca.
1981

WITH ONE HEART BOWING TO THE CITY OF TEN THOUSAND BUDDHAS
VOLUME 8

Printed in the United States of America

ISBN: 0-917512-53-7

For information write to the Sino-American Buddhist Association:

GOLD MOUNTAIN MONASTERY
1731 15th Street
San Francisco, California 94103
(415) 861-9672

CITY OF TEN THOUSAND BUDDHAS
P.O. Box 217
Talmage, California 95481
(707) 462-0939

GOLD WHEEL TEMPLE
1728 West Sixth Street
Los Angeles, California 90017
(213) 483-7497 (213) 358-6177

ACKNOWLEDGEMENTS:
    Edited and Reviewed by Bhikshunis Heng Tao and Heng Ch'ih

    Proof-reading: Bhikshunis Heng Chü and Heng Bin
    Paste-Up: Cultivating Virtue High School students
        Sari Epstein, Kim Samay, and Jade Turgel
    Typing and Layout: Bhikshuni Heng Chia
    Cover Design: Bhikshuni Heng Liang
    Cover Back Photograph: Kuo Kuei Nicholson

"He concentrates and seeks only proper enlightenment,/To take across all living beings./ And never, even for an instant, does he ever abandon this heart."

"Ten Thousand Buddhas' City welcomes you.
Ten Thousand Buddhas are near you, too."

The Great Assembly Unites to Recite Mantras and Sutras during The City's Once-a-Month Liberation of Life Ceremony

AMERICAN BUDDHIST PILGRIMS

CONTACT: RELEASE:

Los Angeles: While current
Gold Wheel Temple
223-2522

Two American Buddhist Monks from San Francisco's Gold
Mountain Monastery are making a bowing pilgrimage from Gold
Wheel Temple in Los Angeles to the City of Ten Thousand Buddhas near Ukiah. Bhikshu Heng Sure has made the vow to bow
to the ground in a full prostration every three steps along
the road. Heng Ch'au, a novice, has vowed to accompany him
on the journey, to protect him, and assist in the work.

Their purpose is to influence humankind to cease all
hatred and hostility, to stop the creation of destructive
weapons, and to work to prevent disasters, wars, and suffering of all kinds. The monks are dedicating their work to
all beings everywhere.

"Our goal is to endure a bit of hard work on behalf of
others," said Heng Sure. "Our job is to turn our own greed
into balanced, moral behavior, to change our own anger and
hatred into compassion for others and into inner concentration, and to transform selfish, stupid actions into enlightened awareness and wisdom," said Heng Ch'au.

"We hope to generate a response in the hearts of men
and women and among the spiritual beings in the universe. If
our bowing is sincere, then afflictions, calamities, and suffering will gradually disappear, and hatred, hostilities,
and wars will be reduced," said Heng Sure.

The monks began their pilgrimage May 7, 1977, at Gold
Wheel Temple in Los Angeles. Their destination is the Sino-
American Buddhist Association's center for world Buddhism,
the City of Ten Thousand Buddhas.

HENG SURE, May 25, 1978
Thursday

"Science Fiction"

Science fiction. Catch-all genre for the most creative
minds in print. Broad as a rainbow, science fiction spans
serious works of visionary prophecy, wild-eyed, fantasy, sensational futurist adventures, sober, scientific projections,
and many trashy tall tales. Science fiction creates be-
lievable realities we've never seen, and opens doors in the
mind to places we didn't know existed. Buddhist Sutras do
the same, only their realm is real, not imaginary; fact, not
fantasy.
The *Avatamsaka Sutra* describes genuine states of human
awareness, expanded, purified, and exalted. Sutras are not
fiction, not the creation of an individual author. The
Avatamsaka is a technical manual, a guidebook for spiritual
awakening, ageless and authentic. Sutras are a natural re-
source, a treasure-map of the mind, shared in common by all
peoples. Not arm-chair entertainment, the wisdom lore of
Sutras is for cultivating, for digesting. It's meant to be
handled, absorbed, entered, and realized in practice.

*If we are able to actually apply and culti-
vate according to the principles in the Sutra,
we are certain to become Buddhas.*

*Avatamsaka Preface,
Master Hua*

HENG CH'AU, May 25, 1978
Thursday

"BOWING THOUGHTS"

Cultivating the Way, especially bowing, cuts through
the artificial and draws us close to the Nature. We are
able to see cause and effect in our own life clearer, as if
in stop-action. What we once took for chance and coincidence now suddenly connects in a full circle of action and
reaction. An isolated event can unfold before the mind's
eye like the blooming of a flower captured by time-lapse
photography. And like never before you know what counts;
you see what's icing and what's essence, what's good and
what's harmful. Shame and remorse well up for all the past
bad karma we've created, but also a heart-cleansing and child-
like gaiety and wonder for getting another chance at becoming a person.

*Luckily we have heard the teachings of the Tatha-
gatha and his disciples,
And now we wish to reverse the flow and forsake
our impoverished ways.
With proper faith in cause and effect we break
the mind of the disbeliever.
With shame and remorse before heaven and people,
we break the heart that knows no shame.*

*--from the Avatamsaka
Repentance*

* * * * *

Keep food, clothes, dwelling simple. It's best not to have
"the best."

*With one robe to cover you and food enough
to satisfy your hunger,
Keep yourself in shape,
Give wealth away, sacrifice your life and body*

*Without a second thought as when you spit or
sneeze.*

--from "Song of the Skin
Bag" by Venerable Hsu Yun

We do t'ai ch'i to keep our bodies in shape, bow to
cleanse our hearts, sit in ch'an to seek out the pure and
spiritual. A better life no one could wish for. As soon
as we separate from these, reaching for short-cuts and sub-
stitues, we go astray.

*Let there be no dullness and confusion.
Be like fir and cypress, defy the bitter cold..
With clear tea and vegetarian food, the mind
Errs not, enjoying Dharma night and day.*

--from "Song of the Skin
Bag" by Venerable Hsu Yun

Enriched foods, supplements, high-protein "quick" energy
from ginseng and caffeine leave us hollow and disappointed.
There's no *oomph* behind them, no staying power. Add this,
and you become deficient in that. Keep to the Middle Way
where everything is naturally full and complete, and soon
you'll be travelling light and easy, "enjoying Dharma,night
and day." The myriad things are all made from the mind: in
the center you turn dharmas, but leave the center and dharmas
turn you.

* * * * *

Enduring the unendurable is the path saints and sages
walk. The cold and loneliness of rising before dawn to meditate and bow, exercise and chant, is hard at first. The urge
to go with the lazy flow is strong, especially on a cold,
raining 3:30 A.M. when the tiny alarm rings in the car. But
months of bitterness ages sweet, and the taste is unforget-
table. It can't be described, only experienced.

*The wind and light of the original ground have
a special and wonderfully delightful flavor that
is quite inexhaustible. If we wish to try its
taste, we must simply purify our minds.*

--from Water and Mirror
Reflections by Tripitaka
Master Hua

* * * * *

In the morning...

    There are a few moments in the morning when the world
is still and quiet. And right in the middle of the half-
awake,half-asleep state, everything looks different. Maybe
we see the basic emptiness of things, or that impermanence
is the undisputed sovereign and that all dharmas have no self.
A fundamental level-sameness covers all under heaven and the
basic substance and nature of each living being mutually pervades and melds to the ends of empty space. No up or down,
no inside or out, where might it all lead if we followed?
    But waking up,the vision passes, or perhaps we pass
right over it in a frantic sprint through life. Living to
make a living, the day-to-day running around, sweeps us along
a swift river to nowhere. We start with nothing, hold on to
nothing, finish with nothing, as if in a dream, or watching
dust particles swirling and falling in and out of sunlight.
Of a 24 hour day, 8 hours are spent in sleep, 8 at a job, and
another 8 gobbled up in the kitchen and bathroom, by clothes
and a hundred little things. Less than 20% of our lives is
ours. The rest is owned by the clock. Read the paper,
watch the tube, buy groceries and fall asleep in a chair
reading last year's best-seller.
    Most of the people in the world simply work, eat, sleep,
and work, stopping only when the heart stops and the last
breath sighs. Some live in leisure, others labor to live.
But in death's impartial eyes, we all look the same and no
one has a name. In the space of a single yawn, countless
living beings get born and die. The earth is a hotel for
the 10,000 creatures. Constantly checking in and checking
out, there are no permanent guests.
    In the morning there are a few moments when we can re-
cognize it clearly and we wonder, "What's it all about?"
But there are no words for it, only the quiet seeing. This
is the beginning of bringing forth the mind for enlightenment.
It is our nature to seek to penetrate the hearts of things.

> *All dharmas are apart from words and speech.*
> *Their nature is empty, still, extinct and*
>   *uncreated.*
> *Because he wants to thoroughly and clearly*
>   *penetrate this true meaning,*
> *The Bodhisattva first produces the resolve.*
>
>   *Ten Dwellings Chapter,*
>   *Avatamsaka Sutra*

* * * * *

Mind and body crying for a party. I've got a few pulled muscles. It's hot and dirty, and months of highway dust and black tar are deeply imbedded in our pores. Every fiber wants to run out and blow off the steam, release the internal heat and pressure required to temper the heart. "Be really careful at this stage," advised the Abbot in our last meeting.

As we finish our last bow of the morning, a beautiful young woman riding a bareback horse rides up and offers us a special invitation to be her guests in a nearby mineral hot springs bath. Like it says,

Everything's a test to see what you will do...

We declined and washed up with cold water out of the plastic jug and then took a ch'an bath instead.

All morning I was experiencing a huge oppressive energy on me while bowing. Pounding headache, constricted breathing, painful muscle spasms. Finally it broke while sitting in meditation. I had a vision of thousands of arms and hands encircling and protecting me, also cleansing and healing. After, I felt light and clear, happy and freed of the weight, whatever it was. It had something to do with past karma and a particle of desire that swelled as we bowed. Then the woman on the horse appeared and immediately I felt a sphere of energy, a presence surround me. As she approached I sensed a test and did a couple of the 42 Hands and Eyes of Gwan Yin Bodhisattva. Then we sat and I saw myself enveloped by all these golden-hued hands and arms. Felt better than any bath I've ever taken. All pain and spasms vanished.

> *A thousand hands pervade the body, wonder*
>   *beyond compare;*
> *He vanquishes the demon hordes, protecting*
>   *the trichiliocosm.*
> *Causing the deviant to return to the proper*
>   *and cultivate wholesome dharmas,*
> *He proclaims the Mahaprajna which is apart*
>   *from words.*

>   *--verse by Venerable Master*
>   *Hua for "The Uniting and*
>   *Holding Thousand Hands and*
>   *Eyes"*

* * * * *

The Lees,from Pacifica, drove out to offer lunch and
supplies. During lunch the Pacific Valley "Childrens' Action-
News Team" piled out of their school bus to do a video tape
interview. They watched the Lees make a traditional offering and peppered us with questions about the Buddha, about
being afraid at night, and the "exactly right way to bow."
One little girl who had quietly watched and listened,
finally asked her question; one she had obviously been mull-
ing over for awhile,
"Do you have any desires?"
"Sure we do," I answered, "But we try to turn them around
and chase them instead of being chased by them."
"Like how?" she asked.
"Like always wanting something better is being chased
by desire. No matter what you get, as soon as you get it,
you're still not satisfied. There's always a better one you've
got to have or something else catches your eye. You are unhappy until you get it and unhappy after you get it too. So
desires are suffering." I told the story of Shakyamuni
Buddha, who grew up as a prince and had everything he desired.
Then one day he saw that life was suffering,from birth, through
old age, sickness to death. So he said, "No way!" shaved
his head, and went off to cultivate the Way. Kids ask the
best questions.

HENG SURE, May 26, 1978
Friday

"WHAT IS HAPPINESS?"

What is happiness? Learning Buddhadharma. Holding
precepts purely. Giving, keeping faith in instructions, following them like a lighthouse beacon in a storm. Doing hard
work. Cultivating according to Sutra Dharma, feeling it
open in the heart and take root like a plumb-line, like a
ridge-pole, solid, real, eternally true.

To learn and constantly refresh: isn't this
delightful?

--Confucius

HENG CH'AU, May 26, 1978
Friday

Guilt can be assuaged, but karma is inescapable. A clever lawyer can win us an acquittal, an expensive therapist might calm our nerves, a cheap bottle of wine obliterates the pain, but when it's time, we still get what's coming to us.
Impartial and unmannered, the law of cause and effect nails us to every offense and transgression committed by body, mouth, and mind. Karmic offenses are invisible, lacking shape or form, yet when we die and everything is left behind, only karma will escort us past the grave.
"Why is my life such a mess!?" someone asked us yesterday. Karma. Our lives are whatever we make them. Break the rules, follow desires, hold to deviant views, we plant a mess of causes that reap a mess of results. Why do all Buddhas appear in the world? To help us clean up our mess and to break the chains of karma.

All Buddhas, World Honored Ones, appear in the world because all living beings have no wisdom and do evil. They claim there is a self and what belongs to self. They are attached to their bodies and upside-down; full of doubts, deviant views and discriminations. They are constantly involved with things that bind them up and tie them down.

Universal Worthy's Conduct,
Chapter 36, Avatamsaka Sutra

* * * * *

"WHERE YOU GONNA' RUN TO?"

Squeal of tires, varoom of high r.p.m. engine. A small, fast sports car skids to a stop. The driver, a young man in sun glasses with a broad smile. With one hand on the 4-speed floor shift and the other reaching out to shake hands, he says,
"Man, I saw you yesterday doing this. Wow! Is this some kind of pilgrimage?"
I explain briefly.
"Hey, that's beautiful. Really beautiful. You keep up the faith and now I'll rush on my American way," he said almost apologetically, as if he would like to slow down but

can't find the throttle in his mind.
    Varoom, squeal, a cloud of dust, a hand salute of good
luck, and he was gone like the wind. I thought, as he sped
away, "Fast or slow, American way or ancient way, it doesn't
matter. None of us is ever outside the Way."
    We people are like leaves and flowers; however much
we flourish, we all return to the root from which we grew.
The Buddhadharma includes the Way (Tao), and the Way embraces
all things between heaven and earth. Buddhadharma is the
teaching of the entire Dharma Realm. It is "vast, great,
and totally complete." Although it is vast and measureless,
it is also non-dual, and so the True Mind of each living
being is perfectly interfused with the Dharma Realm; and the
Dharma Realm is not apart from the True Mind. So it says,

> There is nothing which does not flow forth from
>   this Dharma Realm;
> And nothing which does not return to this Dharma
>   Realm.

> --from the Shastra of Gathering
>   in the Great Vehicle

    Whether we unite with our basic nature or fight with
it, nevertheless, we never separate from it. Even if a
person ran to the ends of empty space, he would still be
within his own mind and within the Dharma Realm. Fast or
slow, near or far, sudden or gradual, eventually each of
us returns to what we never left.

> "To the Tao all under heaven will come
> As streams and torrents flow into a great
>   river or sea.

> --Lao Tzu

HENG SURE, May 27, 1978
Saturday

    Bodhisattvas "accord with potentials and dispense
the teachings," to teach and transform living beings when
the time is right. Sometimes bowing in silence speaks
Dharma for people whom words could not reach. Everybody
seems to receive a message of faith and humility as they
watch the ritual k'ou t'ou to the Buddhas and Bodhisattvas.
If we tried to explain our devotions in words, few of the
Spanish-speaking ranchers and pickers would understand. If

we used words for children's ears, the adults would be bored. When we let the bowing speak for itself, angry people cool off; shy ones find encouragement. Dissatisfied Christians "come from the bushes" as Connie in Cambria put it, and we all get a gentle reminder to slow down and look within.

HENG CH'AU, May 27, 1978
Saturday

Rule of the road: Patience, patience, yet again more patience! The only way to handle it out here is real slow and gentle. Keep life regular and simple, and be as patient as empty space, as forgiving as the sea. The mad mind wants to grab and climb, but what is there to get a hold on? The smart bugs inside want to put it into words and come up with theories but, "What still has words is false." Nothing to hold, no place to stand, sometimes makes me nervous. Why? Because I am stupid. A Bodhisattva, upon hearing all dharmas are empty, jumps for joy, his heart knows peace and calm, But,

Common people are ignorant and can't see anything...They dote on their dwelling places and upon hearing that all dharmas are empty, their hearts know terror and alarm...Amid all existences, they hold on tightly and do not let go.

Ten Conducts Chapter,
Avatamsaka Sutra

When Bodhisattvas see how pitiful we are they only want to increase their feelings of compassion for us. They are willing to,

...Pass through an ineffably ineffable number of aeons in every country in all worlds in the ten directions so as to teach and transform and bring to maturity just one being alone.

Ten Conducts Chapter,
Avatamsaka Sutra

Truly, compassion can pluck out suffering.

* * * * *

Sat in meditation on a grassy knoll on a high cliff
overlooking the sea. Sunset, quiet moment. Sometimes a message comes straight from your heart in simple, almost child-
like candor, when the day's pieces settle and the heart-guard
is down.
"Stop finding fault with people. Be good to others;
treat them with kindness. If you don't stop being so petty
and proud, you will have wasted your life. With a mind always slighting others, one can never end suffering or know
peace." said a friend inside.

* * * * *

A young man camped in some bushes next to us. He
played his guitar in a sleeping bag until he fell asleep
under a crescent moon.

HENG SURE, May 28, 1978
Sunday

"WISDOM"

Wisdom is not a heap of static knowledge, or a shelf
full of wordy ideas, bound by language, fixed in time and
space. Prajna-wisdom is dynamic, alive, neither empty nor
definable. Wisdom is practiced, not discussed. It is the
basic share of Buddhahood in you and me.
Hear the Sixth Patriarch:

> *The capacity of the mind is vast and great,
> encompassing the Dharma Realm. Its function is
> to understand clearly and distinctly. Its cor-
> rect function is to know all. All is one, one
> is all. Coming and going freely, the mind's sub-
> stance is unobstructed. That is Prajna-wisdom.*

> *Sixth Patriarch Sutra*

Wisdom *awaits* discovery within our nature, but we have
to cultivate it, uncover it, operate it. My first steps in
cultivation followed a decision to empty my belly of the
desire for tasty food and to empty my mind of the desire for
fame.

HENG CH'AU, May 28, 1978
Sunday

"GHOST TOWN"

The road sign reads "Lucia, 8 miles." We just bowed through Lucia and I couldn't recall one thing about it. How the temporary flies!
Travelling so slowly while "returning the light to illumine within" has the combined effect of making the world look like a big ghost town. The cities appear as neon-tinsled department store Christmas displays and desert mirages floating in thin air. Days come and go like the whiskers on the face; towns fade from memory one step outside the city limits. What isn't in sight is forgotten; what we can see isn't real. Driving back to fetch water, the ground we had just covered looked like a foreign country on first visit. We could have been here yesterday, years ago, or not at all. We are all strangers in a strange land. This world isn't our true home and time is just a four-letter word. The past is dead, the future's blind and where is now? As soon as you say, "now is now," it's already over and gone by.
All towns are ghost towns. The Ghost of Impermanence lurks behind everything that looks real and solid, even our own bodies. In the Three Realms, (or Three Existences), of desire, form, and formlessness, there is no place to dwell and nothing to rely on.

He contemplates the three existences and not one of them is reliable; he vows to constantly get to see all Buddhas and Bodhisattvas; he follows along with and remembers all of the Buddhadharma; he knows the body is empty and false and does not exist--there is nothing about it to be greedy for or concerned about.

Ten Transferences Chapter,
Avatamsaka Sutra

An old monk once said, "The very best is to vow to be reborn in Amitabha's Pure Land. Because when the fires of the kalpa burn up the world, even the heavens in the formless realm don't escape disasters. But in the Western Land of Ultimate Bliss, there are no disasters and you can come back to save boundless living beings in the Saha World."
This world and all the other measureless worlds are

like the leaves of a forest: some are hanging, some fall
down, some are budding, others are rotting or extinct. Our
bodies are the same. As I stood on a bridge, I saw a person sitting in full-
lotus in a deep wooded canyon. Hours later he was still
there. Two days later he hadn't moved. Turns out he's an
art nouveau polyurethane statue that looks more real than
life and is certainly a lot more durable and permanent than
any of us. Even plastic outlives people. So the Sutra says,
"There is nothing about the body to be greedy for or concerned
about." I vow to join the assembly of all Buddhas and Bodhisattvas, to "follow along and remember all the Buddhadharma."
Everything is bio-degradable except the Buddha.

* * * * *

"Why bother?" asks a cynic.
Because life is suffering, and life without cultivation
is meaningless. Because not to cultivate the Way is just like
being dead. Although you eat, sleep, breathe, and wear
clothes, inside is a wasteland, a hollow shell. One dies
at age 20, but gets buried at 60.
One's own suffering is a small matter. It is the suffering and anguish of all humankind that is unbearable. The
Buddha said all suffering is caused by ignorance. Until I
end my own suffering, how can I possibly hope to end the suffering of others? Cultivation is the work of transforming
dark ignorance into bright wisdom. So the *Avatamsaka* says,

When ignorance is ended, suffering is all over.

But when ignorance is present, then suffering can't be stop-
ped. So we cultivate.
"Who told you to get rid of all your ignorance and bad
habits? Who asked you to try and make the world peaceful?
It's hopeless, it can't be done. Who says you've got to
run yourself ragged to help people out of all their suf-
fering!?" shouts the cynic.
Nobody.
In the "Ten Conducts Chapter" of the *Avatamsaka*, the
Bodhisattva answers the cynic's question like this,

*If I don't cause all beings to dwell in the
unsurpassed, liberated Way, and I attain ultimate enlightenment by myself, then I have be-
trayed my basic vows. I can't let this happen.
Therefore, I will first cause all beings to ob-*

*tain Supreme Bodhi and Nirvana Without Remainder.
Only then will I myself accomplish Buddhahood.
And why?
Living beings did not ask me to express this
resolve. On my own I act as an unrequested friend
for all living beings.*

*Ten Conducts Chapter,
Avatamsaka Sutra*

Like a very compassionate elder monk once said, "If I
have to wait for people to ask me to help them, it's already
too late."

* * * * *

On the occasions of the Master's monthly lectures in
L.A., we bow on the sidewalk in front of Gold Wheel Temple.
One Saturday afternoon, two street-seasoned, burly toughs
stopped to check us out. They boldly slouched over the
front porch railing to leer at us. It definitely felt like
there was going to be trouble. They were itching and building
for a go at us.
Just then the Abbot walked out the front door to the
porch. The men turned, saw him and braced. But the Abbot
grinned a big smile, shuffled gently over and joined the
men at the railing just like they were old friends.
"Hello. Did you come for lecture? You can come inside
if you want," greeted the Abbot.
The tension melted. The men relaxed, smiled like little
boys on their best behavior, and not certain if it was the
right thing to do, they stuck out their hands to shake. The
Abbot stuck his hand out as if to say, "Sure, I'm willing,
but you'll have to show me how, as this custom is new to me."
Leather jacket, tatooed hands, vigorously pumping a long,
yellow-sleeved arm, big smiles all around.
Buddhists have no enemies. People that come to hassle
us are just old friends we treated badly in the past. Show
no anger or fear and the grudge is likely to be forgotten;
the bad karma neutralized by kindness. Where do enemies
come from? From thoughts of hatred, anger and harming.
When thoughts of ill-will and hostility disappear inside,
then enemies stop appearing outside. Bodhisattvas by nature
are apart from hatred, so wherever they go they meet no foes.

*The Bodhisattva always thinks of all living
beings with kindness, with thoughts of benefit-*

*ting, pity, happiness, harmony, and gathering
in.
He has forever left behind anger, hatred,
animosity and harm. He always thinks of getting along with others, of being kind and humane,
and protecting and helping them.*

Ten Grounds Chapter,
Avatamsaka Sutra

* * * * *

I used to think happiness was getting what I wanted;
now I find happiness in not wanting to get. No one ever
truly gets what they want and only occasionally, what they
need. At the place of desiring nothing, you get both.

They know contentment with few desires.

Entering the Dharma Realm,
Chapter 39, Avatamsaka Sutra

I keep getting lost in the dust of the world, forget-
ting to be simple and follow my nature. Trying to be famous,
powerful, clever, #1, isn't natural. Striving and climbing
robs our health and youth, upsets the mind and cheats the
soul. What's natural? Our nature is the Buddha's will, the
Tao.
"The nature is the foundation of a person. It is not
produced and not destroyed. It is full and perfect. It's
also called the 'Great Perfect Mirror Wisdom,' and the 'Wonderful Contemplating Wisdom,' and the 'Wisdom of Accomplish-
ing What Must Be Done.' All are manifestations of the nature.
But not recognizing it, you defile it; you turn your back on
enlightenment and unite with the dust."
The Abbot spoke these words in L.A. to a packed room of
world weary disciples looking for a way back to our true selves.
"By cultivating pure dharmas, we get rid of defilement.
So cut off evil and cultivate good. This means cut off
desire. When desire is cut off you give rise to wisdom.
This is the Great Reversal. Turn around! Reverse the flow.
Don't just go along with things."

* * * * *

The road is full of temptations, some enticing, some
repulsive. Survival depends on the wisdom and maturity
to be indifferent (in Chinese, *she* 捨, literally, "to
renounce, to forsake, to give away"). All states, pleasant

or abhorrent, good or bad, according or opposing, are basically no states at all. The unmoving, single-mind is what
endures and enters the true Path. Anything you can obtain
and attach to is false. So it's said,

> There's not a single dharma that once ob-
> tained, provides entry into the Dharma-nature.

> Bodhisattva Asks for Clarifi-
> cation Chapter,
> Avatamsaka Sutra

This week's tests took the form of many women coming
out offering us food, lodging, hot baths, rides, dinner in
a restaurant. Women would appear in the early A.M. and walk
around, staring at us while we did T'ai Ch'i. "Sticky" men
showed up who wanted "to talk" and pressured us to break
the vow of silence--some even threatened us if we wouldn't
sit and rap with them.
When the Youth Good Wealth arrived at the City Wondrous
Light to seek out his teacher, he encountered magnificent
and splendid sights and sounds. The City was literally overflowing with sensational pleasures and allurements--anything
and everything that could delight the body and move one's
mind. But,

> At that time, towards all these rare treasures
> and wondrous objects, up to and including the
> states of men and women and the six dusts--the
> Youth Good Wealth was completely without love or
> attachment. He solely and properly reflected upon
> the Ultimate Dharma. With a single mind, he wished
> to see the Good Knowing Advisor.

> Entering the Dharma Realm,
> Chapter 39, Avatamsaka Sutra

We get a lot of strength and guidance from this ancient
text. No matter what situation arises, the Sutra is always
there with an answer, a key to unlock the Wisdom-door of
our own minds. It is said that the Buddha never stops
speaking the Avatamsaka, that it is being spoken at all
times, in all places, completely unhindered by time and
space. I can believe it. It certainly must be so. It
is the most important, most used thing in our belongings.
We drive the car ahead and leave it parked for the day, but
we carry the Sutra with us in day-packs on our backs.

HENG SURE, May 29, 1978
Monday

> *Too much is the same as not enough. Keep to
> the Middle Way in all things.*

> *Venerable Abbot Hua*

The Tao does not respond to force. It changes effortlessly, naturally. Each time I push too hard I end up afflicted. With too much planning and too much thinking, I
paint myself into a corner.
For example, we observed that eating less created a
light, high meditation state. Desire appears to shrink when
one eats less. I quickly attached to the state and established a vow. I vowed to eat only one bowl of food per day--
fixed, and rigid. Eating a fixed amount of food is a beneficial ascetic practice for some people. I discovered it is
not suitable for me on the bowing pilgrimage. Sometimes it
worked fine. More often it led to obstacles and to unhap-
piness. I found I could squeeze a bucket of food into my
"elastic bowl," and overeat all the same. Some days one
bowl didn't fill me. The result: uptight and false thinking
about food. If there was more than I needed, I worried. If
there was less than I wanted, I got unhappy.
Fuel needs are different each day. According with conditions is the Tao. I survived this experience and after
some solid scolding from the Master, relaxed my strict,
one-bowl vow.
"Put effort into ending desire. Don't attach to ex-
ternals. Use effort in the mind. If your cultivation creates
more affliction, then you are cultivating a deviant practice.
The Middle Way of the Buddha is the way of non-attachment.
Don't force it, let it be natural. Go towards the good and
don't get afflicted," urged the Master.

HENG CH'AU, May 29, 1978
Monday

The highway is a school. It teaches patience and step-
by-step gradualism. It's said,

> The journey of a 1,000 miles begins with
> the ground under your feet.

The building up of bowing muscles and callouses on the knees,

elbows, hands and forehead, takes time. So does melting
away bad karma and growing in wisdom. Manjushri Bodhisattva
asked Wisdom Leader Bodhisattva,

> *Disciple of the Buddha, in Buddhism, wisdom
> is foremost. Why does the Thus Come One praise
> giving for some living beings, and to others,
> holding precepts? Or for some he praises pa-
> tience and vigor, while for others he praises
> dhyana samadhi and wisdom? For others he praises
> kindness, compassion, joy and giving. And yet
> ultimately, none of those exist. Only by means
> of a single dharma can one make good one's escape,
> and that is by Utmost, Perfect, Proper and Equal
> Right Enlightenment.*

> *Bodhisattva Asks for Clarifi-
> cation Chapter,
> Avatamsaka Sutra*

Wisdom Leader Bodhisattva answers that all the Guiding
Masters, that is, all Buddhas, didn't just speak of one way
to gain the Path. Why?

> *The Buddha knows the thoughts of living beings
> And their natures are all different.
> According to what each should rightly receive,
> In that way, he speaks the Dharma.*

> *Bodhisattva Asks for Clarifi-
> cation Chapter,
> Avatamsaka Sutra*

Of all the people who see the bowing, no two see it the
same. The questions, comments, and reactions are as varied
as people's hair color or finger prints. It is just because
Buddhism is the teaching of all beings that the Dharma is
not fixed. What is fixed is dead; people are alive. And so
the Buddha,

> *Praises charity for stingy people,
> Praises morality for the dissolute.
> He praises patience for those with much
>   hatred,
> And for the lazy, he praises vigor.*

> *Bodhisattva Asks for Clarifi-
> cation Chapter,*

Avatamsaka Sutra

It is just like food. Some people prefer salty flavor, others sour. Some like sweet, some bitter, or hot spiced. There are 84,000 different Dharma flavors and whichever one suits you, that one is the best.

He praises Ch'an samadhi for those with
scattered minds.
The stupid ones hear wisdom praised.
For unkind ones he praises kindness and pity.
And for the angry he praises great compassion.

> *Bodhisattvas Ask for Clarifi-*
> *cation Chapter,*
> *Avatamsaka Sutra*

Those who are grieved and sorrowful receive the Dharma sounds of joy; and twisted, crooked, minds hear about equanimity,

And in this way, cultivating sequentially,
One can gradually perfect all Buddhadharmas.

All Dharmas are designed to stop the flow of false thoughts and break attachments. Although the Dharma doors differ, they all eventually enter the same wisdom ocean, just as the myriad rivers flow into the sea or leaves return to the root. Each person hears the Dharma's single sound 10,000 different ways, like the infinite reflections of a full moon scattered over 10,000 waters. And yet, they are all in complete, harmonious symphony; no one obstructs the other. This is the wonderful principle of,

Progressive gradation does not obstruct
perfect fusion;
Perfect fusion does not obstruct progressive
gradation.

> *--from Hua Yen Prologue by*
> *National Master Ch'ing Liang*

It's best to deeply enter one dharma door and not hop around from method to method. This is like standing on one hill gazing across at another thinking the grass is greener on the other hill. The secret of having accomplishment is focus. So it's said,

In single-mindedness there is efficacy;
But scattered, everything's ruined.

If you are greedy and bite off more than you can chew, you'll suffer indigestion. A young disciple, Kuo Dzai, after a few months as a Buddhist, wanted a special Dharma, but was afraid to ask the Abbot. Finally he mustered the courage and got an immediate response.
"You've got your Dharma name and no one is scolding you. Don't be greedy."
(His Dharma name means, "The result of being vegetarian").

* * * * *

Before the Buddha entered Nirvana, Ananda asked him four questions. The third was where the disciples should live when the Buddha goes to Nirvana. The Buddha answered,
"When I enter Nirvana, all Bhikshus, Bhikshunis, Upasakas and Upasikas should dwell in the Four Applications of Mindfulness: Mindfulness with regard to the body, feelings, thoughts, and dharmas." The fourth is the contemplation of all dharmas as without a self. That's our home.
It means we don't exist apart from all that exists. Our peace and happiness in the Way is a gift to all living beings. Suffering and troubles that come our way we swallow and keep to ourselves.
Our teacher is the Pratimoksha, the precepts. Our Way-Place is a straight and pure mind. Our work is to universally cross over all beings with kindness, compassion, joy, and giving. We fight with no one; we seek for nothing. Reducing desires to live simply, we guard the Middle Way and return the light to illumine within, whether walking, standing, sitting, or lying down.
We rely on the Buddhadharma, and take refuge with the Triple Jewel of our own self-nature; the Buddha, which is awakening, the Dharma, which is right, and the Sangha, which is pure.
We renounce our lives to do the Buddha's work.

In our actions we understand the principles
So that principles are revealed in our actions.

We are the Sangha: harmoniously united, eternally dwelling.

HENG SURE, May 30, 1978
Tuesday

Recalled a scene from the film "Midnight Cowboy." Ratso
Rizzo, the hard-luck, petty hustler, finds himself at an
open-buffet party in Greenwich Village. He stuffs his mouth
full of food. He can't fill it full enough. He grabs as
much turkey, cheese, and salami as his hands can hold. He
looks around like a thief and crams the food into his coat
pockets. A drunken woman bawls, "Hey, man, it's free. Eat
all you want. You don't have to steal it."
Sitting in meditation I caught my mind behaving like
Ratso Rizzo, stuffing its pockets full of thoughts.

> To sum it up, be single-minded. Don't have
> that second thought.
>
> Master Hua

Originally, the mind is pure, still, able to reflect all
things. Greedy desire arises and "second-thoughts" appear;
false thoughts of self, of me, and of mine. Second thoughts
are discontented thoughts, they disturb the concentrated
mind.
In Ch'an tonight every thought prompted an echo. Memories, wishes, rejections, plans, and regrets, endlessly rising and falling like waves on the sea. The mind's false
chatter steals energy the way Ratso stole salami and cheese.
Cultivation is for the purpose of getting the mind to listen to orders and be still.

> He universally gathers in all conditioned and
> unconditioned dharmas; among them he lifts
> no false thoughts.
>
> Ten Transferences Chapter,
> Avatamsaka Sutra

HENG CH'AU, May 30, 1978
Tuesday

Subduing a greed-demon in my own mind. While sitting
in meditation I saw something:
I realized that men and women, self and others, and
absolutely everything else in the world is created from a
single thought of desire. With no desire, there would be

no "doing" (karma), and everything would cease to exist. All in the world would be seen as it really is: level, equal, pure and still.

> All in the world,
> With the many kinds of different karmic retribution,
> None of it is not completely created by the power of deeds.
> If one takes away the doing, then
> All in the world ceases to exist.

> Ten Transferences Chapter,
> Avatamsaka Sutra

* * * * *

"CROSSING OVER"

I met something today that's hard to take. It was more than "something," it was "someone," an entity or being within my own person that's been the source of much affliction and obstruction in my life. I call him the emperor, a ghost perhaps, from the past.

Usually I'm not consciously aware of him, but cultivation illumines within and with a little patience, these inner beings get nervous and blow their cover. You hold on, hold on to the fire until without warning, the ghost panics and surfaces. It's as real and exciting as when Moby Dick first breaches from the depths into view and suddenly myth is alive and breathing down your neck.

You hold on and don't move until you can see the whites of his eyes, ugly and uptight, and then look right at him and say, "I see you. I see you. Come on, let it go. Cross over."

Are there really such living beings inside of our minds, dwelling in deeper recesses of consciousness? Who or what are they? The Sixth Patriarch gives a clue,

> Good Knowing Advisors, the "living beings" within your mind are deviant and confused thoughts, deceitful and false thoughts, unwholesome thoughts, jealous thoughts, vicious thoughts: all these thoughts are "living beings." The self-nature of each one of them must take itself across. That is true crossing over.

*--from the Sixth Patriarch's
Dharma Jewel Platform Sutra*

Seeing one's living beings is one thing; crossing them over is another. "Cultivation is just taking what's hard for you to take" said the Abbot last visit. Facing the deviant beings within my own mind is hard to take. "Anyone can do what's easy, so that's why you want to go and do what's hard, otherwise how can you get free?" he asked, rhetorically.

Today as the meal offering praise ended, I closed my eyes to do the Five Contemplations and I saw him--the "emperor." About 40 years old, polished, almost slimy, he was powerful, selfish, and seeking. He was hungry for a "fix" of the five desires, like a nervous junkie, and couldn't wait for the meal prayer to end. Blowing his cover of politeness, he leaped out for the food and I saw him.

He was dark and slippery, like the oily, braised gluten he went for on the tray--pure *yin* concentrate. (Ghosts are said to be masses of *yin* energy which have shadows but no form, or a form and no shadow). He was negative energy, full of arrogance, contention, fault-finding. He doesn't like losing out or taking second place. He was greedy and aggressive, not at all kind or compassionate.

The vision stopped me. I couldn't eat. Knowing that being lived inside of me was sobering and scary. Was he in charge, covertly running the show of greed, anger, and ignorance, hidden from my eyes? Did I control him or was he controlling me?

I just got a glimpse. He slipped back into the inner shadows like a startled fish diving for the bottom. It took a lot of bitter, hard work and the compassionate guidance of a Good and Wise Advisor to even get a glimmer of my "ghost." What will it take to cross him over!?

What is meant by "the self-nature taking itself across"? It is to take across by means of right views, the living beings of deviant views, affliction, and delusion within your own mind. Once you have right views, use Prajna Wisdom to destroy the living beings of delusion, confusion, and falsehood. Each one takes itself across. Enlightenment takes confusion across; wisdom takes delusion across; goodness takes evil across. Such crossing over is a true crossing over.

--from *the Sixth Patriarch's
Sutra*

During lunch it felt as though an oily, black tumor
of poisonous bile had been dislodged. Dislodged, but not
removed. This dark being was running wild and scared, fighting for his life and desperate for a place to hide. He would
settle for any escape, any attachment or false thought for a
shelter.
At first I experienced surprise and fear to find something so dark and powerful in me. Then came lunch--mob hy-
steria and cruelty. "Hey, he's out of his hole, let's get
him, nail him to the tree!" But then I felt sorry for him
and a flood of compassion and caring came over me. I let up.
I asked the Buddhas and Bodhisattvas to aid me in crossing
over this deviant living being of my own mind; to take him
across without harming and cause him to feel secure and unafraid, as if he were my own child.
"Why don't you try bowing?" I suggested.
"No way! I couldn't hack it" he protested.
"Suit yourself. But that's all I'm doing these days.
This body is a Way-Place now, no longer a palace," I said.
Then I went out to bow. He must have joined in, or at
least sat and watched, because it got real quiet and calm
inside for the first time in months.
Kindness crosses over suffering; bowing crosses over
pride. Round #1: a draw.

HENG SURE, May 31, 1978
Wednesday

"THE HUA T'OU SONG"

I've been working on my *hua t'ou,* all the live
    long day.
I've been working on my *hua t'ou,* my afflictions
    fall away.
Who is mindful of the Buddha?
Form is empty, emptiness is form.
Stop the thoughts where they're arising,
And you won't be reborn.

(sung to the tune of "I've Been Working on the Railroad").

HENG CH'AU, May 31, 1978
Wednesday

Lots of strange dreams lately of unfamiliar places
with bizarre people--all of them dangerous situations. Without fail, the Master and members of the Sangha show up right
in the middle of these threatening dreams and I join up
with the Assembly, thus escaping unknown perils and demon
snares. Last night again, the Sangha swooped down in a big air-
plane to rescue me. The Master showed up after everyone had
nearly left and asked me a direct question. I fumbled with
an answer. The Master then looked right at me and said,
"You know, if you would just learn how to concentrate, you
wouldn't get into all this trouble and I wouldn't have to
keep coming. Concentrate!"
I was being told to do something I could handle, but
simply wasn't using effort. A Good Knowing Advisor never
"abandons" his disciples until they are strong and clear
enough to travel safely on their own. A Good Knowing Advisor crosses over, he is not a place to dwell. He is like
a ship's captain.

He is just like a ship's captain who does not
live on this shore, nor does he live on the other
shore; and neither does he live in mid-stream. Yet
he is able to ferry beings across from this shore
to the other shore, going back and forth without
rest.

Ten Conducts Chapter,
Avatamsaka Sutra

We are learning to stand on our own feet, to be unattached and independent, yet at the same time learning to
never abandon or forsake any living being.

The Bodhisattva Mahasattva is also like this.
He does not live amid Samsara, nor does he live
in Nirvana, and neither does he live in the flow
of birth and death. However, he is able to take
across the beings on this shore and set them on
the other shore, secure, free of fear and trouble.

Avatamsaka Sutra

"CROSSING OVER: Round #2"

My "emperor " ghost showed up again for lunch. The
dark aura and wild-eyed edge was gone however. He looked
bathed, shaved, with combed wet hair, like a kid after his
evening bath. No light yet, but he was subdued, almost
sickly pale, as if convalescing. The dark, pompous clothes
and airs were absent, too.
    He sat quietly with bowed head during the meal offer-
ing chant. But towards the end of the meal, he started to
get loose and unruly, just unable to be good for so long.
I compromised and gave him an extra orange. He wasn't happy, but didn't quibble. A tie.
    I put him on a "diet" this week--reducing his desire
intake. The "emperors diet" consisted of: giving away the
remainder of my favorite clothes (some "excellent things"
like sweaters, a parka, wool shirt, all leftovers from lay-
life, not monks' clothes issue); trading a sleeping bag for
a blanket and taking precautions to sleep in lotus posture
and not lean against anything for support; pulling back my
thoughts of fault-finding and false superiority; eating less
than full and only for fuel, not for flavor.
    Of all of these, the emperor was the least happy about
food regulation. The following day, while I was bowing, a
crazy-eyed, freakish man walked up. He was disheveled and
dark, hidden behind a tangled mass of long hair and a full
beard.
    "Do you have food to share?" he asked me.
    "Not with me now. Why, are you hungry?" I asked.
    "No, I'm not hungry," he said with a weird smile.

    Then he began to make strange hex signs and gestures
with his arms and hands--a set of secret, whammy-looking
finger locks and arm twists performed over me. After, he
walked 30 yards ahead to a point on the curve, and turned
towards us, continuing the ritual, home-made sorcery. I did
a couple of the "42 Hands and Eyes" and he left. I believe
he was somehow related to my internal state of subduing my
living beings. Everything is made from the mind alone.

    *There are no dharmas that the mind does not
    create.*

                        Praises in the Suyama Heaven,
                        Avatamsaka Sutra

Teaching and transforming is a gentle give-and-take;
not a purge or harsh repression. Kindness and compassion
universally cross over all. Crossing over begins at home.

*Living beings of my self-nature are boundless--
I vow to save them all.
The afflictions of my self-nature are endless--
I vow to sever them all.*

It begins at home, but has no end because the self-nature
is just the Dharma Realm and ultimately includes all living
beings.

*The Dharma Realm and the realm of living
beings are non-dual.*

> *Ten Transferences Chapter,*
> *Avatamsaka Sutra*

* * * * *

"KEEP IN TOUCH"

A man who lived in a seminary for ten years, stopped to
wish us well and offer support. He left the priesthood and
is now working with drug addicts.
"I'm just into a different mode, but I still try to
keep in touch," he said.

*Giving, pleasing words, beneficial practice,
and identity in actions--all such karma that is
created is not separate from mindfulness of endowment with the wisdom of all wisdoms of all
modes.*

> *Ten Grounds Chapter,*
> *Avatamsaka Sutra*

Mode is the way or manner in which something is done.
The "Wisdom of all wisdoms of all modes" means that one
knows absolutely everything there is to know about the ways

and methods of doing things; worldly and transcendental. It refers to the wisdom state of a Buddha, but Bodhisattvas also obtain this wisdom commensurate with their level of spiritual accomplishment. Thus a First Ground Bodhisattva acquires a wisdom enabling him to "skillfully estimate what should be done and what should not be done." He knows the potentials and capacities of living beings and can take on a body to fit the mode suited to cross them over.

> Whatever body is needed to cross them over,
> He manifests that kind of body and speaks
> Dharma for them.
>
> Ten Grounds Chapter,
> Avatamsaka Sutra

However, he clearly knows his own strengths and limitations and doesn't force it or bite off more than he can chew. Everything he does is "only done according to his strength and proportionately."

With genuine wisdom a person can turn modes; lacking wisdom, the mode turns the person. For example, before entering the monastery, I worked as a counselor for emotionally disturbed children. The disturbed children were just a sprout, the visible outcropping of a far-reaching and pervasive underground root system that went back to the disturbed homes, to disturbed parents, to a single disturbed thought of the mind. Past the families, the courts and the agencies, past the sociological and psychiatric jargon, were minds that were caught up in a web of afflictions stemming from bad karma. Had we been able to discern the cause and effect of broken rules, unfilial behaviors, precept violations, past offenses of killing, stealing, sexual misconduct, as they create present retribution of sickness, poverty, family enmity, estrangement from loved ones, mental illness and the rest, had any of us possessed that wisdom-power, we could have used the mode to turn the tide. But we didn't have that wisdom and so we got turned instead. The work, with its headaches and emotional intensity, drained our energy and sapped our spirits. Once I saw that it was all made from the mind and knew I didn't know what I was doing, I couldn't stay in the mode. I had to find out about my own mind before attempting to straighten out others'.

The priest left the seminary to work in the world, but he still tries to keep in touch. I left the world to work on the mind because there's nothing in the world the mind doesn't touch. It's said that when one is enlightened, discriminations cease. Outside and inside, worldly and holy are no longer seen as different or distinct. This is skillfully entering the Buddha's wisdom, and keeping in touch with the ultimate mode.

Understanding all dharmas' true real nature
And yet not making discriminations regarding
    their nature,
Knowing that all dharmas are without a nature
    or distinctions,
This person skillfully enters all Buddhas' Wisdom.

Living beings falsely discriminate: this is
    the Buddha, this is worldly.
But one who penetrates to the Dharma-nature
Knows there is no Buddha and there is no worldly.

Ten Transferences Chapter,
Avatamsaka Sutra

HENG SURE, June 1, 1978
Thursday

Don't be pleased if Buddhas come;
Don't be angry when demons come.

The Master spoke these words as we left Gold Wheel on the first day of the pilgrimage. They take on meaning only as we progress into our minds. At first the occasional words of praise we heard tasted sweet and the scoldings bitter. But now the opposite is true. Sharp criticism often reveals hidden faults; it's an unexpected gift, if the tender ego can bear it. Honeyed words and praise always puff up the self. Retribution for pride and self-satisfaction is severe

and bitter. Listening to praise is poison. Pretty talk
often hides a dagger.
   The *Prajna Sutra* warns Bodhisattvas to ignore voices
from space. Visions of Buddhas manifesting before one's
eyes to bestow predictions or lavish praise are often demons in disguise. They try to inflate the cultivator's
pride and cause a fall. Or such appearances may be actual
Bodhisattvas or gods come to test the cultivator's samadhi
and sincerity. Does he still have a face to keep? Does
slander sting and nice talk please him? If so, he's got
more work to do before his skill matures.

> *Regarding all beings...I do not seek a thread's
> worth of approval or a single word of praise...I
> only want to save and to liberate all beings, to
> make them pure and to forever make good their escape.*
>
> *8th Practice "Difficult
> Attainment", Ten Conducts
> Chapter,
> Avatamsaka Sutra*

HENG CH'AU, June 1, 1978
Thursday

> *When the Way grows an inch,
> The demons grow a foot...*

   Attempts to curb selfishness and correct bad habits
meet with stiff resistance. Heavy dreams last night, rich
with temptations of all kinds of worldly desires, coupled
with voices while bowing telling me to quit, that I haven't
got what it takes to be a cultivator of the Way and a
Sanghan.
   In the dream, however, the Abbot and Venerable Dharma
Master Hui Seng, appeared to encourage me to hang in there.
"Keep the Bodhi mind, cultivate deep inside where there
are no words and nobody can see or know. Don't move your
mind!" they said, stern and clear.
   There's a place inside that's indestructible and unmoving. No demon can touch it and only faith can enter.

> *If one always believes in and serves the pure
>   Sangha,
> Then one obtains a mind of faith which does
>   not retreat.
> If one obtains a mind of faith which does not
>   retreat,*

30

Then the strength of this one's faith is immovable.

Worthy Leader Chapter,
Avatamsaka Sutra

* * * * *

Still and quiet, the surf hissing hundreds of feet below; bowing and contemplating how I don't exist.
An All-American-looking father and son on a camping trip tip-toe up to make an offering. Big deep smiles, no questions. They were just having a good time together and somehow what they saw in the bowing was part of it.
Minutes later, a speeding car skids and screeches to a stop right behind us. A disturbed man walks up and lets go with hideous, hysterical screaming and mad howling. We didn't turn to look, and soon he left.
Still and quiet, the surf hissing hundreds of feet below; bowing and contemplating how I don't exist.

*All disciples of the Buddha in this way know:
The nature of all dharmas is forever empty and still.
There is not a single dharma which can be created,
And just like all Buddhas, they enlighten to no self.*

Ten Transferences Chapter,
Avatamsaka Sutra

* * * * *

"CROSSING OVER: Round #3"

The "emperor" bowed a stretch this A.M. and tried looking into the *hua t'ou* "who." He couldn't find a who anywhere, which alternately brought deep peace of mind and freakout panic. Wanting to climb, but there was nothing to climb on; wanting to go back, but the bridges have been burned. "It's boring!" he said finally in exasperation, but no matter what alternative presented itself, all suddenly seemed empty and meaningless. So he reluctantly presses on, crossing over. Not to be trusted an inch though.

*The Buddha said, "Be careful not to believe
your own mind: your mind cannot be believed...
Once you have attained Arhatship, then you can
believe your own mind."*

--from *the Sutra in 42
Sections*

* * * * *

I bowed around a curve and came upon a large snake lying
in front of me. It wasn't moving or startled in the least,
and just stretched out staring up at me. There was a strange
and unusual presence around the snake. I looked at its eyes
and simultaneously got a whammy feeling as I realized I
shouldn't look. Too late.

HENG SURE, June 2, 1978
Friday

*From beyond worlds in number like tiny dust-
motes in ten thousand Buddhalands in each of the
ten directions...*

*Ten Practices Chapter,
Avatamsaka Sutra*

A Sage can gaze upon millions and billions of worlds
existing simultaneously in space. But even without spiritual
penetrations we can enter numberless worlds within this world.
This morning the foggy coastline was deserted as a tomb. Beneath my knee, a shale shard rattled on the tarmac. Overhead a hungry heron gull cried one time. The mist muted the
sounds. We bowed alone in an empty world.
Suddenly a grey sedan slid to a stop on the shoulder. A
Shramanerika in a tan precept sash and two laywomen in long
black robes greeted my startled eyes as I rose from a bow.
Faces alight they said, "C'mon. The Master brought the Assembly on a bus from Wan Fwo Ch'eng. They're waiting for us
in San Luis Obispo!"
Instantly transported to a world on wheels, we whizzed
past roadside landmarks we had inched by with tedious effort
weeks before.
We spun down the road to the south, and pulled in at
Ranger Berry's Salmon Creek Station. Trim flower beds, tidy,
whitewashed cabins gave striking contrast to the stark, moon-

like world of rocks and tides we had just left. The easy
smiles and happy chatter of the rangers and the laypeople
echoed in ears grown accustomed to surf and to silence.
Worlds within worlds.

> ...*came Buddhas in number like motes of dust
> in ten thousand Buddhalands.*

> Ten Practices Chapter,
> Avatamsaka Sutra

HENG CH'AU, June 2, 1978
Friday

"SNAKE DREAMS"

Frightening nightmares last night. Ghosts and demons
transformed into powerful snakes, hassled and pursued me.
The snake could change size from larger than a house, to
small enough to fit through a crack in a window. Disappear
in one place and immediately appear in another. I couldn't
subdue or defeat it. The serpent was indestructible and immune to injury. It engulfed me, creating an omnipresent
feeling of danger, loss of control, and fear. It made appear the killing and harming of family and friends while
locking itself around me so I couldn't go to help them. All
the while a demonic laughing and heavy breathing filled the
air.
Right at the point of succumbing to the snake, the Master
and Assembly appeared in the dream. They were immersed in
light, healthy laughter, and proper energy. They walked
around me in a circle until all the darkness of the snake
vanished. I woke up feeling I had just recovered from a long
illness; subdued, weak, and quiet. Fresh in my mind was a
quote from the Sutra that we read last night:

> *He vows that all beings be born from the wisdom
> state of the Thus Come One, and be circumambulated
> by all subdued and mellow people.*

> Ten Transferences Chapter,
> Avatamsaka Sutra

What a surprise in the A.M.! While bowing, a car pulled
up with Shramanerika Kuo Jing, Kuo Wu, and Kuo Yun. "Come
on. The Master and a whole bunch of people are coming down
in a bus. We came to pick you up and rendezvous in San Luis!"

In San Luis, in a small park by the historic Mission, out steps the Abbot and all our Dharma-friends from a big yellow school bus. They were brighter than the bus and singing a song the Master wrote for us in English on the trip down. The whole assembly did an impromptu, stand-up, bus-side concert in downtown San Luis, raising the spirits of two road-weary monks and the scores of local people who happened upon this happy occasion.

We climbed aboard the yellow dragon bus and amid lively Dharma talks, laughter, songs, gentle scoldings, and deep affinities, headed south to Gold Wheel Temple in L.A. As we drove through Santa Barbara, the Abbot shouted, "Time for evening recitation. Shake a leg! Wherever we go we cultivate." Someone in the back of the bus hit an empty pop bottle for a fish, and the sounds of the *88 Buddha's Repentance* drifted from the bus windows along the crowded rush hour main drag of Santa Barbara.

As the bus rolled along towards L.A., in a quiet moment looking out the window, the Sutra quote returned and I realized, in some ineffable way, the dream I had last night wasn't a dream at all.

> *He vows that all beings be born from the wisdom state of the Thus Come One, and be circumambulated by all subdued and mellow people...*
>
> *Ten Transferences Chapter,*
> *Avatamsaka Sutra*

HENG SURE, June 3, 1978
Saturday

On the bus on the way to L.A., the Venerable Abbot wrote a song for us. He dictated the lyrics in English. When the Ten Thousand Buddha's Vehicle reached San Luis Obispo's Mission Park, two bowing monks were suddenly surrounded by light and music as the Assembly sang:

> Goody, goody! Cultivators, you two!
> The City of Ten Thousand Buddhas welcomes you.
> Be careful in everything that you do,
> Every step you take, be true.
>
> The City of Ten Thousand Buddhas is near us.
> Vigor! Be more vigorous,
> With Patience. Patience! Do not rest.
> The last step--your first success.

Ten Thousand Buddhas' City welcomes you.
Ten Thousand Buddhas are near you, too.

HENG CH'AU, June 3 and 4, 1978
Saturday/Sunday

Attended Abbot's lectures at Gold Wheel Temple. Bowed outside during the day and slept in the garage behind the temple with some well-behaved black widow spiders and a dismantled Chevy engine. Took few notes. No interview this time or specific instructions. On the surface, the visit seemed uneventful, but it was a sleeper. The Dharma is that way. Often the teaching seeds are silently, imperceptibly planted in the field of the mind. Then, like time-capsules, they sprout and blossom in the future.

For example, before the Venerable Abbot speaks Dharma, an incredible, purple-white, pure light washes the room, filling up every space and bathing the audience. There's a feeling of imminence as before a tornado, an earthquake, or before lightning strikes, only not of impending danger, but of approaching joy and revelation. People sit on the edge of their chairs and minds, anticipating some kind of energy exchange. During the lecture the hard soften, the old become younger, and everyone has less worries, wrinkles and shadows. After, people are as if intoxicated, and so buzzed-up with wholesome current that they glow with a light of peace and goodness.

> The Tatagatha's great wisdom light
> Purifies the entire mundane world.
> Having purified the world,
> He then gives instructions in the Buddha-
> dharma.
>
> > Praises in the Tushita Heaven
> > Palace,
> > Avatamsaka Sutra

Or maybe it's like when Good Wealth visits Upasika Unmoving in the City of Peaceful Dwelling,

> Upon entering that residence, he saw that the hall was filled with golden light which universally illumined everywhere. Those who encountered this light became clear and cool

*in body and mind. When the light touched the
body of the Youth Good Wealth, he immediately
attained five hundred samadhi doors...and because of those samadhi doors, his body and mind
became pliant and supple, like a seven-day old
infant.*

> *--from Entering the Dharma
> Realm Chapter of the Avatam-
> saka Sutra*

I don't know exactly how it is. My scientific,near-
sighted mind can't begin to grasp things spiritual. The
light is there yet it's not; it's not there, yet it is. I
am coming to understand that what is true and real is invisible and what is visible isn't true and real. The Sutra
clearly states that realms of wisdom are not entered by
looking at forms and seeking in sounds. Nor are they attained through thought.

> *The ways of the Thus Come Ones, great im-
> mortals,
> Are subtle, wonderful, and hard to comprehend.
> Not thought, they are apart from every thought:
> Those seeking them in seeing can't attain them.*

> *Ten Grounds Chapter,
> Avatamsaka Sutra*

It was that kind of weekend: nothing you could point to or
touch happened, but one would have to be a block of wood
to say nothing happened.

HENG SURE, June 3-6, 1978
Saturday-Tuesday

"GOLD WHEEL DHARMA-TREASURES"

I. The Venerable Abbot gave us a recipe for turning
people into cultivators:

> 1. Have a face like a car tire. With skin so
> thick that nothing can puncture it or cause it
> to lose air.
> 2. Have a beggar's body. Nothing that anyone
> could care for or love. Eat to live, don't live

to eat.
3. Have a belly like a Prime Minister's.
Able to swallow great oceanliners or entire
oceans. Both insults and praise, fortune
and calamity vanish within, never having a
trace of emotion or views.
4. Have a heart like Lord Buddha's. A heart
that is never angry but always shows kindness,
compassion, joy, and giving to all beings.

2. "The hardest thing to give up are our afflictions.
Who could you give your miseries to? Give them to
empty space. By holding on to fears and doubts you
obstruct yourself and block others' light from reaching you. Bodhisattvas give away their doubts, fears,
and afflictions. Then they get on with the purpose
of their coming here."

3. "Invite the spirit of happiness into your heart.
When you reach the place of seeking nothing, you
have no more worries. Don't seek enlightenment.
Don't seek peace. Bow in empty space; 'Ride the
clouds and drive the mist.' When you bow, have no
self. With no self, who can get enlightened? With
no self, who is not at peace? Do you understand?"

4. "What's spoken is Dharma; what's practiced is
the Way. Speak it well, speak it wonderfully. If
you don't truly practice, it's still not the Way."

I heard it straight this weekend from the Ven. Abbot.
If you want to be false, then wear a phony mask,
cover up your true face. But true Disciples of the
Buddha don't tell lies, don't wear false face masks.
True Disciples are cultivators, not phonies.

5. Mrs. Chen: "The Master told me that he is always with you, he never leaves your side. I told
him that you both deeply respect him. He laughed
and said, 'Oh, you mean they don't scold me?'"

6. Coyotes howl on three sides of our South Pasadena Way-place garage. Neighborhood dogs uptight,
frenzied barking. Coyotes in L.A.? Yes. There is
a gossamer, a thin tenuous line between civilization
and wilderness, between life and death. We forget.
The coyotes remind us.

7. Layman to Assembly at Gold Wheel:

"Our temple is not a place to throw money
at the Buddha, light up stacks of incense, and
tell fortunes. Our teacher tells us how to cultivate the Way and how to end birth and death. This
is not only special in Los Angeles, it's rare in all
the world."
    A Dharma lecture in South Pasadena, California,
U.S.A. There's excitement in the air as we listen
to the living principles of ancient wisdom brought
to life, vital and full of meaning.
    You can see the gears turn as half-understood,
half-forgotten truths of the highest and oldest cul-
tural heritage on the planet, connect with the heart
of everyday experience.
    The principles of filiality, Way-virtue, self-
lessness and wisdom once again, fresh and vibrant,
transcend East and West, penetrate ancient and modern.

8. A fellow Dharma-Master speaks from the heart:

"I cry a little bit each time I give up control
to the intent of the Buddhas and Bodhisattvas, but
until I die to wanting to be #1, to being boss, I
haven't truly lived.
    Giving my self to all living beings is the
same as giving up to the Buddhas' and Bodhisattvas'
intent. They are not two."

9. "Go one step at a time towards the right road.
Don't seek. Don't seek progress, don't seek enlightenment, don't seek Buddhahood, don't seek anything. You will certainly become a Buddha."

10. "If you boil over, you won't make it. In a
pure state of stillness, the ideal state manifests
spontaneously, without effort. Wanting even the
most precious jewel is still greed. You've got to
cool down and take it as it comes."

11. "How do you cultivate blessings and wisdom?
Don't go after your own benefit. The blessings
that should come to you, give away to others. This
way you will never fall or retreat. If you are
really sincere about benefitting the entire world,
you will never fall. Vigor keeps you from getting

lazy and retreating. Vigor in both body and mind.
If your body bows to the Buddhas but your mind
doesn't, this is not true vigor."

12. "Enlightenment is seeing a thing to its ultimate point. Enlightenment is not resenting heaven
or griping about others. You take charge of yourself and never blame others for what goes on."

HENG CH'AU, June 5, 1978
Monday

*In every Buddhaland in the ten directions and
the three periods of time, exhausting the Dharma
Realm and the realm of empty space, in each and
every tiny mote of dust, there are Buddhas equal
in number to all the tiny motes of dust in all
worlds. In each and every place of these Buddhas
is an ocean-wide assembly circumambulating.*

*Using my deepest and best understanding, I will
appear (in every place) to know and see them all.*

*Universal Worthy's Conduct
and Vows Chapter,
Avatamsaka Sutra*

On the drive back to the Big Sur from Gold Wheel Temple, I experienced a state of finding a "light switch" to
an immense sun within. The light of the sun billowed and
expanded, dispersing all the darkness in my mind and seemed
to light up infinitely, endlessly. This happened nine or
ten times and each was followed by an understanding, a vision past words. The heart of it was this: When one is
pure and singleminded to the extreme, the Way and response
intertwine. One becomes a Dharma-vessel able to hold and
receive, unite with and behold all Buddhas, Bodhisattvas,
Sages and worthies of all time and all space. There is no
outside and no inside, no big or small, no boundaries or
limits at all. It is just as the Sutra describes--Buddhas
and Bodhisattvas in number like motes of dust in every single mote of dust pervading the universe; worlds in number
like motes of dust entering into hair pores. Moreover, there
was a merging of minds as well and all the enlightened states
and spiritual powers of all these Buddhas and Bodhisattvas
simultaneously manifested and could be seen in one's own
mind. Understanding after understanding unfurled, layer

upon layer; too rich, too profound, too subtle to remember or hold. There was a message: "All one need do is purify oneself of all greed, anger, and stupidity; sweep out all dharmas, cast out all marks; be really sincere and straight and all these enlightened beings would constantly appear before you. They are always there waiting only for you to put it all down and in every thought, bring forth the great Bodhi-mind. They are waiting for you. What are you waiting for?"

I felt a mixture of inexpressible, boundless joy and excitement as well as deep shame and unworthiness. My petty attachments, faults, and offenses stood out like black ink on white satin. I repented that night as I meditated outside. What was I waiting for?

With my body, mouth, and mind karma completely purified, I constantly cultivate making bows in respect to all Buddhas. In each and every place where Buddhas are, I make my body appear in number like motes of dust in an inexpressible, ineffable number of Buddhalands. Each and every body simultaneously bows to an inexpressible number of Buddhas like motes of dust in that many Buddhalands.

Universal Worthy's Conduct and Vows Chapter, Avatamsaka Sutra

* * * * *

Shramanerika Kuo Jing, Kuo Wu, and Kuo Yun drove us back to the bowing site. We left our wagon parked behind the Ranger's cabin at the Salmon Creek Forest station in Los Padres National Forest. Ranger Howard had washed the Plymouth and came out to greet us with a big smile. "I've been watching your progress closely" he said, strong and clean.

We drove another 30 miles to Anderson's Landing where we had marked our bowing spot with a rock cairn. After Kuo Jing and the laypeople left, a fox came to sniff us but turned and high-tailed it up the hill. Then, as I was locking the car and putting on my backpack to go bow, a pick-up truck travelling at high speed left the road, skidding out of control, and heading straight for me. There was no time or place to run. "I'm a goner for sure this time," I thought. But within a few feet of hitting me, the truck suddenly veered off-course and crashed through a fence into a tree. The truck was smashed up, but no one was injured. The men left in a hurry. Strange vibes.

Right after, a bright-eyed, happy family of five came
to make an offering. They stood together, smiling, respect-
ful, rosy-cheeked, holding recitation beads in their hands
while the youngest child placed the fresh food and flowers
in front of us.
Minutes later, a car careening wildly nearly wiped out
in a head-on collision next to us. The driver slammed to a
stop and walked back to us saying,
"Yeah sure, okay! There's beer and cigarettes in the
car, help yourself," mumbling to himself as he walked into
the woods.
"M' name's Crazy Horse, but some people just call me
Crazy."
We transferred at sundown and camped under a stand of
tall fir trees on a cliff above the sea. Quite a day.

HENG CH'AU, June 6, 1978
Tuesday

> *You need only be pure, peaceful, and happy,*
> *and you will not lose the Way.*

Sutra in 42 Sections

Pure? Pure is just no sexual desire. Pure is knowing
contentment, not constantly craving more. Peaceful means
equanimity. It is simply not getting angry or losing one's
temper. If you are patient, then every moment of your life
will be peaceful. If you are content with what you have,
then everyday will be happy. Happiness is reaching the
place of seeking nothing. Happiness is purity.

* * * * *

As we recited the Shurangama Mantra before sleep in
the car, a loud, piercing scream from outside broke the
mountain stillness. It was pitch dark, late and no houses,
cars, or towns nearby. We kept reciting. Wonder what it
was?

* * * * *

Ed and his wife, Cunio, stopped to offer us food and
lodging at their Inn in Big Sur. We explained our vow to
stay outside and politely declined their offer.

"City of Ten Thousand Buddhas? Well, you'll make it all
the way, I'm sure," said Ed enthusiastically.
 "We will *all* make it all the way," I said.
 "Yes we will,"said Ed and then as if the idea slipped
down deeper inside, "...hmmm. Yeah! We will, won't we."

> *If I don't cause all living beings to dwell in
> the unsurpassed, liberated Way and I attain Annut-
> tarasamyaksambodhi by myself, then I have betrayed
> my basic vows. This should not happen. Therefore,
> I will first cause all beings to obtain supreme Bodhi
> and Nirvana without Remainder. And only then will
> I myself accomplish Buddhahood.*
>
> > Ten Conducts Chapter,
> > Avatamsaka Sutra

"We look forward to seeing you," said Cunio. "Maybe
we can offer some food if you can't accept lodging?"

HENG SURE, June 7, 1978
Wednesday

> *Not thought, they are apart from thought.*
>
> > Ten Grounds Chapter,
> > Avatamsaka Sutra

Reality is too complex, too magical to think about. All
I can do that feels real anymore is bow, meditate, transfer
merit,and quiet my thoughts. Thinking about anything is
wasted energy; it turns into thinking about thinking every
time. Reality gets smothered in the dusty echoes of my mad
mind. The magic of the universe waits within for the singleminded returning from false to true.

> *With not one thought produced the entire substance
>   manifests.
> When six organs suddenly move, you're covered by
>   clouds.*

* * * * *

"BOUND IN FUR, CAPPED WITH HORNS"

"You two be really careful on this leg of the trip,"
cautioned the Master. "Have you been seeing wild animals?
Have the birds begun to talk to you? Are there lots of trees
nearby?" he asked, mysteriously.
The *Earth Store Bodhisattva Sutra* describes the causes
for rebirth in the evil destinies. After reading about the
laws of karma, I felt pity and sympathy for animals as never
before. I recognized the reasons for their sad, brief lives
"bound in fur, feathers, or scales, and capped with horns."
"Greedy desire causes people to fall into animals' bodies,"
said a wise Sage.
"Animals are people who in previous lives didn't believe
in cause and effect and became animals."
Chills ran up my spine tonight during standing meditation.
I finished the last mantra and dropped my arms. Six feet
away, a slinky, black shadow leaped and turned, then disappeared into the pines. It was large as a dog, silent and
quick. After ceremony, Heng Ch'au saw a large silver fox
dash away from the manzanita and vanish up a vertical cliff-
face. Later that night we heard a fatal combat outside the
car: A harsh, metallic snarl, a hawk, maybe, or a hunting
cat. Then heavy thuds, scrambling feet, and falling rocks,
then silence.
We recalled the Master's advice the next morning as we
bowed past a freshly-killed, 3-foot red, black, and white-
striped snake. We both instinctively registered "poisonous"
vibes as we saw it. Namo Amitabha. I believe in cause and
effect.

HENG CH'AU, June 7, 1978
Wednesday

"SMELTING NOTES..."

*The Buddha said, "People smelt metal to refine
it of impurities in order to make implements of
high quality. It is the same with people who study
the Way: First they must expel filth and defilement from their minds. Then their practice is pure."*

--from Sutra in 42 Sections

You've got to have "juice" in the battery to turn over
the car engine. Smelting is the same: to expel filth and
defilement requires the juice of wisdom that is generated
from precepts. Smelting takes fire, an internal fire stoked

and tended by cultivating non-outflow wisdom. Precepts are
the fuel of blazing wisdom. At some point, precept-practice
transforms something inside into light-power, and from this
light-power flows forth the mind for the Dharma and the mind
that can smash through all the demonic obstacles that stand
in the way.

> He gives rise to the mind of liberation from
> all demons' bondage.
> He gives rise to the mind to smash the hosts
> of demonic armies.
> He gives rise to the mind for the unsurpassed
> Dharma and the wisdom light it radiates.
>
> Ten Transferences Chapter,
> Avatamsaka Sutra

The filth and defilement are just desire thoughts and
accumulated bad habits growing out of greed for food, fame,
wealth, sex, and sleep. Each attachment, every bad habit,
has a demon ruling it, and if you decide to go towards the
good and refine the impurities from body and mind, then
sooner or later, you're going to meet up with that demon.
Demons don't want you to leave the dirt and darkness. They
want to drag you back into the pit of desire. When you encounter your demons they say, "Don't cultivate. It's too
difficult." They are like a salesman shark, or slick defense
attorney that can make hell look like paradise, and murder
like an act of kindness. If you've got the wisdom-light,
you flip the switch and let it shine and the demons are subdued on the spot. They can't face the light, and purity's
power makes them curl up and tremble.
Smelting isn't a head-trip or sterile metaphor--it is
a total mind/body transformation of greed, hatred, and stupidity, into morality, concentration, and wisdom. It begins
with faith, is sustained by sheer will-power and vows, and
aided by a little something more you discover when you go past
the point you felt you couldn't go.

* * * * *

Camped near Partington Point. The road continues to
run close to the sea and over countless creeks and streams
flowing down from mountains that rise abruptly to our right.
Light traffic, long quiet stretches and lots of time to look
deep within and watch the mind.
The Avatamsaka says the nature of the mind does not

exist at all. It's neither inside or outside the body
and is ultimately like an illusion and a transformation.
Sometimes after a good day of bowing next to sea and mountains, the normal, narrow boundaries of our bodies and minds
break down and dissolve into the immense and infinite. And
right then, for a few undefended and subdued moments, one can
see what the Sutra describes must be so. It's "like peering
through a keyhole, and seeing endless space." Most of the
time, I can only see my self.

HENG SURE, June 8, 1978
Thursday

Crazy Horse.
His car was hard to miss; for a week I'd heard a thun-
dering exhaust just before the gravel spattered, too close
for comfort. Then I heard a voice cursing in a sing-song
cadence, unclear above the roaring engine. Every day he
buzzed us, testing nerves and concentration. He flew by so
fast I never got a close look at him, couldn't tell what he
said but it seemed generally hostile. We've learned not to
judge people by first appearances. Sometimes the louder
the bark, the softer the heart. Tough acts conceal tender
souls. So it was with our mysterious assailant. Even at
second look, Crazy Horse was a character.
He switched abruptly one afternoon from cavalry charge
to infantry assault, still testing. I turned a steep, winding curve on a deep arroyo switchback and came upon his car--
convertible top down, idling and hot.
"There's beer in the back seat, you two clowns can have
all you want," he said, then hopped out and vanished into
the trees, carrying a heavy box. I heard him shout to an
invisible party on the hill above,
"Ray! Ray, I'll be up to fix your pump next week. It's
C.H.,Ray. I'll get the part in San Luis and install it next
week. You'll have water in a week. Okay, Ray?"
Striding out of the woods on parade march, he hopped
over the driver's door and gunned away, cursing again in a
manic monologue.
"So you don't drink beer, eh? You creeps."
Today we passed the test. C.H. appeared after lunch
from a cloud of dust and squealing tires, holding a jug in
his hand, a toothy, lunatic smile on his face.
"The name's C.H., Can't Hack It, they say, or Crazy
Horse, if you like. Course some call me Crazy As Hell, but

C.H. will do. You two look pretty dry, here's some spring
water, good and clean. It'll cool you off. Course you
look pretty cool already. Hope you enjoy it." He seemed a
little apologetic, as if to say we'd passed his test and he
now considered us part of the Big Sur family-scene.
    C.H. didn't stop buzzing us for weeks. The curses
turned to sing-song cheers and the roaring passes and flying
gravel had a friendly atmosphere. He stopped twice more to
offer water and to point out the good running springs flowing
down the steep cliffs under the road and cascading to the
sea level far below.
    Patience and not contending subdue all comers. A peace-
ful mind turns foes to friends. This part of the highway is
rugged, the road twists and changes abruptly, the few in-
habitants we've met feel the same way.

> *Bodhisattvas enter into the uniform and equal
>   nature of all dharmas.*
> *They have no thought of any living beings not
>   being family or friends.*

> *Ten Transferences Chapter,*
> *Avatamsaka Sutra*

HENG CH'AU, June 8, 1978
Thursday

> *He vows that all beings be covered by whole-
>   some dharmas and eradicate the hubbub,
>   dirt, and dust of the mundane world.*

> *Ten Transferences Chapter,*
> *Avatamsaka Sutra*

    Driving out of L.A. in the dust, dirt, and clamor of
the freeways and big city perpetual rush hour, I could see
worlds of people, animals and all kinds of sentient beings
caught up in the buzzing madness of birth and death; all of
us "like fish in evaporating water." Renewed my vigor to
cultivate the Way and then return to save and take across
living beings beyond number.
    This world is so false and empty and yet amid it, we
get so confused and can't find the road to liberation.

> *I only want to save and liberate all beings,*

*to make them pure and forever make good
their escape.*

Ten Transferences Chapter,
Avatamsaka Sutra

The common and sagely in each of us is kept apart only
by a thin shadow of ignorance. The pure and the holy lie
dormant, as if hibernating within the ice of our defiled
attachments. But our eyes are covered by a film, the ca-
taract of karmic obstacles, and so, standing next to the
river, we can't see the water.

*He vows that all living beings cast off the
bonds of desire and forever leave behind all the
greedy desire of the mundane world and have no
defiling attachments within the Triple Realm.*

Ten Transferences Chapter,
Avatamsaka Sutra

The Dharma was spoken for all living beings. It pulses
and rings out from the supermarkets, shopping centers, asphalt alleys, and suburbs. It says, "Basically, who is
binding you up? No one. We create our own chains and sentence ourselves to prisons of our own making. When the
mad desire-mind stops you are free; free beyond your wildest
dreams. It's all made from your mind alone."

* * * * *

Patience is:

*The thought of cultivating for hundreds of
thousands of millions of nayutas of kalpas.*

Ten Transferences Chapter,
Avatamsaka Sutra

Buddhist sense of time is mind-boggling. It's a contemplation in itself that can calm the frantic clock-bound
world we live in. For example, one kalpa is roughly equiva-
lent to 16.8 million years. A thousand kalpas makes one
small kalpa. Twenty small kalpas makes a middle-size kalpa;
and four middle-sized kalpas make one great kalpa. *Nayuta*
is a Sanskrit tally, alternately translated as ten million
or hundred million. Add it up. A Bodhisattva brings forth

the thought to cultivate for that long! For hundreds of thousand of millions of hundred millions of 16.8 million years.

There is a Dharma door that exclusively uses this kind of numerating and reckoning to enter samadhi. Basically there's no way the tabulating of these enormous Sanskrit numbers can be exhausted. They challenge the mind to go beyond itself and enter what lies above the intellect and beyond the uncomputable.

Good Wealth learns this Dharma door from his teacher the Pure Youth Comfortable Chief in the *Avatamsaka's* "*Entering the Dharma Realm*" Chapter. Sometimes while bowing, I let my mind enter this number-adding contemplation--expanding, expanding the measure of my shoestring thoughts until all sense of size and time and space vanish. It levels the highway and my petty ups and downs.

HENG CH'AU, June 9, 1978
Friday

Face to face with one's own mind. The mind that climbs on conditions and thinks itself in circles; the mind that chatters and babbles non-stop; the mind that wants to contend and attack; the mind that refuses to see all dharmas are like dreams and illusions, and that the things of this world are false and empty affairs. Face to face with one's own mind. Bowing, the silence, the vast solitude of this mountainous highway, and "the wildest, most rugged land in California" brings the mad mind front and center.

At the end of the bowing day I wanted to grab and scamper, but there was nowhere to go, nothing to hold. I reached for the Sutra instead and read the first passage that appeared.

> He vows that all beings dwell in the dharmas of non-contention, and understand that all dharmas are uncreated--the no-nature is their nature.
> He vows that all beings leave behind all unbeneficial speech and constantly delight in solitary places, their minds without a second thought.

> Ten Transferences Chapter,
> Avatamsaka Sutra

I sat in meditation, sat and sat until the dust settled. "That's just how it is" said the Good Advisor within. "Un-

created, no-nature. No place to dwell, nothing to lean on.
The 'solitary place' just means the truth: the truth of no-
self, the truth of taking what's hard to take. It's the
precepts, no rapping and running outside; it's the perfection of patience; it's the price of independence. Wonderful
existence is born from true emptiness; enlightened beings
come through the gate of loneliness. Don't have a second
thought."
    The test follows immediately. Can you really delight
in the solitary place and leave unbeneficial speech? Three
men walk up full of sticky smiles. They want to talk and
visit, camp the night, have a campfire cozy. We gesture
"no talk." They leave.

* * * * *

    Ken Wright, of the CHP, stopped at sunset to go over
the route and discuss logistics.
    "They made these roads before there were bicyclists
and bowing monks. Now there are both!" he laughed.
    Officer Wright was really helpful and supportive. "All
clear ahead, be careful."

* * * * *

    Three more men stop who "want to talk." Again we re-
fuse.

HENG SURE, June 10, 1978
Saturday

    Three thousand years ago in India, the Buddha first
turned the Dharma Wheel. Six centuries later, the Good Law
flowed East to China. Now in the Twentieth Century, the
Lion's Roar resounds in the West.

> *Buddhism is the gasoline that powers the
> changes for goodness in the Universe. Buddhism
> is the proper energy for the world. Buddhist
> disciples who cultivate the Way change the flat
> tire on the world. We are mechanics in service
> to all beings throughout the Dharma Realm.*

> *Venerable Master Hua*

HENG CH'AU, June 10, 11, 1978
Saturday/Sunday

Big Sur. Got $10.00 worth of gas. Lew Kuo Shr and
her mother drove out to offer lunch. Kuo Shr told us about
her son, Melvin, age 15, who can't find the answers about
birth and death in encyclopedias or at school.

Mad mind continues to do cartwheels and crazy, sense-
less antics while bowing--all manner of bizarre states, images, memories, skits and movies--anything to exercise its
main function: to discriminate and create the ten thousand
things. The conscious "thinking" mind holds a dual filter
over the vast, big, non-dual state so that everything comes
out in twos. The wind is easier to control than the mind's.
A Bodhisattva removes the minds filter, and,

> He clearly sees the Dharma Realm, how it
>   is vast, big, and peacefully set up.
> He knows the entire world as well as all
>   dharmas are level, equal, and non-dual.
> He leaves all attachments behind.

> Ten Transferences Chapter,
> Avatamsaka Sutra

There's no product in cultivation, only process. "No
attaining or non-attaining," nothing sought, not even seeking to be one who seeks nothing. This too is an attachment.
"Every step you take, be true" says the Master's song.
That's all there is: no mind, no thought, no self, no times,
just deeply entering the Way with a single, free-'n-easy
mind.

HENG SURE, June 11, 1978
Sunday

Bowing past the Chevron Station in Nepenthe, a grizzled
cowboy leaning on a tilted-back chair, shouted from the
porch,
"I been here a long time but I ain't never seen anything the likes o' these two. Hey Bob! These are the two
biggest screwballs we've ever had in Big Sur."
Even by avant-garde, anything-goes, Berkeley standards,
Big Sur was fabled as home of the heaviest weirdos and far-
thest-out freaks in California. How can two harmless bowing
monks be Big Sur's #1 oddballs?

*They seek no offerings from others but only
to give to living beings. Therefore, they have
no fear of a bad reputation.*

*Ten Grounds Chapter,
Avatamsaka Sutra*

HENG SURE, June 12, 1978
Monday

"VIGOR BEATS THE SLUMP"

*The disciples of Gautama are always awake,
day and night thinking of disciplining the body.
The disciples of Gautama are always awake,
day and night delighting in pure meditation.*

Dhammapada

My vigor slumps in the evening. I've caught a bad habit
of napping after bowing. There's no reason to indulge in a
nap at sunset. Vigor brings happiness; after desire comes
suffering. The Sutra says that just as sturdy walls protect
the citizens of a capital city, so do patience and vigor
protect Bodhisattvas. I want to cultivate vigorously like
the Bodhisattvas in the Sutra, so I've added more martial
arts in the evening. I'll kick my way to wakefullness.
Beating the sleep-dive takes persuasion. To break out
of the five o'clock slumber I have to go through a song and
dance routine in my mind:
Reach for the t'ai ch'i shoes, say "Well, maybe I'll
do a few exercises and then go "meditate" (translate: sleep).
After ten minutes breath circulates: "Hey, I was tight
as a drum. Guess I'll do all the exercises, not skip the
sinew-changers like "chin-to-toe." Do it right." The Master
says,

*Just because it's a difficult practice, that's
the very reason to do it.*

After thirty minutes, basics completed, entire system
feels refreshed and alive. "That didn't take long. Shao
Lin next; how did that new movement finish?"
Relaxed and alert, the nap is forgotten. I'm concentrated and ready for vigorous Ch'an meditation. Vigor and
hard work beat the lazy demons every time. It takes an
expedient sales-pitch to move my bones to action, but life
is movement, death is inert, the practice of Ch'an ultimately
unifies motion in stillness, stillness in action.

They have much liking, much happiness,
And much pure faith as well.
They have courageous vigor to the utmost
Along with much elation and rejoicing.

Ten Grounds Chapter,
Avatamsaka Sutra

HENG CH'AU, June 12, 1978
Monday

When the mouth opens, the body's energy
scatters.
When the tongue moves, rights and wrongs
arise.

Cultivation breaks attachments to self and to
dharmas, and yet does not harm either. In the midst of
the myriad things, one is nowhere bound up or confused by
them. Liberation and enlightenment are not dwelling in no-
thingness, they are a state of true self-mastery gained by
nowhere-dwelling.

For example, I am coming to a place where talking and
writing seem totally empty and useless. The mouth opens
and energy disperses; the tongue wags and gossip appears.
Words and language artificially freeze the natural, never-
fixed flow. They create differences and barriers where none
existed before; they confuse by adding a head on top of a
head. Words turn the wonderfully ineffable into a lifeless
corpse. Words and speech are like picking a flower--it soon
dies.

And yet the Middle Way says, "Don't attach to what is,
don't fall into what is not. Neither nihilism nor eternalism is the true and actual meaning." This means that even
though words and language themselves are false and empty,
they are used to point to what is true and real. It is just
as wrong to attach to no communication as it is to be constantly bantering and looking for someone to talk to. Unattached to the body, the body suddenly obtains a wonderful
function. Unattached to the mind, the mind transforms into
a wisdom mirror and gains the use of spiritual powers. Unattached to words, words can become a key to opening up the
prison of birth and death in the world.

52

He does not seek what living beings can speak
of.
These are all conditioned, false, and empty
matters.
Although he does not rely on the path of
words and language,
At the same time, he does not attach to not
speaking.
...And although he again appears in the world
with a body, yet his mind is not in any way
attached to worldly dharmas.

Ten Transferences Chapter
Avatamsaka Sutra

Standing on the mountain we can't see the mountain.
And so sometimes we need to leave behind the things that are
hardest to leave behind and travel far before we can find
ourselves. Just as seeds blow away from the plants in order
to sprout and flower, people break attachments in order to
grow and to enlighten.

HENG SURE, June 13, 1978
Tuesday

Two laymen met us near the Big Sur River at the end of
the day. We stood briefly without speaking. The air was
crystalline, shafts of gold lit the tops of redwoods and firs.
The shallow river rippled by; three husky crows perched above
the Plymouth and croaked a sundown tune. It was a special
moment. Kuo Chou offered bread and peanut butter, Kuo Ch'au
Lee offered blankets and canned vegetables. I felt content
as never before.
Bhikshus hold no personal wealth and do not seek the
necessities of life. Their minds are free to contemplate the
important matters: "Where did I come from? Where am I
going?"
None of the food, clothes, and shelter provided by
donors has a name on it. Just like the flowing Big Sur River,
all conditioned things float by. We use only enough to satisfy our needs. The goods change our shape as we change
theirs; neither of us last long.
Why do I weary the mind with concern for my body? Dharmas come and go infinitely, without boundaries.

The strength of the thinker and what is thought give birth to all kinds of dharmas. They quickly pass away without an instant's pause. In thought after thought, that's how it is. That's how it is in every thought.

The Bodhisattva Asks for Clarification Chapter, Avatamsaka Sutra

HENG CH'AU, June 13, 1978
Tuesday

Entering change of terrain from rocky, mountain slopes slanting into pounding surf, to thick, flat forest land. The Big Sur River drops down from the Santa Lucia Range and runs parallel with the road which leaves the coast and heads inland. Tall stands of pine, fir, spruce and redwoods, line the flat river bed landscape about 4 or 5 miles wide between the seashore and the foot of the mountains. Got some room to move sideways now instead of the perched-on-a-narrow ledge feeling of the highway. Since April, for over 2 months, we hugged ground that constantly slanted up, down, or sideways and wasn't wide enough for 2 cars and a pedestrian to pass at the same time. We are off the "slide" now.

Just as abruptly and dramatically as the geography changes, so does the demography, the "carve and cut of the people." A time to be especially alert and careful. We have learned from past experiences that when the land and water and wind change, so do our visitors. Some are friendly protectors, others are not.

HENG SURE, June 14, 1978
Wednesday

Memorizing the *Ten Practices* Chapter of the *Avatamsaka* and eating with wisdom and restraint have cured me of chronic indigestion in the belly and in the mind. I've always eaten too much and chewed too little. I'm now eating a measured portion once a day and chewing slowly. Indigestion has vanished; my body feels light and alive.

I've always read too much, stuffing my mind full without digesting the information. While in school, my literary shelves were packed with books but my overloaded mind went hungry for wisdom. Memorizing the text of an ancient Sutra, word by word, has transformed mental indigestion and has brought deep satisfaction.

Small bites of food,
Small bits of wisdom--
Chew both thoroughly.

HENG CH'AU, June 14, 1978
Wednesday

We camped alongside the Big Sur River last night. At dusk a strange, half-naked beggar appeared,walking towards us out of the tree-shadows from the river bank. He was barefoot, no shirt, and wore only thin, tattered pajama pants bottoms and an old yellow-rubber rain jacket that would not fasten in front and was ripped up the back. We gave him food, clothes, and our two warm blankets. The more we gave, the more he wanted.

After loading up with all he could carry out of our supplies, he demanded disdainfully, "Is that *all* you can spare!?" We dismissed his rudeness and arrogance as a test of our Bodhisattva resolve, fancying him to be maybe a Bodhisattva or deva in disguise come to check out our sincerity and non-attachment.

Heng Sure had just come to a section in the *Ten Practices* Chapter of the *Avatamsaka* where the Bodhisattva practices being a great benefactor who can give away all his material objects without even thought of regret or stinginess. His only wish and concern is to cause others to leave suffering and obtain bliss. Thousands upon thousands of beggars come to this Bodhisattva and say,

Oh kind one, we are very poor and have no means of support. We are starving and emaciated and in dire straits. We are next to death. Would you be so kind to give us your body's flesh to eat so we might live on?

Heng Sure stood by the side of the car in the river-chilled night air reading the passage to me while I salvaged through our gear to find something to keep us warm that night.

Hundreds of thousands of beggars come to this Bodhisattva and he doesn't flinch, but only increases his mind of kindness and compassion. He thinks,

I am getting good help. All these beings

(beggars) are a field of blessings for me. With-out being asked, they are coming to instruct me about entering the Buddhadharma. I should now cultivate and study in this way, and not counter the thoughts of these beings.

Ten Practices Chapter,
Avatamsaka Sutra

Heng Sure closed the text and wrote a note: "He was probably a Bodhisattva. We should have emptied our pantry and bowed to him!" Maybe so, but in our minds there was a pinch of doubt, regret, and a vague feeling of having "been had." This feeling was later bolstered when a Park Ranger drove up in a jeep with the "beggar" in the front seat, hugging his new warm blankets, clothes, and food bag.

"He says you gave this to him, that he didn't acquire it illegally. Is that right? asked the Ranger.

We nodded. He scratched his head, lifting back his hat.

"You sure you want to give him all this stuff!?" he asked.

We nodded "yes." In our minds we thought maybe the Ranger was part of the divine test script and that we were showing true giving and unflinching kindness. In retrospect, the Ranger probably thought we were plain stupid and as out-to-lunch as the beggar. The one virtue missing in the whole experience was common-sense, something no cultivator should be without.

Luckily, David (Kuo Chou) Rounds and Arnold(Kuo Ch'au) Lee, came out the same evening with an offering of food, warm clothes, and blankets, or we would have spent the night shivering under a paper-thin, old nylon tent fly.

HENG SURE, June 15, 1978
Thursday

"SONG FOR KUAN SHIH YIN"

1. Homage to the Bodhisattva Kuan Shih Yin
    Who's made a vow to save us from the troubles
        we're all in.
    Though he travels everywhere, saving as he
        goes,
    Ten Thousand Buddhas' City is the Bodhisattva's
        home. (chorus)

2. Namo Bodhisattva who observes the world's
   sounds.
   Every place your name is heard happiness
   abounds.
   Contemplating freedom, compassionate and
   kind,
   Saving all from suffering, bringing peace
   of mind.

3. Namo Great Compassion Mantra, holy magic
   spell.
   Gives goodness inconceivable to those who
   hold it well.
   Miracles more wonderful than words can
   ever tell.
   Healing sickness, stopping evil, lucky,
   as-you-will.

4. Called by many different names, in many
   different lands,
   A thousand eyes, thousand ears, to rescue
   those in need.
   Recite the name of Kuan Shih Yin, he comes
   to set you free.

5. In transformations thirty-two, he reveals
   his light.
   Manifesting different bodies when the time
   is right.
   Now appearing as a beggar, solving someone's
   plight.
   Now appearing as a king with awesome, royal
   might.

6. Now a monk and now a maiden, now a nobleman.
   Teaching in a way each different being can
   understand.
   Compassionately bringing joy and ending
   suffering.
   That's the greatness of the Bodhisattva
   Kuan Shih Yin.

7. Homage to the Bodhisattva Kuan Shih Yin.
   Bringing joy and ending sorrow, say his
   name again.
   Homage to the Great Dharani, holy magic
   spell,

> Healing sickness, stopping evil, lucky,
>   as-you-will.

(Chorus)

> Namo Kuan Shih Yin Pu Sa
> Namo Kuan Shih Yin Pu Sa

HENG CH'AU, June 15, 1978
Thursday

Bowed long and strong this A.M. Light body and a clear mind. Ate too much at lunch. Bowed less this afternoon. Turbid, heavy body and a murky mind. Cultivation is right here.

> *The superior person thinks of the Way, and*
> *   does not think of food.*

Confucius once said that a person who does not go on eating until he is sated may be said to have some taste for learning. The converse is equally true.

HENG SURE, June 16, 1978
Friday

Bowing past the Big Sur Inn today, I recalled a sojourn here six years ago, a last worldly fling before entering the monastery. I tried to fill every orifice in my head with sense-pleasures. Greed for the good life overwhelmed good sense. No matter how much delicious food, chamber music, rare wine, and conversation I consumed, I found no peace, no contentment, no joy at all. You pay a high price for gluttony: the body gets sick, the mind runs mad, the spirit goes bankrupt.

Six years later, my heart has changed; so have my habits. I eat one meal a day of simple food. I used to eat three, and of gourmet fare. I feel content, refreshed, energized, and clean. Meditation tonight will be tranquil and unobstructed by the fire of greedy desire.

> *He vows that all beings will obtain the food*
> *of wisdom; that their minds will not be obstructed;*
> *that they will understand the nature of food and*
> *not be greedily attached to it, and that their*

58

only delight will be in Dharma-bliss and the food of transcendence.

Ten Transferences Chapter,
Avatamsaka Sutra

HENG CH'AU, June 16, 1978
Friday

Food is one of the five desires that can obstruct the
Way. It is also a basic requirement for staying alive. Buddhism is straightforward and sensible about food and simply
says, "in all things, keep to the Middle." Neither too much
nor too little, don't grasp for existence, don't fall into
emptiness. Greed for flavor is as off the mark as trying
to starve your way to enlightenment. "Eat as if you didn't
eat a single grain of rice," our teacher advised us, meaning:
the very best is to just "fill your belly with tasteless
food," to avoid the sickness of hunger. Have no thoughts of
whether you ate or did not eat, whether it tasted good or
bad, was well-balanced, not enough of this and so forth. In
cultivation you want to have a pure mind, free of extraneous
thoughts and hang-ups.
So far on the pilgrimage we have found:

-- If we hold the precepts and stay away from defiled dharmas, we don't need a super-charged, pro-
tein-packed, Whole Earth diet. Purity is the source
of natural health, not protein.

-- Simple vegetarian food eaten in silence is best
for cultivation. Avoid rich foods, heavy oil, deep-
fried, spicy items, all prepared for flavor and to
enjoy mouth blessings. The better it tastes, the
worse thoughts it creates and the more trouble it
brings.

--Sweets and dairy products like butter, cream,
cheese, cottage cheese, yogurt, etc., or the
"roasted-toasted," mouth-watering foods, increase
desire and obstruct proper reception and proper
concentration (samadhi). If offered, it's okay
to accept a token amount, but never seek after
them. On the other hand, by leaving even that
much of a loophole in your thoughts that, "Well,
if it's offered, then it's okay," it's for certain

the pies and ice-cream, milk and "just like real
meat" substitutes will start showing up by the
bags full. Everything is manifested from the mind
alone.

   "How should it be? If you can be unaware of
whether you ate, dressed, or slept, then this is
best. 'Did I eat? I don't know. Did I dress or
not? I don't know. Did I sleep or not? I don't
know.' If you can remain unaware of these matters
then your practice approaches the state of wonder-
fulness...No false thoughts is purity."

                    --Instructions en route
                    from the Venerable Abbot,
                    March, 1978

                  * * * * *

   We ate lunch in a dirt pull-off outside the Inn next
to the Big Sur River. A platoon of tourists from Europe
piled out of a sight-seeing bus to snap pictures and stick
their toes in the cool river. Foreign visitors don't find
two monks bowing on a pilgrimage and camping on the road at
all strange or out-of-the-ordinary. They hardly notice us
and often treat us like part of the scenery or like parking
meters. Strangeness is only made from the mind.
   After lunch, Mike and Joe, two Park Rangers, stopped
their green jeep to ask about the trip.
   Joe: "The only reason I can see for doing something
so incredible is for eternal life. Is that it? Are you
seeking eternal life?"

   *In all countries, in every direction, they
   rely on nothing and dwell nowhere. They do not
   seek life itself or any of the other host of
   dharmas.*

                    Ten Transferences Chapter,
                    Avatamsaka Sutra

   Monk: "We don't seek anything."
   Joe: "Then why do it?"
   Monk: "We just do it because it needs to be done. The
world is full of suffering and disasters. We do our work
and transfer it to the world."
   Mike: "Do you think things will get better because of

this? I mean, are the good vibes increasing in the world
from what you do?"
    Monk: "We don't think about whether our work has this
or that effect and response. That would be like giving a
gift expecting something in return. We just try to bow
with a single mind and not be scattered."
    Joe: "Yeah! That's true. I can see that. But are
you really happy?"
    Monk: "Yes."
    Joe: "Not just kidding yourself and escaping from
things?"
    Monk: "Everyday we come face-to-face with things. If
you're looking for escape from reality, this isn't the way
to do it. There's no kidding yourself in Buddhism and no
place to hide."
    Mike: "Then you're going completely on faith! That's
all you have!"
    I never thought about it that way, but it's true. We
are going completely on faith. It's all we have; all we
need. The ancients had a saying,

> *If a person has no faith, what can be done
> with him?*

    With faith there's nothing you can't do; without faith,
you can't do anything. Faith isn't blind belief; it's ne-
glected wisdom's blurred vision. Faith keeps us from blowing away.
    The most famous Buddhist saying on the power of faith
comes from the "Worthy Leader Chapter" of the *Avatamsaka
Sutra*. I sat on the tailgate waiting for some hot water to
boil and read it as the Rangers drove away,

> *Faith is the source of the Way, the mother of
> merit and virtue. It nurtures and raises all
> wholesome dharmas. It cuts through the net of
> doubts and leaves the flow of love. It opens up
> the highest road to nirvana..."*

begins the lengthy eulogy.
    "Then you're going completely on faith! That's all
you have!" echoed the astonished Ranger's words. I thought
of the Abbot's essay on "The Importance of Faith,"

> *The Buddhadharma is like a great ocean; only on
> faith can we enter it. The single word "faith" is
> the essential secret to resolving the matter of*

birth and death."

Tea was ready; time to go bow.

* * * * *

Bowing corrects arrogance. In flash after flash I've
been facing my pride all day, each bow like a line-drive
to the nose. One bow produces an indescribable feeling of
purity as if seated peacefully in the center of blossoming
spring flower. The next bow leaves one feeling as rank and
dirty as falling into a cesspool. Back and forth on the
teeter-totter of repentance and reform. Past karmic shadows
and ghosts, future glimpses of deliverance and pure white
dharmas. Big Sur River rolls and flows along beside us as
we bow, washing clean the land. The Dharma washes clean the
heart.

> *I sincerely repent of my offenses and vow never
> to create them again...May the long-flowing river
> of Dharma wash away the defilements of my mind.*

> *--from Avatamsaka Repentance
> Ceremony*

HENG SURE, June 17, 1978
Saturday

"THE FOOTBALL EXPEDIENT"

It's funny, the things you remember while bowing. Even
before we meet the Dharma, the Dharma is still constantly
speaking to us. I was 12 years old, it was my birthday.
"Do you like it?" asked my father, handing me a brand
new football.
"Wow, it's really neat!" I said, reaching for it with
eager hands. It was an imitation leather football with
white, plastic laces. My Dad let me toss the ball around for
a time, imitating Johnny Unitas throwing the long touchdown
bomb to Raymond Berry, the glue-fingered end. Then Dad spoke
Dharma.
"I planned to get you a better football for your birthday, one that will last. This is a good one but not the best.
Jamra's was sold out of the ball I had in mind, but Jerry
said they'll get more next week. So the choice is yours.
If you can be patient and wait, you can have a football like

the pros use, a football to keep for years. But if you want
the best you'll have to return this ball now; once you use
it, it's yours. You decide and let me know," he said.

The Buddha appears in the world, and
Universally contemplating what living beings'
    hearts enjoy,
He brings them to maturity with many expedient
    means.
This is the liberation gate of the Grain Spirit
    Pure Light.

> *World Rulers' Wonderful*
> *Adornments Chapter,*
> *Avatamsaka Sutra*

At the time I didn't have words to explain, but I recognized a test of desire versus principle. It was October,
football season. To wait a week meant getting my birthday
present late. But something told me my Father hoped I would
be patient and not greedy for short-term happiness. I swallowed and handed him the plastic-laced ball. "I'll wait,"
I squeaked.

I was patient all week, counting the days that seemed
to drag on forever. Finally, Monday, the shopping day arrived. Dad returned from work with empty hands. He took off
his coat and shoes and sat down to read the paper. I didn't
want to ask, but I couldn't help wondering if he had forgotten our bargain. I stood by his wing-backed chair quivering in silence, anxious for my birthday present after
an endless test of patience for a twelve year old. Surely
my Father wouldn't forget--but how could I ask without
sounding like I couldn't be patient?

"Oh say, I left my briefcase in the front seat. Would
you get it for me?" he said, looking up from his newspaper
with a broad smile. My shoes struck sparks as I raced out
the back door to the blue Pontiac. There, on the front seat
by the briefcase, was a brand new official N.F.L. football
emblazoned with "Wilson. All pro-model." It weighed a ton
and hurt my toe with every punt and place-kick for years.
But to me, the ball was most special. It spoke the Dharma
of patience and the reward of controlling greedy desire for
small benefits. My Father's expedient lesson returned to
mind each football season through the years of my childhood.

Cultivators endure bitterness now in the same spirit;
put down worldly desires and physical comforts to practice

the Way. Patient cultivation, when mature, yields the Bodhi-
fruits' never-ending bliss. So it's said,

Enduring suffering ends suffering.
Enjoying blessings exhausts blessings.

I played football as a child with an innocent, carefree
heart. The ball was made of pigskin and spoke the Dharma of
patience of short-term pleasures. Now I play the game of
life and death in a bag of skin that will outlast the football
by only a few years. My body speaks the Dharma of past causes
and conditions. How fortunate to be able to walk the path to
the end of suffering!

Disciples of the Buddha, this Sagely Truth of
the path to the extinction of suffering may be called
the most victorious principle...it may be called the
Great Expedient.

Four Sagely Truths Chapter,
Avatamsaka Sutra

HENG CH'AU, June 17, 1978
Saturday

"RIVER TOLL GATE"

We call them "tollgates"--a place where there's a sudden
change in geography marked by a confluence of new energy and
intense vibes (atmosphere). There's usually a lot of action,
strange people, tests, and sometimes trouble, as we file
through an invisible, but unmistakable corridor of inspection
and appraisal by the local spirits.
We call them "spirits"--beings who embody the feel or the
spirit of the area. Rough and harsh as the sea, playful and
quick as a waterfall, unpredictable as a curving mountain
road, hard and powerful as mountains, they appear by bridges,
valleys, mesas, rivers, with nightfall, with the winds, and
on the edge of every town. They can be cold and dark or
bright and warm, jovial or surly, threatening or alluring--
as varied as the land and weather itself. We have found our
best response is no response. If we are not seeking anything
and don't talk to them, we pass through the toll gate, otherwise we pay a toll.
As we bowed over the Big Sur River into a small village,
a crazy man with wild, frizzy, electric hair descended on us.

He rolled and spun on the ground at our feet, making weird
gestures and sounds, shaking his hair violently and mock-
bowing. He jumped onto the highway and lay flat on his back
with a cigarette in his mouth, blocking traffic in both directions in front of the Inn. Getting up he played traffic cop,
directing and harrassing motorists. We bowed around him and
he went away.
   Some "spirits" are lighthearted and impish, others mean
and nasty, but they are always mischievous and pranky.
There's no time to think. If you are false thinking, you
flunk their test. They appear when least expected, thus evo-
king an instinctive knee-jerk response that shows exactly
where one is really at. Always the encounters are lessons.
Often they end in an air of enigma and shoulder-shrugging
puzzlement, like the "leprechaun lady," that came tonight.
   It was dusk. Heng Sure sat inside the car while I meditated on the lowered tailgate. We were camped in a small
clearing, a wooded glen, next to the river. Suddenly, I was
aware of a woman standing next to me. She was 50'ish, emotional, weeping and nearly hysterical--taken to melancholy.
   "I'm not from this planet. I'm from very far away.
Does that sound strange?" she asked.
   "Nothing is strange," I answered.
   "It's said, 'the superior man doesn't ask where or why,
but simply perfects patience.' But...(her voice breaking)...
what can I do? I can't kill myself, that wouldn't free me.
Can you tell me? How do I get back? Can you tell me?" she
sobbed and shook with emotion.
   I closed my eyes, envisioned the Abbot, and silently
recited Gwan Yin's name. The woman changed. Her face lit
up and she dried her tears, saying,
   "I just gave myself the answer! It's okay now."
   She requested what I was reciting. I wrote out "Namo
Gwan Shr Yin Pu Sa" on a card and handed it to her.
   "That's it! That's my friend," she exclaimed. "God-
dess of Mercy. That's my friend!"
   She offered cheese, crackers and a shamrock plant that
belonged to her recently deceased mother.
   "The 'little people' are all over here," she said, mat-
ter-of-factly. She left reciting Gwan Yin's name.

   *If you view what is strange as not strange,
   then all strangeness disappears and everything's
   okay, no problem.*

                              --Venerable Abbot, Instructions
                                en route

* * * * *

*He dwells in great kindness and practices
great compassion. His intent is to happily benefit living beings.*

Ten Transferences Chapter,
Avatamsaka Sutra

A young man named Dave, from San Luis, stopped. He's
a college student who devotes his spare-time to caring for
the disabled and the handicapped. Danny, a paraplegic, accompanied him. Dave lifted Danny out of the car into a
collapsible wheel chair and pushed him over to where we were
bowing.
"We both are really interested in your practice," said
Dave. "I'm coming from the Christian tradition, but just now
discovering meditation. There's a mystic school in Chris-
tianity, but most people don't know about it. That's the
only thing keeping me in the Church."
We talked briefly about the bowing and Buddhism. Dave
lit up when he heard about Great Compassion and the Bodhisattva Path. He said,
"There is something here that's very appealing and true.
You know, of the priests who went into the cities to do social work, only the contemplatives stayed on long after all
the others burned out. So there's got to be something here
in contemplation. Helping others and meditation go hand-in-
hand, huh?" said Dave.

*Not for himself does he seek happiness,
But only because he wants to save all beings.
This is how he brings forth the heart of Great
Compassion.
And he quickly enters the unobstructed ground.*

Ten Transferences Chapter,
Avatamsaka Sutra

"There's got to be more to life than work and football
and cheeseburgers," said Dave. Danny liked that comment.
He smiled and gave a big nod of "right on!" from his wheel
chair.

* * * * *

Officer Ken Wright of the CHP stopped to check our pro-

gress.
      "My wife wants to bake you something. What do
monks eat?"

HENG SURE, June 18, 1978
Sunday

"*SONG OF THE DHARMA-DOCTOR*"

I. I thought I would a doctor be,
         foremost in all the land.
     I would eradicate disease,
         with skillful healing hands.
     I saw a lot of suffering and began
         to wonder why,
     We worry so about our health, when
         in the end we die.
   (Repeat last line)

II. I asked the question high and I asked
         the question low:
     Where do we really come from? At
         death, where do we go?
     A man said, "Buddha answered that
         3000 years ago.
     Go ask the Dharma-doctor for what you
         want to know.
   (Repeat last line)

III. I found the Buddhist temple and a
         monk with merry eyes.
     Why do we get sick? I asked him; why
         do people die?
     "Everything's impermanent," he said,
     "I think you'll find that birth and
         death's the big disease. It all
         comes from the mind."
   (Repeat)

IV. "It's evil thoughts that hurt," he said,
     "It's what you say and do.
     It's called the karmic law. What you
         send out comes back to you.
     As is the seed, so is the fruit; like
         cause so is effect.

And when you break the rules, you hang
    a rope around your neck.

  V. If you kill and steal and lust, if you
      drink and lie,
    You'll get reborn again until your
      karma's purified.
    When the bag of bones gives out, your
      suffering's not done,
    Until your karmic debts are paid, you'll
      get another one.

  VI. Even though your spirit leaves this
      fragile bag of skin,
    Until you purge the poisons three, you'll
      get reborn again.
    How can you stop your evil ways and do
      what's good instead?
  "Just put an end to poisons three," the
      Dharma-doctor said.

 VII. "The poisons three are greed and anger,
      and stupidity.
    Greed for wealth and sex and fame and
      food and sleep," said he.
    With Five Desires unsatisfied our angry
      thoughts appear.
    And stupidly we break the rules--all sick-
      ness begins here.

VIII. Living beings are upside-down, our
      habits hard to break.
    The Doctor gives us medicine, which
      we forget to take.
    The Buddha tells us many times, we
      walk a dead-end road.
    We nod and say "I understand,"
    But that's the way we go.

  IX. The Buddha left three medicines for living
      beings to take.
    Precepts heal the mind of greed, samadhi
      conquers hate.
    Wisdom is the perfect herb to cure
      stupidity.
    That's the Buddhadharma's way, to end
      the poisons three.

X. Precepts are the rules, a shield to guard
      our energy.
    Samadhi means to fix the mind. Wisdom
      sets you free.
    So keep the rules and fix the mind,
      wisdom manifests.
    When all your karma's purified,
      you've ended birth and death.

XI. Buddhadharma is a tonic. Medicine superb.
    It's like a panacea, like a cure-all heal-
      ing herb.
    It gives us wisdom and compassion, for all
      living things.
    That's the state of perfect health, the
      Buddhadharma brings.

XII. The Buddha is the Healing King with cures
      for all our ills.
    But he doesn't sell us potions and he
      doesn't send us bills.
    His medicine is Dharma. It's not on the
      drugstore shelf.
    The Dharma-doctor shows us how, and then
      says "heal yourself."

XIII. Well since that day I met the monk, my
      whole new life began.
    I used to want to heal the body, now I've
      changed my plan.
    I'm going to cultivate the Way and leave
      desire behind.
    I'm going to cure the poisons three, in-
      side of my own mind.

(Repeat)

* * * * *

"BUDDHA CITY BOUND"
by Heng Sure & Heng Ch'au

(To the tune of "Can't Help but Wonder Where I'm Bound")

It's a long and dusty road,
It's a hard and a heavy load,
And the folks I meet ain't always kind.

Some are bad, some are good,
Some have done the best they could;
And some have tried to ease my troubled mind.

(CHORUS)

To the City of the Buddhas I am bound,
   I am bound.
To the City of the Buddhas I am bound.

Had a life it was fine,
Lots of food and fun and wine.
Spent m' blessings till I plumb went insane.
But I was too blind to see,
It was only grievin' me, and
Good times are just another kind of pain.

--CHORUS--

Met a friend good and wise,
He could open up your eyes,
In the Golden Mt. by Frisco Bay.
And sometimes when my heart is true,
His light comes shining through;
His kindness ain't easy to repay.

--CHORUS--

So if you see me passing by,
And you stop and you wonder why,
And wish that you were a pilgrim too,
Shave your head and don the *yi*
Take the precepts and you're free;
In this world, ain't no better thing to do.

--CHORUS 2X-- (trail off)

HENG CH'AU, June 18, 1978
Sunday

"BOWING THOUGHTS..."

   Quiet Sunday morning, long beams of sunlight slant down
through the tall corridor of pines lining the road along the
river. A few chirping birds, an occasional woodsman's ax,
punctuate the soft, forest-muted stillness. We bow deeply
absorbed, always looking within.

The hardest thing in the whole world is to get rid of the self and to cultivate to Buddhahood. It is the hardest thing for everyone. We all possess the inherently enlightened wisdom of the Buddha. Our true nature is identical, pure and bright. Mine is not less than yours, nor greater than the tiny sparrow's perched on a branch above. It doesn't increase in the Sage or decrease in the common person. All differences are illusions that fade away like the morning dew, leaving level equality through and through.

We are all on a pilgrimage, on a return. We are in this world to go back and awaken to the knowledge and vision of the Buddha. It is the one great matter.

> It is also as THE DHARMA FLOWER says, "Only due to the causes and conditions of the one great matter did he appear in the world. That is, to open, to disclose, to make enlighten to and enter the knowledge and vision of a Buddha." Living beings possess it equally, and so it says, "Only one."

> --from the Avatamsaka Sutra Prologue

Dreamed last night of the Abbot and the Sangha assembly. Cardinal Yu Pin was there, also. The 42 Hands and Eyes encircled and weaved throughout. Everyone bathed in a sea of light and big, glowing, radiant happiness as they did the pure work of the Buddha.

> With wholesome, clever expedients they are able to do the Buddha's work and release the Buddha's light which universally illuminates the world without limit.

> Ten Transferences Chapter, Avatamsaka Sutra

* * * * *

While bowing in the pristine stillness of these woods, suddenly I found myself wrestling with a gnarling demon of affliction. Who could I blame, who could I pass the buck to out here? The wilderness solitude became an immense mirror, forcing me to return the light and illumine within.

I traced my miserable state back to a single thought of pride and a self-satisfied wish for fame. Just one small thought of self-seeking turned this tranquil paradise into a grating hell. Outside nothing had changed, only my mind had changed. It was as if the forest and cool river were speaking Dharma for me, saying,

"Look within, return the light, everything's made from the mind. Whatever you long for will bring you trouble; whatever you seek will obstruct. Look at your faults, weed out your pretensions. Be unattached, pure, and selfless.

We are all on a pilgrimage, a return. We are all in this world to go back and awaken to the knowledge and vision of the Buddha.

72

Leave no place for trouble to stand and nothing for worry
to hold, then what can impede your wandering?"
    Ah, the Middle Way! So close to home, so easy to lose
and yet it never comes or goes. It's held without clutching,
followed without going, seen without straining, and fathomed
without a thought. Like a fool I forget the secret: go
light and carefree, simple and empty. Follow the Tao and
don't false think. The Way is effortless and innocent; clev-
erness and striving never find it.

* * * * *

    *He vows that all living beings in the Buddha's
presence be without jealousy or malice; that in
their hearts they will constantly plant roots of
goodness and joyfully seek the Buddha's wisdom.*

                            *Ten Transferences Chapter,
                            Avatamsaka Sutra*

    Molera Beach, Sunday noon. Two groups of lay donors
arrive within minutes of each other: one group, Chinese-
Americans, who drove up from L.A.; the other, Vietnamese-
Americans came overland from San Jose. There was a moment
of tension and disappointment, thinly held in check behind
social awkwardness and strained smiles. We are all part of
the Buddha's family and the Buddha's family fights with no
one, especially among ourselves. Yet we are people, too,
with human desires and emotions which trip us up in our
search for wisdom. Of these snares, jealousy is one of the
worst.
    Suddenly someone breaks the silent, icy stand-off and
says energetically,
    "Let's have a big group picture! C'mon, everyone
squeeze together." The ice melted and the kinship emerged.
Soon everyone was sitting together on mats, sharing food and
laughter, backs huddled against a stiff wind blowing up
dust and sand from the State Beach.
    The Buddhadharma is vast and inclusive, without discri-
mination or limits. All beings are gathered in and made
happy and harmonious--just this is the Buddha's mind. Last
month in L.A. the Abbot said,

    *The measure of our minds should be so vast
that it exhausts empty space and pervades the
Dharma Realm...We should help others and be*

glad to take a loss. We never can be jealous.

Tonight the winds continued to howl and whistle through the cracks in the car as we read from the *Avatamsaka,*

The strength of this Bodhi-mind is vast and great like the Dharma Realm and ultimate like empty space...Their hearts are vast and pervasive, the equal of All-Wisdom.

> *Ten Transferences Chapter,*
> *Avatamsaka Sutra*

Wisdom does not compete. Wisdom is being one with everyone.

* * * * *

"THE 'LIGHT': MISCELLANEOUS QUOTES"
(Not for any particular happening except to raise our spirits when the world gets dark and the shadows cross our minds. The AVA-TAMSAKA is our map to the City of 10,000 Buddhas).

Everywhere he gathers together conditioned and unconditioned Dharmas,
But among them he has no false thoughts.
He is the same way toward mundane dharmas.
The Lamplight which illuminates the world is awakened in this way.

> *Ten Transferences Chapter,*
> *Avatamsaka Sutra*

Universally practicing all purified karma of the Bodhisattva, they enter inconceivable comfortable samadhis. With wholesome, clever, expedients they are able to do the Buddha's work and release the Buddha's light which universally illuminates the mundane world without limit.

> *Ten Transferences Chapter,*
> *Avatamsaka Sutra*

*He vows that all living beings attain a pure light
to illuminate and view the mundane world in
its extremely fine and subtle forms.
He vows that all living beings get a light which
is not screened-off and understand the realm
of living beings as empty and non-existent.
He vows that all living beings obtain a boundless
light body which produces a wonderful light
which illuminates all things.*

> Ten Transferences *Chapter,*
> Avatamsaka Sutra

HENG CH'AU, June 19, 1978
Monday

We have been bowing through wilderness terrain for
months--gravel, debris, hot sand, thistles, ditches, pas-
tures, through woods, on the edge of cliffs and over wind-
blasted mountain slopes and shoreline. Our robes, hands,
and knees look the same as the road shoulder and chaparral-
covered foothills.

During lunch yesterday, one of the laypeople from L.A.--
the biggest cement-asphalt spread in the world--stood up and
scanned the vast, wind-swept coastline and tall waving grass-
es. She looked up and down the narrow Cabrillo Highway and
then said in disbelief,

"And no *sidewalks* to bow on!?"

* * * * *

A white convertible that's been hazing us all week
finally tried to run us over. There was no other traffic.
We perched like sitting ducks on a wide, flat shoulder
along a straight, open stretch of road. I heard the engine
gun into overdrive as it left the pavement and bore down
on us from behind. We continued to bow.

"Get 'em. Wipe 'em out!" someone yelled.

But suddenly, a few feet before hitting us, the car
began to spin and slide out of control as if tripped up. It
squealed and screeched three times completely across the
highway from shoulder to shoulder, throwing up a cloud of
smoke and dust so thick I couldn't see Heng Sure 10 yards
ahead of me. Finally it smashed through a rail fence and
plunged into a ditch. Fortunately, no one was hurt. The
two men, now pale and subdued, quietly, slowly, drove away

with a wobbling rear axle and lots of dents.

The Buddha said, "When an evil person hears about virtue and intentionally comes to cause trouble, you should restrain yourself and you should not become angry or upbraid him. Then the one who has come to do evil will do evil to himself."

--from *the Sutra in 42 Sections*

HENG SURE, June 20, 1978, Tuesday - June 28, 1978, Wednesday

"BIG SUR WIND WEEK"

DAY 1

In the Avatamsaka, "The practice of steadfastness," the Fourth Practice, talks of vigor in the face of hardship. Road too narrow to bow safely; counted and paced off nearly a mile. Passed a Caltrans workcrew in flourescent orange vests; after 468 bows, found a tiny elbow turn-off between two high banks. The wind blows hard today, funneling through the coastal valleys and lashing like "the tail of the dragon of Northern California," as Heng Ch'au put it. The highway crews packed up and went home, too cold and windy to stand up safely on the precarious shoulder. Not even sandbags kept their "men at work" signs in place, as they blew all over the road.

Opening the door of the Plymouth took real effort; climbing out after lunch to begin the 468 bows in place felt like staring at point-blank range into the Quaker Oats cannon: wind-volleys "shot from guns." Head-on gusts rock the car on its springs like a leaf in a whirlpool. Hard to bow down, hard to plant the feet and stand, fighting the rushing air that pushes like a football tackle. Sudden noises deafen the ears, darting shapes whistle past, every body-cell is cold and tense, every nerve is bow-string tight.

At first it's a challenge, invigorating. After five hours, with hundreds of bows remaining, it's misery. Feeling hassled, sorry for myself, then slowly, I recognize it as a test. Principle says,

"Don't be turned by any state, inside or outside. Take all states as they come; be vigorous through thick and thin alike."

The text of the *Avatamsaka's* Fourth Practice had the
Dharma-medicine I needed to hold my mind steady in the wind.
I recited the text to reverse my attitude of self-pity.
What's a little hard weather compared to:

> *Can you, for the sake of living beings,...*
> *pass through numberless aeons in the Uninter-*
> *rupted Hells and endure all of that suffering?*
> *The Bodhisattva answers, "I can!"*

> *Ten Practices Chapter,*
> Avatamsaka Sutra

It's right, in some inexpressible way, to be bowing on a
narrow, dusty highway shoulder in a mad windstorm somewhere
in Big Sur, California as spring turns to summer in 1978.
Let the wind blow right through.

Day 2.

Head-on winds blow us off our feet; fill every crevice
of the body and crack of the car with flying grit. The
Plymouth dances on its springs like a string-pull toy. We
wipe streaming noses on grimy bandannas and squint bloodshot
eyes into the endless stream of air.

Situations beyond my control quickly become personal
affronts, sources of anger and affliction. Why? Because
I'm attached to having things go my way. I'm attached to
a big view of Self. My pride takes a loss when the wind
blows me down. Opposing states counter my wishes and bruise
my Ego.

Big lessons this week in impermanence. When the body
falls apart it doesn't ask permission, it simply scatters
like the dry grass whipping past a forsaken turn-off near
Pt. Sur Lighthouse.

Day 3.

Buddhadharma teaches methods to deal with states. They
boil down to this: maintain Proper Mindfulness no matter
what situation you meet. The body is falsely set up and
empty of self. How can we learn to leave confusion in the
midst of the howling wind?

> *They vow that all living beings leave all*
> *distinctions that come from being moved from*
> *mindfulness, and enter the unmoving wisdom-ground*

of level equality.

*Ten Transferences Chapter,
Avatamsaka Sutra*

"THE PRACTICE OF WHOLESOME MANIFESTATION"

Day 4.

To avoid poisoning the mind with greed for flavor,
Granola should be eaten by the thimbleful. Greedy for tasty
variety, I used to pack my lunch-bowl full. I would top the
granola with raisins, nuts, seeds, yogurt, dates, applesauce,
roasted peanuts, bean sprouts, wheat germ, peanut butter,
sliced cheese, mashed bananas, wet it down with hot water
and powdered milk or applejuice, then inhale the bulging
mountain of food without chewing.

Contemplating this gross eating, I can hardly believe
it. I ate this way for months, indulging in greed, unchecked by principle or by concern for the donor's kindness.

"One grain of donor's rice taken with a mind of greed
creates offenses as heavy as Mount Sumeru," said the Buddha.

Desire for good flavor creates a field of offenses, not
the "field of blessings" of a left-home Sanghan. Time to
change my ways, follow the Middle Way, and approach a Wholesome Manifestation.

* * * * *

Changing bad habits is hard work. Attachments have
momentum, they feel comfortable. Change requires constant,
steady pressure on the sore spot, applying good Dharma-medicine with patient courage until the new, proper view replaces
the old way of being. Lift the bandages too soon or leave
the habit alone, and the illness returns.

*He vows that all beings become great kings of
medicine who always remove the many sicknesses
and do not allow them to recur.*

*Ten Transferences Chapter,
Avatamsaka Sutra*

Day 5.

In its fifth day, the windstorm fans the earth and
flails at our faces. The Plymouth dances the shimmy, the

gales whistle, roar, boom, and thunder. To bow, we fall
through air as thick as water. To stand, we rise against
invisible hands. The wind abates, the pressure yields, we
lurch forward. The next clever gust shoves us off-balance,
we stumble back.
I wasted four days gritting my teeth and pouting at conditions. Each time I lost my feet before the wind, my afflictions rose a notch. Staying with the bowing, not giving
in and quitting, is the hardest work I've done.

Day 6.

Six days of big breezes chill the flesh and scatter
the ego's notions of good and bad. Enduring unfavorable
states pressures the limits of patience and stretches the
mind. Fears level out, habitual views of self fall away.

*In cultivation we must have an attitude of
great renunciation. If you can do away with
all attachments to self and to dharmas, then
this is another way of saying you have gotten
liberated.*

Venerable Master Hua

Sometimes help arrives unexpectedly. Ready to collapse
this morning. I used my last fiber of patience just to keep
bowing in the cold wind. At lunch-break I briefly lost control. My emotions flowed out unchecked. I pantomimed around,
imitating the wind for Heng Ch'au, trying to relieve my misery, to prompt a laugh and pop the tension.
Cultivating the Way requires patience. The pressure
of enduring all states, both pleasant and unpleasant, can
transform emotion into wisdom and affliction to Bodhi. But
cultivators must wait out the fire and not flow out into emotion and monkey shines.
Patience reached the breaking point; just then a silent
sedan slid to a stop between the Plymouth and a tall sand
dune. A family of laypeople emerged and silently offered us
food and incense. They had driven hours from the Bay Area
and found us right at lunch time.
After the meal they joined the bowing, heedless of the
stiff conditions. I felt much calmed by their presence and
their faith in the Triple Jewel. My energy returned. By
mid-afternoon, I was back on center, mindful, and recovered
from the morning's ordeal. I recognized my lack of patience,
saw that I had attached to a state and was turned.

All states arise from the ten directions to test you. They are hard to recognize. Recognizing them, you turn the situation. If you don't see it clearly, the situation turns you. Use the perfection of patience. Contemplate that there is nothing you can't endure. No matter what arises simply endure it. Don't get anxious, then you can pass the gate.

Venerable Master Hua

"THE PRACTICE OF BEING HARD-TO-OBTAIN"

Day 7.

Swift mountains of air pounding empty space to bits. After seven days we've learned to cope this way:

1) Cook inside the car;
2) brush the layers of dirt from the Sutras, the eyes, the sleeping bags, and the toothbrushes;
3) exercise in field culverts and cement rain ducts;
4) meditate in a ship-at-sea rocking motion as the gusts wash over the Plymouth;
5) endure constant nervous tension, struggle back to the car's shelter after a bout with the blow, look at each other's raccoon-mask, dust-ringed faces and say "whew!";
6) relieve nature in a jar, then dash outside to dump it in the tall grass, then rinse it from the plastic water jugs wedged beneath the car bottom and the rutted ground. Don't drop the jug cap or the wind whisks it over the cliff instantly;
7) we do not stop. We bow and the wind speaks the Dharma for us.

For example, the BI LAN (毗藍) wind Shakes the entire earth, The Buddha's field of blessings is like this; Shaking all beings in the three existences.

The Bodhisattvas Ask for Clarification Chapter, Avatamsaka Sutra

Day 8.

After lunch as I reviewed our instructions, I found
this teaching:

> *In this life our job is to know contentment.*
> *Then we cast out afflictions all at once.*
> *Strike me and I'll kneel right down;*
> *I only laugh, don't know how to cry..."*
>
> One should learn to be a Big Dummy,
> Then one's uniqueness can emerge.

> Venerable Master Hua

This wind-week in Big Sur is my training ground for
changing into the Big Dummy. Wind gusts strike us left and
right with every bow. Do I have the skill to "only laugh
and not cry?" This is the place to learn. Nearly overlooked a great opportunity!
The afternoon's bowing passed quickly. My heart was
full of laughter at my foolish attachments to the Self. Our
eight-day ordeal became a rare test, a special chance to
grow and to truly change. The wind is a Good Knowing Advisor, come to aid us in blowing away another dusty layer
of Self.

HENG CH'AU, June 20, 1978
Tuesday

Heavy winds continue to pound from the sea. Our bowing
pace is broken and slower, but we bow the same no matter
the weather.

*   *   *   *   *

Two men stop and ask,
"What are you?"
"Buddhists."
"Oh, that's great! You both look so tranquil we had
to stop and find out." they said.

*   *   *   *   *

> The one with wisdom contemplates:
> That everything is impermanent.
> All dharmas are empty, they have no self,

And never do they have any marks.

> The Bodhisattva Asks for
> Clarification Chapter,
> Avatamsaka Sutra

Twigs and dust swirls, bugs and birds go flying by in winds at 50-60 m.p.h. as we bow, juxtaposed in slow motion as in a separate time/space zone. Inside, thoughts of life, memories, and random flotsam fly through my mind without a track or trace like the rustling leaves and passing cars outside. Truly, it's all impermanent.

In none of it is there a place to hold on or stake a claim. The earth itself is like a dry ocean--swirling, rolling, floating, never at rest or quiet. Why be so serious and out for oneself? This life is a dream, the world's like an echo. Success and fame, wealth and honor, family and future plans, are just the shadows on the ground from passing clouds. Why chase shadows and get so uptight? Smile, let it all go, ride the wind and benefit the world.

> *Also it is like the unified nature of wind*
> *Which blows upon all things.*
> *But the wind itself has not a single*
> *thought;*
> *And all Buddhadharmas are the same.*

> The Bodhisattva Asks for
> Clarification Chapter,
> Avatamsaka Sutra

HENG CH'AU, June 21, 1978
Wednesday

"RILEY"

He stood with his back and shoulders pinched against the cold gusts blowing in from sea, hands stuffed in pants pockets, face wide open like a child's. His shining, sleek, new car was pulled up alongside our dull, sun-blanched wagon. The dirt and dust whipped in swirling clouds on our highway pulloff. I was doing lunch clean-up as Heng Sure bowed. Shivering in a thin floral print shirt slapping in the wind, the man stood between us, looking back and forth, hesitant, but inexhorably drawn and held by something.

Slowly he came over, as if tip-toeing into church late.

"Excuse me, I don't mean to disturb your practice but, would it be possible just to ask who you are and what you're doing?" he asked. He said his name was Riley.

I began explaining the pilgrimage and when I said that we were Buddhists, he interrupted me, full of excitement, as if a dam had broke inside.

"Buddhists, Buddhists,,,Buddha, the Buddha. Oh wow!" he exclaimed, now obviously unable to contain his emotions.

"Listen, I was in prison for five years and I read a book called *Zen Flesh, Zen Bones*. It was full of parables and they really talked to me deep inside. It got me through and was the best friend I ever had. I read it over and over, day after day," said Riley.

"But you're Americans--Caucasians," he said.

"Buddhism doesn't have one country or a people..." I began.

"Or one language, or a color or race," Riley added. "It's in the heart, in the mind, right?"

"Right. The Dharma belongs to everyone." I said. He threw up his hands and his voice pitched to vibrato, "Oh, oh, ohhh...!"

"Then you *know* that book!?" he asked, his voice quivering with enthusiasm, tears coming to his eyes.

"Sure," I said.

He broke into tears and wanted to hug me.

"And so here I was speeding by on my way to L.A. and I saw you bowing...and, listen: I've seen Christians, Krishnas, Muslims, Jews, and some no one's ever heard of, but I've never seen anything like this!" He wiped the tears from his eyes, shaking with emotion.

"What I read in that book, it's true, and here you are. I can't tell you what this means to me. You have no idea"-- the tears are rolling down his cheeks again--"It belongs to everyone and it's everywhere," he kept saying, with a face full of joy and light.

> *His faith and understanding are most vast and great.*
> *His resolutions and inclinations too, are pure.*
> *Intent upon the search for a Buddha's wisdom,*
> *He brings forth this thought unsurpassed.*
>
> Ten Grounds Chapter,
> Avatamsaka Sutra

Through the suffering of five years in prison and disappointing years of searching after, Riley never abandoned his faith. He heard the Dharma like it is and knew that the Buddha wasn't apart from his own heart. He knew that *real* Buddhism wasn't just for Asians or Indians or the religion of people who lived centuries ago. He knew Buddhism could be opened up within his own mind. He knew the *real* Dharma wasn't confined to books, to temples, or even to this world. He knew that he could become a Buddha. But he never dared express this faith, this dream. He carried it hidden in his heart like the little book of Buddhist parables he kept in his cell in jail.

Then when he saw two Buddhist monks bowing right before his eyes on California State Highway I in the 20th century, everything burst open inside. He left trembling and full of something he couldn't find words for. His eyes were big and bright as crystal platters.

"You have no idea what this means to me...no idea." He held my hand, smiling and crying. "You have no idea."

> *If one hears the Dharma like it is,*
> *That all Buddhas are born from it,*
> *Although one might pass through*
> *   measureless suffering,*
> *He will never abandon the practices of*
> *   enlightenment.*
>
> *Praises in the Tushita Heaven*
> *Palace Chapter,*
> *Avatamsaka Sutra*

* * * * *

Windstorm into its fifth day. A constant, 24-hour blast that doesn't subside for a second. More than the rain or the cold, more than the blistering heat or the drought, the wind is nature's meanest streak. A howling windstorm can rattle one's nerves and punish the body unlike any of the other elements. And yet from a passing car or looking out from behind a living room window, the wind appears harmless, innocuous. You've got to live in the wind to feel its sting and respect its power. Only direct and prolonged exposure brings an awareness that the wind can make your body sick, drain your strength, exhaust your humor, and mess up your psyche. There is only one way to bow in hard and heavy winds: softly. There is only one way to survive living outside, walking the roads: yielding.

Truly, what is hard and stiff is the companion

*of death; what is soft and weak is the companion
of life...That the yielding conquers the resistant and the soft conquers the hard is a fact
known by all men, yet utilized by none.*

--Lao Tzu

Five days of no control. The wind is boss, not man.
The way of people is harmony; opposition only courts disaster. Either we let go and relax or the weather turns us into
casualties.
A soft and yielding attitude overcomes all obstacles
without the slightest force or effort. "Soft and weak" we
can bow in the winds for hours without fatigue. But with
a "hard and stiff" mind that fights the wind and calls it
a hassle, we burn out in a matter of minutes.
Patience thrives on opposition and difficulty. Our best
understandings and clearest moments come after bitter suffering; the most peaceful, deeply joyful times follow renunciation and enduring what couldn't be endured.
The wind pounds and batters the body, but inside it
speaks a soft and quiet Dharma to the mind. It says,

"Let go, release your hold. There's nothing
to win, so why do you struggle and contend?
There is no you, so who is the wind beating upon?
Happy and content is the Going Nowhere One. The
wind is unobstructed, why aren't you?

*As a strong, swift wind
Whips along unobstructed,
So too does the Buddhadharma
Quickly pervade the world.*

*Entering the Dharma Realm,
Avatamsaka Sutra*

HENG CH'AU, June 22, 1978
Thursday

Near Pt. Sur Lighthouse: Dreamed last night I visited
the City of 10,000 Buddhas. Coming around a corner of
an inner courtyard, I encountered an awesome and lordly
being. A bright, pulsing light (like a soft welder in intensity), blazed forth from this one's forehead. In one
hand he/she held Amitabha Buddha, in the other hand, Kuan

Yin Bodhisattva. I was overwhelmed by the strength and purity of this great being and stood staring up, dumbstruck and humbled by such a display of virtue and spiritual presence. "Who is this? Who is this? Does anybody know?" I asked. But no one answered.

* * * * *

Windstorm now into 6th day. Lots of false thoughts about sleep, food, shelter and the like. The mind that seeks to control things is working overtime. A situation of helplessness and external anarchy throws the mad mind into a high gear of grabbing, discriminating, planning, arranging, scheming and dreaming. In the "Brahma Conduct Chapter" of the *Avatamsaka*, Dharma Wisdom Bodhisattva says that the workings of the ordinary mind are not pure Brahma conduct.

> *If the mind were Brahma conduct, then Brahma Conduct would have to be perception, observation, discrimination, various kinds of discriminations and considerations; various kinds of considerations, illusions, slumber and dreams.*

Facing the truth of no self, the truth of impermanence, the truth of the still and empty nature of all things, the busy mind fights back with thoughts. Thoughts of clocks and cookies, comfort and clothes, thoughts of the past and future, the starting line-up of the 1957 Milwaukee Braves World Series team and the name of my morning kindergarten teacher. I review my life, screened through a half-dozen fantasy motifs, with its petty triumphs, bantam defeats and tall dreams of who I was, might have been, or am going to be. But the wind is unrelenting and keeps bringing me face to face with the here and now. A thousand feelings come and go but none of them mesh with the Way or hit that elusive spot inside beyond all feelings.

> *If the actions of the mind were Brahma Conduct, then one should know that Brahma Conduct would be thoughts, and feeling, cold or hot, hungry or thirsty, miserable or happy, worried or pleased.*

> > Brahma Conduct Chapter,
> > Avatamsaka Sutra

Thoughts and feelings are as empty and hard to get at

as the wind. The elements wear us down by day, the Sutra
rebuilds us by night.

> All dharmas are without a self...
> All dharmas have no dwelling.
> No fixed location can be obtained.
> All Buddhas dwell in this place
> And ultimately they do not move.
>
> Praises in the Suyama Heaven,
> Avatamsaka Sutra

How is it then? Miserable, endless hardships out here?
Not at all. We have never known such happiness. The false
breaks and buckles, the true springs back like the green
grass pushing up through the concrete highway. Our pretensions and coverings crumble and give way each day, in every
bow to something more glad and mysterious than words or
thoughts could ever guess. We fall asleep worn out and full
of wonder.

> I give rise to happiness because I have turned
> away from and left behind all worldly states...I
> give rise to happiness because I draw near the
> grounds of wisdom.
>
> Ten Grounds Chapter,
> Avatamsaka Sutra

HENG CH'AU, Friday June 23, 1978 and
Saturday June 24, 1978

Windstorm continues outside, greed storm howls and blows
inside. Here are some rough notes from an internal 2-day
battle with greedy desire:
Food.

When eating, guard the mind against trans-

gressions, of which greed is the foremost.

—from the Vinaya for Daily Use, "Meal Contemplations"

The Abbot asked the assembly last month in L.A., "How is it then, do we eat to live, or do we live to eat? "We eat to live and live for the sake of,

'Having merit with regard to the world,
Having virtue with respect to the people,
Benefitting the four continents under
heaven.'

We eat to live, We live to cultivate and to benefit the world. Eating with a mind of greed benefits no one under heaven, and creates a mountain of offense-karma. So severe is the retribution for eating out of greed that the Bodhisattva Precepts in *The Brahma Net Sutra* state,

I resolve that I would rather my tongue were cut out by one hundred thousand knives than ever taste the various flavors of pure food with a mind in violation of the Precepts.

—from the Thirty-Sixth Minor Precept

Today I ate "with a mind in violation of the precepts." I savoured the flavor and bathed my tongue in the texture. The manner in which I ate and the defiled after effects, approached mentally breaking the precepts against taking intoxicants. The acts themselves were different of course, but the mind was the same—greedily seeking pleasure and sensation, purely selfish gratification, and escape. The food was cookies and sugar-sweetened yogurt, but the offense was my attitude. I moved.

When the six organs move
One is covered by clouds.

A cloud of affliction-dust fogged me in all afternoon. Bowing was turbid, heavy, and scattered. The *Avatamsaka* says all disasters and evils in the world are caused by greed and attachment to the five desires (food, fame, wealth, sex, and sleep). Another lesson learned the hard way.

* * * * *

Our cultivation is greatly enhanced when we are silent
and sparing with food and clothes. Simplicity and few desires smooth away anger. Patience comes effortlessly like
a gentle rain, and obstacles seem to melt by themselves. Our
bodies travel lighter, our minds are clearer and farther.
When the body is subdued and the heart made straight, then
without seeking, the Way opens and grows。

* * * * *

"Eating and drinking less to avoid
ghostly visitations."

Yesterday's indulgence in dairy products and sugar
brought ghostly visitations in dreams last night. State of
mental harrassment continued all A.M. bowing--little nagging,
demon-voices harping on about good food, rich flavors, and
getting "high" again on greed at lunch. As I firmly said "no"
to them in my mind, a car sped by out of control and wiped
out into the guard-rail behind me. A frustrated demon, maybe? Missed by inches taking me over the side with it. (or
maybe meant to scare the demon away?)
     A few minutes later a kind family of Dharma-protectors
showed up with a meal offering.
     "Today, just simple, light food. Not too much. No
sugar or flavors. Huh? OK?" said the donor with a cheerful,
understanding smile.
     How could these folks have known? We talked to no one,
sent no messages, but here they were with the perfect anti-
dote to food-greed poisoning and an uptight mind. Ate a
bowl of rice and water-boiled vegetables, a banana and 1/2
grapefruit. We get by with a little help from our friends.
Someone is certainly looking after us. Clear and worry-
free afternoon of bowing, demons gone, mind peaceful.

*When people eat a lot, it strengthens their
desire. And when desire is strong, demons run
rampant. However, if you decrease your intake
of food and drink, if you eat less, you will not
have so many eerie things happen to you.*

--Master Hua

* * * * *

Renewed resolves to reduce and regulate food, clothes, sleep and words. Food: eat for fuel, not for flavor. Eat one simple, mindful meal a day before noon as the Buddha recommended. Clothes: dress for warmth, not for plumage. Don't seek the best, don't discard the old and crave the new. Sleep: less than 6 hours, never lie down, no naps. Words: "Manifest a body to speak the Dharma." Write and speak true words, important words. Empty tin cans rattle the loudest. Don't rattle on. Transfer the merit and virtue; seek nothing for yourself. When others are happy, so am I; when others get what they want, so do I.

> The Bodhisattva equally contemplates all beings just as if they were his own children. He wants all to get a body which is purely adorned and to accomplish the world's supreme peace and happiness, the happiness of the Buddha's wisdom, to peacefully dwell in the Buddhadharma and to be of benefit to all beings...When he gives he takes his good roots and transfers like this...
>
> Ten Transferences Chapter,
> Avatamsaka Sutra

Immediately after making these resolves, desire thoughts filled my mind like the wind fills a ship's sails. Greed for forms, sounds, smells, tastes, things to touch—-rose uncontrollably. I found myself looking at people in passing cars, staring off at the beaches and mountains, smelling fragrances, craving hearty teas and sweet juices. Then came anger.

> From limitless aeons past until the present we have accumulated uncountable states of mind in the field of our eighth consciousness. Sitting quietly allows these states to come forth in a way that they can be recognized, just like the moons reflection can be seen in still water.
>
> Tripitaka Master Hua,
> Dharma Talks

The serene Big Sur countryside disfigured before my eyes, marred and vandalized by my thoughts of greed and anger. Although I couldn't purge the poison within, I was determined not to shoot it out or give in to this state. We have found

that the key to turning states is to hold your ground and keep
the light inside--to wait out the fire in full lotus, alone,
determined, and with a patience that never heard of quitting.
Fall asleep to a dream of a beautiful temptress who made
advance after advance. I was emphatic and said "no." Finally,
she turned into a grappling beast and attacked me. We fought
and wrestled all night. Woke up bruised, with sore and aching
muscles. She (it) finally left.

> Don't look at states of mind as true or false.
> Working hard is true. When untaught folks who
> lack this understanding encounter a state they
> are delighted and think they have become enlightened,
> or dread they have been attacked by demons. Don't
> hold on to fear or joy. Don't become attached to
> anything, and you will reach a state of real ac-
> complishment.

> Tripitaka Master Hua,
> Dharma Talks

Slowly we are making headway. The craggy, high, rocky
cliffs and wild shoreline of Big Sur capture the feeling of
the mind ground we covered: "wilderness."

> Wilderness, in contrast with those areas where
> man and his own works dominate the landscape, is...
> an area where the earth and its community of life
> are untrammeled by man, where man himself is a
> visitor who does not remain.

> --from Wilderness Act of
> 1964

We are 10 or 15 miles south of Carmel Highlands, but
already one can feel the tendrils of civilization reaching
out to dominate the landscape, "man and his words" trying
to erase the wordless writing of nature that boldly states,
"man himself is a visitor who does not remain!"
We emerge from the wilderness eating smaller portions
and no sweets; talking less and bowing longer. We feel strong
and healthy, younger, older, cleaner and smaller. Posture
and carriage are more erect, backbone more solid, and our resolve and vigor for the Way grow by the day. Reducing desire
is the door to liberation.

> In a world that's upside-down and full of
> attachments,

May the one with thoughts of permanence,
    bliss, true self and purity,
And the wisdom eye who can leave all this
Disclose for me the door of liberation!

Pure and clear like empty space,
With love and views extinguished,
There is benefit for all beings:
May I ride upon this carriage!

Entering the Dharma Realm,
Avatamsaka Sutra

* * * * *

Day's end...
John, a young man with a pack on his back, found us bowing up a long, steep switchback road carved on the side of a mountain. The wind was blowing heavy; hundreds of feet below, the blue sea shimmered and frothed with white-caps and wind-wrinkles.

John was driving the motorcycle in an accident that occurred in Ventura. Heng Sure and I were the first people on the scene. Cindy, his fiance, was killed and he barely survived. The ill effects showed. John limped, wore a protective plastic hat and still looked in shock. He sat huddled against his pack on the other side of our Plymouth, unnerved by the gusting wind and afraid of the passing cars. He was carrying a load of guilt, blame, fear, and grief. He stuttered now, too.

"I been looking for you for months," he said. "I set out on foot and kept on your trail, asking folks along the way. You're not easy to find."

I'm not sure what John wanted. I don't think he himself knew. He seemed to feel better when we told him that he tried to get up and help his friend after the collision, and that we didn't blame him for her death.

"I'm still together with Cindy in the heavens" he said, trembling. John had a ghost riding on his shoulders and per-haps that's why he stopped--to see if we could help him shake it.

He peered into the car at a picture of the Abbot as we told him,

"It's all over now. Everything's okay. Be happy." A slight smile came to his face, and a weight of darkness lifted off his back.

"Thanks." he said. Shook hands and headed back home.

* * * * *

92

Two Japanese travellers stopped to take photos and to
tape an interview for a Tokyo newspaper. The woman said she
was the daughter of a Soto Zen Priest. They were courteous
and to the point. Made an offering and wished us well.
"This is what Daruma did!" said the woman. They·half-
bowed and left.

* * * * *

"DOOR TO LIBERATION"

*They dwell in the universal boundary,
and they enter the limits of reality.*

*Entering the Dharma Realm,
Avatamsaka Sutra*

Car is parked on narrow, steep ledges etched into the
side of the nearly perpendicular mountains. At night we
prop it up with rocks and timbers under the tires to level
it off. The car groans and shakes all night in strong winds,
perched on the edge of the highway, pushed to the limits
of its own reality.

Each day we too approach our own edge, our own reality
limit. The falseness and phoniness gets honed away by the
bowing, the silence, the solitude. Our minds and bodies
are poised on a thin edge at the boundary of self and what
belongs to self, much like the car, precariously balanced
on boulders hundreds of feet above the sea. The Master's
words come to mind as I gazed up at the stars after checking
the car-tire placements once more before going to sleep.

*Be careful in everything you do,
Every step you take be true.
...Vigor, be more vigorous.
Patience, patience, do not rest.*

HENG CH'AU, June 25, 1978
Sunday
Heavy winds persist. In ancient Chinese medicine the
wind is referred to as "the cause of a hundred-fold ill-
nesses." Our experiences support this "old-fashioned" notion. Once we started wrapping up in hats and scarves, especially keeping the head, neck, and extremities out of
direct wind exposure, we eliminated a host of ailments that
descended on us nearly every time a wind came up. Even
on seemingly warm, sunny days like Spring or Indian
Summer we bundled up, as these winds proved to be the most

deceptive and debilitating. A cold, flu, or fever brought
on by the wind can set in a few hours and stubbornly linger
for weeks. "An ounce of prevention is worth a pound of
cure." No joke.

Some people figured we keep warm with the car heater,
but in our car, the only equipment that works is the engine,
and it only works when it has a mind to. Once we get wet,
cold, or sick, we stay wet, cold, or sick. Out here there's
no place to hot shower and warm up. We learned fast after
a foolhardy attempt to chest-beat our way through the first
winter storm last year. Luckily we found an all-night laundromat in a small seaside village or we might have contracted
a good case of pneumonia and ended the pilgrimage before
wearing out our first pair of shoes.

Living outside instills common sense and deep respect
for the fragile gift of life. The teachings of Nature begin
as punishment, but soon soften into gentle reminders. Its
rigors and restrictions yield a special liberation, and in
its own simple way, Nature bestows a kind of enlightenment
to those who learn to bend and endure. Walking the Path is
the same way.

* * * * *

"A.M. BOWING THOUGHTS ON THE 'ONE GREAT MATTER'"

My first encounter with Buddhism was three words: "Existence is suffering." I didn't want to believe it, yet I
could not deny it. Birth, old age, sickness, and death unfold one after the other, strung together by uninterrupted
pain. From our first breath to our last, if we aren't suffering outright, we are inescapably aware that it's just
around the corner. Man is perhaps the only animal who knows
he is going to die, and also the only one who pretends he is
not.

*Ordinary people lack wisdom. They are at-
tached to Self, and constantly seek its existence or non-existence. They don't look at
things correctly. Giving rise to false practices they walk down deviant roads.*

*Ten Grounds Chapter,
Avatamsaka Sutra*

Living outside instills common sense and deep respect for the gift of life. The teachings of Nature begin as punishment but soon soften into gentle reminders.

A case in point of "not looking at things correctly," is this remark by a modern philosopher, "there is no cure for birth and death, save to enjoy the interval." Pure rubbish! The Buddha spells it out so clearly:

Birth and death from thoughts are made;

When thoughts stop, birth and death are ended.
When ignorance is the condition, suffering can't
   be stopped.
Ending the condition (ignorance), then suffering is all over.

                    Ten Grounds Chapter,
                    Avatamsaka Sutra

   Thoughts means false thoughts. They refer to ignorance.
What is ignorance? Ignorance is trying to "enjoy the interval" between birth and death. Ignorance seeks to end
suffering by increasing suffering.
   Enjoying life isn't the cure to the illness of birth
and death; it is the cause. There is no greater suffering
in this world than the emptiness that comes from trying to
enjoy life. Pleasure never ends in satisfaction, it only
brings more longing and keeps the big wheel turning.

   ...Feeling never satisfied is craving. When
craving grabs hold and one cannot let go, this
is grasping. With the arisal of these branches
there is existence. Birth in turn, arises from
existence. Birth ripens into old age. Old age
degenerates and there is death.

                    Ten Grounds Chapter,
                    Avatamsaka Sutra

   Is life hopeless suffering then? Are we simply born
to die and die only to be born again? Then death isn't
liberation from suffering, it's just a change of locale.
And life isn't a victory over death, merely a postponement.
   Birth and death are a revolving door in the middle of
a prison--no matter where you enter or exit you are always
behind bars. Cultivating the Path is the only way to break
out and forever escape.

   I cause all beings to cultivate the Path
   that can put an end to birth and death.

                    Entering the Dharma Realm,
                    Avatamsaka Sutra

   The "interval in between" is our only chance to get free
and find a cure for suffering. If we waste this precious

opportunity enjoying ourselves, then isn't this too pitiful? Isn't this to live drunk and die in a dream? Each day our life is shorter. We are like fish in an evaporating pond. And for this one great matter, to teach us to make our escape, the Buddha appears in the world.

> *Smashing completely all existences and the*
> *wheel of birth and death,*
> *Turning the pure Dharma Wheel,*
> *Unattached in all the world,*
> *He teaches this to all Bodhisattvas.*

> *Ten Dwellings Chapter,*
> *Avatamsaka Sutra*

The Master always exhorts us, "Don't let this time go by in vain." What time is he referring to? Right now!

* * * * *

> *No one saves us but ourselves,*
> *No one can and no one may.*
> *We ourselves must walk the path.*
> *Buddhas merely show the Way.*

> *--from the Dhammapada*

A.M. bowing, "waiting for Godot." Wake up, what are you waiting for? Return the light, illumine within; seek the fullness of yourself. If we are waiting for someone else to save us, or waiting for wisdom to magically fall from the sky like mana fell in the Old Testament, we have a *long* wait.

I don't believe the people who tell us, "Oh, you don't have to do anything. Jesus did it all. Just believe in Jesus and you're guaranteed salvation. Nothing you could do will make any difference."

Nothing in life works that way. If we followed the logic of that principle in eating everyday, we would have starved to death long ago.

> *As one who prepares succulent treats*
> *And he himself is starving to death but does*
> *   not eat,*
> *When one does not cultivate the Dharma,*
> *Mere study is just like this.*

Bodhisattva Asks for Clarification Chapter,
Avatamsaka Sutra

My first months as a novice earned a round scolding
from the Abbot for being lazy. The words stung, but were
a true gift.

In cultivation, don't worry that you
don't have an understanding. Only fear
being lazy. If you don't understand, that's
not important, but if you don't cultivate,
then you're useless.

HENG CH'AU, June 26, 1978
Monday

Cold, foggy, windy morning bowing on a pull-off. A
station wagon pulls up and out hops a troupe of circus jug-
glers, all decked-out in light-colored tights, sequinned
slippers, capes, and court jester floppy hats. They respectfully offer fresh flowers and then the leader takes off his
hat, crosses it in front with a grand sweep and a deep bow,
and says,
"And now!" he announces like the ring master, "we are
going to juggle for you, 'cause that's what we do best."
And juggle they did. While Heng Sure and I bowed they
flipped and tossed striped balls and star-spangled white
bowling pins over our heads, past our ears and all around
us. "Hip...hup...hup." They shouted in between the clip-
clop, clip-clop rhythmic sounds of the balls and pins, plates
and rings going from hand to hand. When finished, they
smartly snapped together in front of us, bowed and skipped
away into the fog again.

*   *   *   *   *

The wind blew hard all day matching my restless mind.
Finally, in the last half-hour of bowing, I found a little
peace inside--a sunlit meadow, clearing in a thick, dark
woods. Then I noticed the wind had subsided, too. A con-
nection or coincidence? Or maybe because I was concentrating I didn't notice what the wind was doing. The sentence
that calmed my mind was,

98

> *When you reach the place of seeking nothing,*
> *then your troubles vanish.*

We did transference of merit as the sun slipped through
the crack between the sea and the sky. "So that calamities, disasters, and suffering be eradicated from the
Dharma Realm," we contemplated in silence. I then saw that
eradicating my own seeking and worries was the same as eradicating disasters and suffering from the world. The
Dharma Realm is all things, all time, all places. It is
one and we all are it. There is no me.
And right at that moment a passage from the *Avatamsaka*
came into my mind. Ever since first hearing it I couldn't
penetrate its meaning. For weeks I was unable to get it
out of my mind, nor could I make it fit. Now something
clicked and it fell as effortlessly into place as the sun
sinking below the horizon. The passage was,

> *He vows that all beings skillfully enter the*
> *level-equality of all dharmas and understand*
> *that the Dharma Realm and the self-nature are*
> *non-dual.*

> Ten Transferences Chapter,
> Avatamsaka Sutra

* * * * *

When we are not bowing we constantly recite the Great
Compassion Mantra. The mantra has become a close and trusted friend. Wherever we go it goes too, and guides us
through the darkest, strangest, and most difficult places.
The Mantra is a path through the wilderness, a life line at
sea, a ferry boat to the other shore. Whenever I get lost
or weak and weary, the Great Compassion Mantra comes through
like the sun which no storm can move or change--strong,
constant, and dependable.

> *World Honored One, I have a Great Compassion*
> *Dharani-mantra which I now wish to speak so*
> *that all living beings might obtain peace and*
> *delight, be rid of every sickness, and attain*
> *long life; so that they might obtain prosperity,*
> *wipe away the evil karma of heavy offenses,*
> *separate themselves from obstacles and hard-*
> *ships, grow in all the pure dharmas and in every*
> *kind of merit and virtue...*

*The Dharani Sutra, BTTS
Publication, p. 23*

This A.M. my meditation entered a state of chaos, a
dark, twisted forest with no exit. "Stay calm, relax," said
my Good Advisor within, "don't seek and you won't be worried.
Recite the Great Compassion Mantra." So I did. I let go
like a small, trusting child in the arms of a kind parent.
I let myself become the sounds of the mantra. Suddenly I
was stepping lightly along a sunlit arbor-tunnel out of the
murkey, tangled woods, pulled along by the mantra's power
and a refreshing wind. The more sincerely I recited, the
brighter and easier became the path. My fears vanished and
I felt as "dried-up wood is touched by Spring."

*...so that they might create only good roots,
become separate from fear, and quickly fulfill
all their longings. World Honored One, please
be merciful and allow it to be heard.*

Ibid.

I had the thought to keep reciting the mantra even
though I was safely out, so that others could find their
way.

*...with respect to all beings, they should
give rise to a heart of equality, reciting the
mantra constantly, without interruption.*

Ibid, p. 49

The magic and kindness of the mantra is inexhaustible
and boundless. Its compassion puts living beings at ease.
I experienced the mantra as a great assembly of kind and
deeply wise,holy beings, uniting into a vast, spiritual river. The river twisted and wound throughout the ten
directions, unhindered by time or space, picking up and
crossing over countless living beings to peace and happiness.
All we had to do was recite with a single mind and the magic
river appeared to carry us away to another land of joy and
light.

*...World Honored One, if humans and gods
recite and hold the phrases of the Great Compassion Mantra, then when they approach the
end of life, all the Buddhas of the ten direc-*

*tions will come to take them by the hand to re-
birth in whatever Buddhaland they wish, according
to their desire.*

Ibid, p. 30

P.S. The vow power and compassion of Gwan Yin at all times
reaches out to help and support us. This is called "other's
power." But unless the individual reciprocates and extends
himself to unite with Gwan Yin with "self power," the Way
and response can't intertwine. The key is to enter a state
of proper concentration and proper reception, that is, sincere
singleminded recitation of the mantra or Gwan Yin's name,
with no extraneous thoughts. So it's said,

In singlemindedness there is efficacy,
But when you are scattered, there is nothing.

One's own power is often insufficient to generate a
response. The kind, protective, and caring power of Buddhas
and Bodhisattvas is unable to reach us if we are scattered
or insincere. But when the two powers can combine, it is
wonderful beyond words and can enter the inconceivable. Thus
the *Dharani Sutra* stresses,

*...you should recite my name with a sincere
heart and also recite singlemindedly the name
of my teacher, the Thus Come One, Amitabha...*

Ibid, p. 29

and also,

*...They should regulate their minds to one
point, with no other conditions, and recite
and hold the mantra in accord with Dharma. At
that time Sunlight Bodhisattva and Moonlight
Bodhisattva, along with numberless spirits and
immortals, will come to certify and to increase
the efficacy of the recitation.*

Ibid, p. 49

HENG CH'AU, June 27, 1978
Tuesday

Narrow mountain road hanging like a piece of Christmas tree tinsel on the side of sheer cliffs that plunge straight down into the sea hundreds of feet below. The road was built for Model-T's and slower times. Times have changed but the road's the same. Two R.V. campers can't pass side by side and stay on the road. The shoulder is at best two tire-widths wide and often non-existent. People, afraid to get out of their cars to look down, steal cautious glances from rolled-down windows, while tightly gripping their safety-seat belts. Occasionally a courageous soul stops to take pictures with one foot still inside the car. No one goes for a walk.

And yet what in this vast universe is solid and secure? Where's the center? What is the railing attached to or the highway resting upon? Nothing but thin air and an ocean of dust motes.

At that time within the Jeta Grove, the Great Assemblies of Bodhisattvas saw that within all Buddha kshetras pervading the Dharma Realm and the realm of empty space--in every single dust mote-- were Buddha lands as many as dust motes in all Buddha Kshetras.

Entering the Dharma Realm,
Avatamsaka Sutra

Countries within dust motes to the number of dust motes. The solid ground we are standing on is just a mote of dust floating in the cosmos. And within that mote of dust are further countless billions of worlds of motes of dust, loosely and temporarily held together by the wind of gravity. Underneath our feet is a molten sea of liquid and gas.

The center is no-center. We find our roots and foundation in the "unattached, unbound, liberated mind"--the true home of all living beings. Inside the nucleus of a single cell of our body is a tiny speck too small to see with a microscope. Scientists call it a gene. Within this "dust mote" gene is the potential to reproduce the entire human race--people as many as motes of dust in all the world. We are right now living in the middle of the inconceivable and miraculous and all around us the whole world is constantly speaking the *Flower Adornment Sutra*. And so,

The vast and great can enter
where there is no place.

102

*Dust motes and hairs envelope
with nothing left outside.*

Avatamsaka Preface

* * * * *

Bowing breaks loose whole chunks of the psyche's sediment. Memories and impressions rise up from the bottom of the mind and drift by in richly-detailed tableaus, so distinct and vivid they make the present reality seem like the dreamy past. One's life parades by for inspection--an inventory of accomplishments and failures, victories and defeats. Added up and assessed, it doesn't amount to the mist lifted by the wind from a wave breaking on the shore. Not one worldly thing I sought or obtained ever brought me fulfillment or real happiness. Two sentences from the *Avatamsaka* constantly echo in my mind.

There is not a single dharma that once obtained, provides entry into the Dharma nature.

and,

Of all the happiness in the world, there is none that is not suffering.

Conversely, of all the suffering in cultivation, there is none that isn't happiness. We have never been poorer outside and richer inside. So unsettled, yet so deeply at peace. Why? The Dharma is just that way. Cultivation is the only true thing in the world. It's also invisible. To the passing eye nothing appears to be happening; the common ear catches no sound. The Way is flimsy and faded, hidden and silent, yet it fulfills and nurtures all things.

*If one looks for the Way, there is nothing
    solid to see.
If one listens for it, there is nothing loud
    enough to hear.
Yet if one uses it, it is inexhaustible.*

Tao Te Ching

HENG CH'AU, June 28, 1978
Wednesday

This A.M. I saw again that ignorance turns into wisdom naturally when precepts and concentration are sufficient. It does not happen by thinking or trying.

> The Ways of the Thus Come Ones, Great
> Immortals,
> Are subtle, wonderful, and hard to com-
> prehend.
> Not thought, they are apart from every
> thought:
> Those seeking them in seeing can't at-
> tain them.

> Ten Grounds Chapter,
> Avatamsaka Sutra

Our "first thought" instinctive reactions to dangers and tests we meet on the highway prove to be the most telling and true to our actual state. Wisdom and ignorance are total mind-body states, not a question of quick wits or I.Q. deficiencies. However, the state of natural wisdom isn't reached through repression or mere intellectualizing.

> Not thought and leave the path of
> the mind...
> The wise know intellect does not
> reach them.

Only long-term cultivation of precepts and dhyana samadhi turns confusion into enlightenment, the common into the sagely. Long-term, not instant.

When done right we are not even aware it's happening. That's how unconscious and artless this ancient method is.

> If you seek to know the essence of things,
> It takes bitter effort.
> When your skill arrives,
> Then silently the mind penetrates.

> Venerable Master Hua

* * * * *

> The power to subdue all demons.

> Avatamsaka Sutra

> *So demons test you to see if on one hand you*
> *are bowing, while on the other hand, striking*
> *up false thinking. If you pass, okay. If not,*
> *then you'll have to start all over again. If*
> *you do not recognize a situation, then you'll*
> *have to smelt anew.*
>
> > *--Master Hua, instructions*
> > *en route, L.A., 1978*

Demons manifest in many forms. They can appear as
people, ghosts, strange freaks and weirdos, outside, or as
sickness, or as states of your own mind. For example, they
may manifest as "voices of doubt" internally to test your
sincerity and concentration power.

Today while bowing, I heard such doubt voices in my
mind concerning the Buddhadharma and the path to Buddhahood.
I did not decisively cut them off. I half-listened and half-
ignored them. But half-listening opened a crack for a demon
to slip in. Immediately, I lost mindfulness and entered a
daydream state. For an hour or so (a guess, as I lost track
of time, and was totally spaced-out in a trance-like reverie),
my thoughts drifted into a fantasy-movie where I was an
"undercover Bodhisattva" cultivating the Way, but not in robes
and sash--a "maverick monk" without a monastery. In a dream
that night I met nasty demons and suffered a big energy loss.

> *Demons are not necessarily bad. They are your*
> *best Good Knowing Advisors. Why? When Buddhas*
> *retire from their job, they become demons. Demons*
> *want to test you...The more you are tested the*
> *brighter you'll get, until you shine like the Au-*
> *tumn moon. It's like sharpening a knife: demons*
> *rub you until you are sharp and bright.*
>
> > *--Master Hua, instructions*
> > *en route*

The lesson: It's not enough to subdue the body and control
the mouth. One's mind must be solid and pure, too, or you'll
take a loss every time. Cultivation is right at this point:
gather in and guard the mind, don't be lax in thought.
"The mind is dangerous, moreover it is deep," says the *Avatamsaka*. To simply go along with whatever comes into your
mind courts disaster and catches demons. Why? Desire.

*Demon-states come from a particle of desire
or attachment in your own mind which unites with
external conditions and manifests as a demon. The
poison inside unites with the poison outside. Don't
move! Don't move your mind...Act as if they don't
exist.*

> *--Master Hua, instructions
> en route*

P.S. The following day the identical demon-test appeared.
This time I didn't let my mind wander. That night demons
gathered in a dream to have it out with me. But suddenly a
list of my vows materialized in front of me, surrounded by
the awesome might and presence of the Triple Jewel. The demons vanished; peaceful sleep.

*Demons come from selfishness. The root of
all afflictions is desire. At the place of seeking nothing, you have no worries. If you don't
seek anymore, what can the demons do to you? You
have to subdue all the demons.*

> *Master Hua, instructions
> en route; airport conversation,
> 1978*

HENG SURE, June 29, 1978
Thursday

"BIG DUMMY"

I was trained to be #1, to be quick, a go-getter, in
touch, and in charge. No matter the social situation, I
pushed my way towards the top. The result: a big ego, little satisfaction, much greedy contention, and a big desire
for fame. I wish I had dropped the bag of tricks at Gold
Mountain's front gate, but I didn't. It has taken months of
bowing to begin to penetrate this heavy bad habit of fame-
seeking.

*Cultivating until you're like an idiot
is just the wonderful.
Only when your learning approaches stupidity is it truly rare.*

We are learning a new self-image. Being like Big Dummies is not in vogue yet; there are few role-models, but it
feels something like this: no sparkle, no relating, no
charisma, no charm. But *happy*. Happiness is the secret.
The Big Dummy looks more dead than alive. Don't be fooled.
He's busy inside, concentrating his mind on cultivation-
work. He has no time for pleasant social chit-chat. His
dull appearance is not an act, he's fully awake within a
wordless, perfectly-centered world. Without masks, without
pretense, the Big Dummy doesn't contend with others for first
place. He needs nothing, and seeks neither fame nor benefit.

"I heard from my father that when the Venerable Hsu
Lau was asked a question, he usually shut his eyes and didn't
answer. He was always reciting the Buddha's name." said
Laywoman Kuo Wu.

The Big Dummy doesn't worry how he looks, he doesn't
reflect back on himself at all. He's penetrated the illusion
of self, he's resolved to waste not another second in his
walk back home to the Pure Land.

Hard to appreciate, but true in the heart. The world
can use fewer fighters. Nature appreciates her Big Dummies.

> For *it is the way of Heaven not to strive,*
>   *but none-the-less to conquer.*
> *Not to speak, but none-the-less to get an*
>   *answer.*
> *Not to beckon, yet things come to it of*
>   *themselves.*
> *Heaven is like one who says little, yet*
>   *none-the-less has laid his plans.*
>
> Tao Te Ching, #73

By cultivating, we slowly unlearn false ideas of striving for fame. Instead, we learn to value the deeper goodness of yielding, and going slow. Bowing teaches timeless
lessons.

> Fame or one's own self, which matters to one most?
>
> Tao Te Ching, #64

HENG CH'AU, June 29, 1978
Thursday

> *Precepts can open up the foundation for en-*
> *lightenment.*
>
> > Worthy Leader Chapter,
> > Avatamsaka Sutra

Precepts are the "great reversal," the turning around
and heading for the other shore. As each word, thought,
and deed is gathered back and resmelted in the furnace of
morality, the wind and light of the original ground returns.
The noxious vapors scatter and we ascend to the high country,
to the merit and virtue of pure conduct. Just this is ob-
taining the wonderful Wish-fulfilling Pearl. When precepts
are pure then whatever we desire we can get.

> *As by example, in all worlds there is a won-*
> *derful Wish-fulfilling Pearl...If one can always*
> *uphold the precepts, cultivate, and study them,*
> *then one can complete and perfect merit and virtue.*
>
> > Worthy Leader Chapter,
> > Avatamsaka Sutra

* * * * *

BIXBY LANDING, BIG SUR

A soldier offered two red day-packs. They are ideal
for carrying the Sutra, canteen, extra sweatshirt and wind-
breaker while we bow. The bright red color adds a margin
of safety--our bleached and faded sashes and gray robes are
almost invisible to a speeding motorist especially at dusk
or on a gray, foggy morning. Even people who know where we
are and are looking for us have trouble spotting two slow-
motion figures clad in camouflage. The Buddhist Sangha tra-
ditionally wears earth-color tones to represent the Middle
Way which doesn't fall into the extreme views of nihilism or
eternalism. Red belongs to fire and to the south, not to the
Middle. But,if wearing a little red "fire" keeps us from getting run over, then it respects the spirit of the Middle
which is: accord with conditions. Don't fall into emptiness,
don't cling to existence.

108

* * * * *

...life is but a dream.

Dreaming and waking seem only to be different speeds
of the same motor, the mind. Whatever we false think about
and attach to makes waves on the mind's waters. The principle applies equally--asleep or awake. It is just that when
awake, we are too busy to notice the waves. But in sleep,
when our sense organs are allowed to cool off, we get a
fleeting look at a small corner of our mind-ground. "Conscious thought" or "the unconscious," "reality" and "dreams,"
don't describe the mind as much as they reveal our lack of
understanding of our own minds. The mind is always awake and
conscious. It doesn't sleep and is not confined to the body
or any other place or dimension.

> *The mind doesn't dwell in the body.*
> *The body too, does not dwell in the*
> *mind...*
> *The mind is constantly non-dwelling.*
> *Measureless, it is hard to conceive of.*
> *It reveals and manifests all forms*
> *Each of which does not know the others.*

> *Praises in the Suyama Heaven,*
> *Avatamsaka Sutra*

Dreaming is just false thinking while the body takes
a rest--eventually not different from the "upside-down dream
thinking" we do while "awake." The body itself is a borrowed, bio-degradable motel room, but the mind is forever and
all-pervasive. Living beings, the mind, and the Buddha are
the same. We only get glimpses of the Thus Come One because
we close our eyes and forget we are only dreaming. The capacity of the mind is vast and great but we try to confine it
to a small apartment.

> *As is the mind, so too is the Buddha,*
> *And living beings are all the same.*
> *One should know that the Buddha and*
> *the mind*
> *In substance and nature are inexhaus-*
> *tible.*

> *Ibid.*
> *Avatamsaka Sutra*

HENG SURE, June 30, 1978
Friday

"SOME DAYS EMPTY, SOME DAYS FULL"

When I see an empty bowl I vow that living beings will attain ultimate purity and be empty of afflictions.

> Pure Conduct Chapter,
> Avatamsaka Sutra

Kind laywoman works her elbow as she packs our bowls full of white rice. She would be horrified to know she's filled our minds with afflictions, totally the opposite of her intention. Lots of humor here. The laypeople brought a Dharma lecture along with the meal today.

Heng Ch'au and I are subduing our greed for food by eating a regulated amount of food per day. It's a tough practice but we decided our bellies needed strict discipline. The Dharma, however, is not fixed. Real skill calls for flexibility and gentle compliance. Our practice became a big attachment today, a source of false-thinking and confusion.

Being novice cultivators we haven't learned how to accord with situations. It's called "holding a view of restrictive morality," one of the Five Quick Servants. Instead of leading to peace, purity, and happiness, our stiff, fixed ideas of cultivation today brought us grief. The laywoman filled our bowls with rice. Our silence vow prevented the explanation, "Wait! We're eating only a fixed amount, no matter what it is." She doesn't know our practice. She gave us a normal portion of rice and then showed dismay when we refused any other food.

When I see a full bowl I vow that living beings perfect the fullness of all wholesome Dharmas.

> Ibid.

So not only did we not accord and get along with people, but we didn't know to appreciate the good fortune of

simply having a bowl of food to eat. We felt we had it
tough eating only white rice, but at least we got to eat.
In India, mendicant monks ate what appeared in their begging bowls without comment. Some days empty, some days full.
Many people in the world regularly go to bed hungry; we two
rarely eat less than our fill.
  "I don't know how many days in this life I've gone without eating; too many to count," said our teacher.
  Many lessons today.

HENG CH'AU, June 30, 1978
Friday

  More lessons: Don't attach to anything, inside or outside. At all times and in all places return the light to
illumine within.

> *Inside and outside, and in all worlds*
> *The Bodhisattva is attached to none*
>   *of them...*
> *In all countries in every direction,*
> *He relies on nothing and dwells nowhere.*

> *Ten Grounds Chapter,*
> *Avatamsaka Sutra*

  Everything has to be renounced, even private thoughts,
doubts, and desires. The smelting has to be that thorough
and pristine or the Dharma-vessel won't pass the test of
fire. Everything that belongs to self is jettisoned to
speed the inward journey. More than the miles we cover with
our feet, the pilgrimage is the changes we make in our hearts.
Freedom is won by losing, by truly letting go. Leaving home
is a state of mind. When one leaves the "home" of desires,
afflictions and improper views, this is truly leaving home.
I still try to hang on to what I've got until I'm absolutely
certain that what lies ahead is safe and secure. Consequent-
ly, I have one foot in the boat going upstream and the other
foot clinging to the shore. The few times I mustered the
courage to let go and make the "leap of faith" I felt like
a bird leaning on the wind, soaring above the waves.

> *The Buddhadharma is like a big ocean,*
> *Only on faith can we enter it.*

111

Venerable Master Hua,
Water-Mirror Reflections

* * * * *

End of day. A tall, old white-haired man with a long
snowy beard slowly walked around the car a couple of times,
absorbed in thought, scrutinizing every inch of our mobile
Way Place. Then he strolled over to us, folded his hands,
half-bowed reverently and left.
Fresh drinking water, compliments of Pt. Sur Naval Base.
We were on our last few cups--a timely and welcome offering.
This trip is making us appreciate the simple things in life,
like water. I always took water for granted, nothing special. But plain old drinking water is a treasure. We can
go indefinitely without newspapers, meat, coke, T.V., a
bathtub and a bed, but we can't go a day without water. The
Dharma is the same. As an old monk told us,

> A cultivator can go a day without food, a day
> without sleep, a day without warm clothes, but he
> can't go a day without the Dharma.

We were forced to bow 400 times in place on a small
dirt pull-off on the North side of the Rocky Creek Bridge.
The road leading up to the bridge had no shoulder at all,
and we never bow over bridges, so we walked it off and added 10 per cent to cover any missed paces.
During lunch a strange man came out of the bridge. He
looked like a playful Pan, had a genie feel about him, and
the temperament of a fairy-tale pixie.
"Did you know there's a way to get *inside* the bridge?
C'mon, I'll show you," he said, with a mischievous grin,
peeking in the open car door.
"I think *you'll* really enjoy it. Those four pillars
have a secret passage and you can stand inside of them.
C'mon, c'mon," he coaxed with merry eyes and beckoning arms
as he tip-toed backwards to the large stone bridge.
We declined. We don't bow across bridges because they
are said to be inhabited by particularly strange and often
troublesome spirits, and essences (like trolls and goblins
in folklore and popular "myths"). I believe it. Both times
we stopped to rest and eat too close to a bridge, strange
"people" showed up. Last time it was two satyr-type sprites
with an offering of fresh goat's milk. They turned white as

sheets and ran away when we began reciting the Great Compassion Mantra. We didn't even recite aloud--just in our
minds. Today's bridge "elf" appeared at the sign saying "End
of Big Sur," same as when we met the "ocean spirits and mountain weirdos" at the start of Big Sur.

* * * * *

The wind and sea don't cry or laugh. Heaven and earth
don't fear or covet. Why should I then? Rocks and trees,
the great rivers, mountains and deserts all are free of a me.
The things of nature are free of a me and mine. And so should
I, so should I.

*Free of self and what belongs to self, devoid of
knowing and awareness, with no doer and receiver,
like grass and woods, like rocks and walls, and also
like reflections.*

*Ten Grounds Chapter,
Avatamsaka Sutra*

The earth doesn't pause to thank the rain, tall mountain peaks don't obstruct the floating clouds, winter yields
again to Spring without signing any papers. No self is to
be in harmony with the Way; one substance with all things.

Since the start of the pilgrimage, I've had a recurring
dream where an old friend appears as an evil advisor to lead
me and many others down a wrong road, down a path of selfish
desire and pleasure seeking. The road is lined with dark
caves and small, shadowy rooms. He encourages self-expression,
individual freedom, and doing whatever feels good at the moment. Morality, filiality, and common decency are flagrantly
abused and scoffed at. Last night he appeared again, but I
was able to stand up and say "no." I found myself speaking
true principle to his retinue.

Everyone stopped. The dream stopped. People froze and listened, saying, "Right on!" The momentum turned and another night of bacchanalian orgies and rebellion was reversed. It was as if someone turned on the lights at a candle-lit mood dinner party and stopped the music. I know this was a result of bowing in repentance and reform. Otherwise I would never have been able to stand up and stop it in a dream. While bowing that day I had asked for help and made a sincere wish to end this karmic obstruction once and for all. The dream came that very night. The power of repentance and reform is wonderful and deep.

If you can spit it out, then do so. Why chew on your offenses again? With this thought of repentance and reform we reverse and break the mind that constantly remembers evil deeds.

> *Avatamsaka Preface, By*
> *National Master Ch'ing Liang*

* * * * *

Sometimes we reach a point where we feel we can't go on. Faith wavers and it looks like there's no way. Maybe it's the wind or a pounding winter gale. Maybe it's the blazing heat or a bitter cold that cuts to the bone and hangs on day after day. Maybe it's a state of mind, thoughts of doubt, tests of willpower and sincerity more treacherous and gruelling than any of the elements. Today I reached that point, a mental end of the rope. Then out of the clear blue I remembered an incident from childhood in Wisconsin:

During a 5-day snowstorm, a farmer took a lantern and went to check his cows. On the way back from the barn, the wind blew out his light. The drifting snow had covered his tracks. Although the house was less than 75 yards from the barn, he got lost. He walked and walked, then gave up and lay down in a snow drift. They found him the next A.M. frozen to death only a few feet from his back door.

If I stop and lay down in the snowstorm of my mind, I may freeze to death a few feet from my door. A cultivator's door is the mind that never lays down; the thought that dwells nowhere. The single thought to go on when you feel you can't go on anymore releases enough energy to go on forever. The Dharma Wheel ever rolls, the Bodhisattva path is eternal.

In all worlds to the exhaustion of all future time they will dwell in the Bodhisattva

114

Path without fatigue...They produce the Bodhi
mind and never retreat.

Ten Transferences Chapter,
Avatamsaka Sutra

*   *   *   *   *

A Christian "preacher" came out to convert us. I tried
to talk with him, but it was pointless. He was "gone." He
stood on top of a Cal Trans gravel pile, bible under one arm,
the other pointed straight up in the air, shaking and warning. Red face, full of emotion, he didn't even know I was
trying to talk with him. I went back to bow.

Not for an instant do they give rise
to a thought of foolish debate,
But only contemplate all dharmas
as empty and without a self.

Ten Transferences Chapter,
Avatamsaka Sutra

HENG SURE, July 1, 1978
Saturday

Travelling from sunlight to shadow, from bow to bow.
Having no plans is a kind of liberation. Dharma enriches
the heart, fills each space created by reducing excess food,
clothes, sleep, words, thoughts.
Failure and success lose their meaning. Life grows simple, turning in constant change, a never-stopping lesson in
adapting and harmonizing.
Our bowing space, gear, car, even our lives, could all
vanish in the next instant. The gift of life itself is like
a bubble on a pond, like a mirror reflection, like a dream
that's over in a turn of the head. An ancient Worthy said,

If one does not seek the Great Way to
escape the paths of confusion,
Can blessings, nobility, or talents pro-
duce a Great Hero?

One hundred years of life is brief as a
flying spark.
This body lasts no longer than a bubble
on the sea.

Wealth must be put down, it does not belong
    to you.
But offenses truly own us, it's hard to cheat
    on karma.

Reflect within: can stacks of gold heaped
    higher than the hills
Buy off the Ghost of Impermanence when it's
    time to go?"

HENG CH'AU, July 1, 1978
Saturday

"MERIT AND VIRTUE--SEEK WITHIN"

*His wisdom clearly penetrates the ocean of
all dharmas,
And he always feels happy to cultivate the
dharmas that leave ignorance far behind.
Having perfected the accomplishment of merit
and virtue which transcends the world,
He never again cultivates worldly dharmas.*

*Ten Transferences Chapter,
Avatamsaka Sutra*

When I first read this verse one afternoon, sitting on
a sand dune off the highway near the sea, I was nearly moved
to tears. Why? Hard to express. It evoked a deep feeling
of liberation and left me with a vista of a new road opening
before me--a pure road leading out of the triple world. I
also knew shame and remorse for wasting so many years of my
life on trifles and pursuing worldly dharmas.
"But what is merit and virtue?" I asked myself. The
term appears repeatedly in the Sutras, Shastras, and in our
en route teaching from the Master. He told us, "How should
we conduct ourselves? Our attitude should be,

'Having merit with regard to the world,
Having virtue with respect to the people,
Greatly benefitting the four continents
under heaven.'"

Establishing merit and cultivating virtue is the purpose
of being a person and the foundation for becoming a Sage.
The pivotal point in all three schools of ancient Chinese
thought was the instilling and refining of virtue. Confucius, in the *Great Learning*, calls virtue the pinnacle of
education and the root of everything else besides.

*The Tao of the Great Learning lies in illu-
mining oneself with radiant virtue; renovating the
people; and dwelling in the highest goodness...Cul-
tivating the person is the root of all things...*

Confucius held that just as riches adorn the house, so does
virtue adorn the person. And, therefore,

> *The superior person first and foremost
> takes pains about his own virtue.*

Mencius maintained that all men were endowed by nature with the virtuous qualities of the Sage. "All things are already complete within us," he said, and "Sages differ from common people only in that they don't squander their endowment. Seek and you will find, but neglect it and you'll lose it." So Mencius stressed,

> *The path of virtue should be pursued without
> turning back and without a thought for reward.*

> *The wise embrace all knowledge, but they are
> most earnest about what is important. The humane
> embrace all in their benevolence, but what they con-
> sider of the greatest importance is to cultivate an
> earnest regard for the virtuous.*

> *He who rises at cock crowing and diligently
> applies himself to the practice of virtue is a
> disciple of Shun.*

Lao Tzu, in titling his most famous work, the *Classic of Way Virtue*, left no doubt about the preeminence of virtue in cultivating the Tao.

> *The Tao gave them birth,
> The virtue of Tao reared them,
> Shaped them according to their kinds,
> Perfected them, giving to each its
>   strength.
> Therefore, of the ten thousand things
>   there is not one that does not revere
>   the Tao and cherish virtue.*

> *Tao Te Ching*

But in Buddhism, merit and virtue receive the deepest treatment and reach their highest expression in the Bodhisattva Path. The ultimate fullness of merit and virtue is the Bodhi mind, the unsurpassed resolve for Buddhahood.

> *Desiring to know all Buddhadharmas
> One should quickly bring forth the
>   Bodhi mind!
> This mind amongst all merit and virtue*

is the supreme.
One will certainly obtain the Thus
Come One's unobstructed wisdom.

The Merit and Virtue of First
Bringing Forth the Resolve,
Avatamsaka Sutra

I realized that day on the coast highway that I had no
real understanding of genuine merit and virtue. In the West we
learn of inventors, adventurers--men who pitted themselves
against nature of other men, and won. Missing are the wise,
Guiding Masters for the inner journey and for the spiritual
path of the great hero.
I hear it. I read it, but I don't truly understand
merit and virtue. It's new ground, and yet the oldest ground,
the native soil of our true mind. The Tao and its virtuous
qualities never leave us for a moment. The Buddhanature
does not come or go, does not increase or decrease, we simply
forget. Thus Confucius said,

The Tao may not be left for an instant.
If it could be left, it would not be
the Tao

Doctrine of the Mean

The Buddha's wisdom is that way:
Pervasive in the mind of living
beings.
By false thinking we are bound and
tied.
Unaware of it, we do not know.

Manifestation Chapter,
Avatamsaka Sutra

Merit and virtue is the root from which all the branches
flow forth; it is the sea to which all the lesser streams
return. It transcends all differences of time and place,
uniting East and West, ancient and modern, into a single
here and now. The teachings of Confucius, Mencius, Lao Tzu,
all contain excellent descriptions of merit and virtue. But
the most concise and thorough "hammer on steel" statement
I've found is in the *Sixth Patriarch Sutra.* These quotes
from the Great Master Hui Neng have been extremely valuable
and dear to me. Time and again while bowing I find myself

turning to them for sustenance. They guide, inspire, and most of all function as a proper mold to pour my mind into, casting and forging a new person from the foundry of proper knowledge and views. I finally copied my favorite passages into a notebook and carry it in my pack. I pull them out while sitting on the side of the road or in an all-night laundromat and contemplate the best part of being a person and the basics for becoming a Buddha.

"MERIT AND VIRTUE--'SEEK WITHIN'"

*Merit and virtue are in the Dharma body, not in the cultivation of blessings. Seeing your own nature is merit, and equanimity is virtue. To be unobstructed in every thought, constantly seeing the true, real, wonderful function of your original nature, is called merit and virtue.

*Inner humility is merit and the outer practice of reverence is virtue. Your self-nature establishing the ten-thousand dharmas is merit and the mind-substance separate from thought is virtue. Not being separate from the self-nature is merit, and the correct use of the undefiled (self-nature), is virtue. If you seek the merit and virtue of the Dharma body, simply act according to these principles, for this is true merit and virtue.

*Those who cultivate merit and virtue in their thoughts do not slight others, but always respect them. Those who slight others and do not cut off 'me and mine' are without merit. The vain and unreal self-nature is without virtue, because of the 'self,' and because of the constant slighting of others.

*Good Knowing Advisors, continuity of thought is merit, and the mind practicing equality and directness is virtue. Self-cultivation of one's nature is merit and self-cultivation of the body[1] is virtue.

[1]Note: 'Body' means "no lust, hatred, or delusion. If you do not kill, steal, or lust, you cultivate the body. That is virtue."

*Good Knowing Advisors, merit and virtue should be seen within one's own nature, not sought through giving and making offerings. That is the difference between blessings and merit and virtue. Emperor Wu did not know the true principle. Our Patriarch was not in error.

*...the eyes, ears, nose, tongue and body are the gates. Outside there are five gates and inside there is the gate of the mind...The Buddha is made within the self-nature. Do not seek outside the body. Confused, the self-nature is a living being; enlightened, it is a Buddha.

Sixth Patriarch's Sutra

* * * * *

To be complete in oneself, and not rely on what is outside, is virtue.

Venerable Master Hua, L.A., May 8, 1978

* * * * *

The ancients taught that society can only be well-ordered when the mind and nature of its people are well ordered. The country pacified and regulated only when the rulers have learned to rule themselves by cultivating their persons and 'seeking the fullness of self.' When the foundation in virtuous conduct is solid, and the inner merit round and full, then it produces a wholesome and righteous energy that naturally flows forth to nurture and to guide all that lives.

The principle to which the superior person strictly holds is cultivating his person, then everything under heaven is thereby pacified.

Mencius

Merit and virtue lies in self-cultivation. Self-cultivation means purging all faults, selfishness, pettiness, and afflictions, and correcting all errors, bad habits, excesses, and deficiencies. The person is cultivated by rectifying the mind. Rectifying the mind lies in cutting off desires. The highest and most complete merit and virtue comes forth effortlessly when the mind is proper, like a gentle rain, and as inexhaustibly as a mountain spring. And the proper mind lies in producing the thought that is nowhere attached. This is the basic nature of people, and what is meant by "cultivating the person" and "returning to the root." The ancient Worthies and Sages differed slightly in their emphasis and approach, but their agreement on this method of cultivating virtue by means of proper thought and pure conduct is clear and unquestionable. Purity is the root of merit and virtue; wisdom is its branches.

> To nourish the mind there is nothing better
> than to make desires few.

> Mencius

> If there is something a man desires, he
> won't obtain what is proper.

> Confucius

> Only he who rids himself forever of desire
> can see the secret wonder of things
> (essences).
> He who never rids himself of desire
> can only see the outer boundaries (outcomes).

> Lao Tzu

> Your basic purpose in cultivating is to trans-
> cend the wearisome defilements. But if you do not
> renounce your thoughts of desire, you will never
> be able to get out of the dust.

> Shurangama Sutra

* * * * *

Cultivating the person is accomplished by rectifying the mind. The mind is rectified by chasing away desires. Desires send themselves away as thoughts are cleansed and stilled. When desires vanish and thoughts stop, then our natural state of enlightened, pure stillness reappears, just as the sun shines when the dark clouds scatter. The highest state of mind turns back on itself to the place where there

is nothing to seek, nothing to obtain. And the fullness of
merit and virtue comes from simply knowing to be content.
And so an ancient author wrote,

> The perfectly complete fruit of
>   enlightenment,
> Returns to where nothing is obtained.
> To be complete in oneself and not
>   seek outside
> Is the fullness of virtue.

* * * * *

"THE ROAD NOT TAKEN"

> Two roads diverged in a yellow wood,
> And sorry I could not travel both
> And be one traveler, long I stood
> And looked down one as far as I could
> To where it bent in the undergrowth.

Robert Frost

End of Big Sur. We re-enter civilization on the plush fringes of the Carmel Highlands.

"Hey Marty! Hey Marty!" someone shouts from behind as we bow close to the sea. It takes awhile for the name "Marty" to register. That was my layman's name--haven't heart it in over a year. (A year of cultivation is longer than an entire lifetime).

A car full of old friends wave and smile.

"Bet we surprised you, huh?" They say. If they only knew. There are awkward pauses, long stares, maybe a little shock as we take each other in and grope for a common ground, a familiar groove. The groove is gone and the old ground grown over.

These are close, old friends. We share years of affinities and deep experiences in this life: marriage, children, college, communal living, birth and deaths, divorce, hard times and good times, tears and songs--all the human bonds and emotional ties. We could never forget each other, and yet as we stand face-to-face on this windy coast highway, silently, intuitively, we all know--it's changed for good this time.

> ...And both that morning equally lay
> In leaves no step had trodden black.
> Oh, I kept the first for another day!
> Yet knowing how way leads on to way,
> I doubted if I should ever come back.
>
> Robert Frost

We began fifteen years ago in the back room of a little Italian restaurant, vowing around a candle-lit checkered tablecloth, "to follow the truth no matter where it leads." We were young, idealistic, and high-spirited. We went into battle together, but the battle of the soul is always fought alone and the best of friends soon must take different roads.

> Those who follow the Way are like a single person who goes to battle alone against ten thousand. Donning his armor, he goes out the gate. Perhaps his resolve is weak; perhaps he gets halfway to the battleground and retreats, or perhaps he is killed in combat; perhaps he returns victorious.
>
> Sutra in Forty-Two Sections

It was hard concentrating after they left. Lots of
memories stirred up, lots of thoughts. Coming out of the
wilderness to a car full of old friends was a double shock--
one culture, the other identity. "Marty" was itching to
come forth again. The fragile, new Heng Ch'au felt clumsy,
not confident and crisp, but rather dull and unsettled.
Quiet, soft-spoken, maybe even a little cold. It's not
easy changing skins.
And yet, the monk, the solitary one who "mounts the
wind and rides the fog," is my true home, my real face. My
heart knows the happiness of leaving-home, of being true
and natural, of losing everything to find all. My mouth
couldn't find nice words and polite talk, but inside I deeply
care for all of them and all mankind.
I am a beginner, a clay Bodhisattva yet, barely able to
hold my own at sea--one wave and I crumble. But when the clay
turns to vajra, then I will return to take all living beings
across the sea of suffering.

*I now for all these living beings, cultivate
blessings and wisdom, and the dharmas which aid
the Way. On my own I resolve my mind and do not
seek companions. I use this merit and virtue to
cause all beings to amass ultimate purity up to
and including the Thus Come One's Ten Powers and
unobstructed wisdom.*

Avatamsaka Sutra

Part of me wanted to shine a big smile, crack a joke, slap
a back, and make it like old times again. But we have done
all the old times and they don't bring deliverance; they
don't chase away the shadow or fill the echo in the heart.
Time to move on. Growth is on the branch-tip buds, and so
is Spring. We turn our backs on the dust to reunite with
enlightenment. How else can we be true friends to each
other except by being true to our souls? Cultivating the
Path is lonely and free, full of joy and wonder--it is the
road less travelled by and that makes all the difference.

*I shall be telling this with a
sigh
Somewhere ages and ages hence:*

Two roads diverged in a wood, and
I took the one less travelled by;
And that has made all the difference.

--From *"The Road Not Taken,"*
by Robert Frost

HENG SURE, July 2, 1978
Sunday

"BE PREPARED"

In that way, always do they practice
Day and night, and are not lazy or
*   fatigued.*
Good roots brighten and become more pure
Like gold which has been smelted in the
*   fire.*

Ten Grounds Chapter,
Avatamsaka Sutra

Coasting on the bliss of cultivation. I got lazy this morning and earned a test. Came in from bowing feeling care-free and drunk with the beauty of the coast. Full of lax-ness, I didn't use patience and vigor in Ch'an. Popped out of meditation too soon, before I had gathered back body and concentrated thoughts. Ate lunch with scattered mind. Un-settled and off-center, I resumed bowing in the afternoon's bright sunlight. My test arrived before I'd taken nine paces.

Gray sportscar stops in a cloud of dust, inches from my head. Door clicks open. Husky female voice purrs, "You looking for a ride? I'm going to the Hot Springs. Want to come with me?"

Amazon queen strides from the driver's seat. 5'10", bleached-blonde, swinging matron in her 50's. Puffy-face, long slit side, black silk dress. Silver Navajo jewelry dangling from ears, wrists, throat.

"C'mon, I'll buy you lunch and we'll take a bath. You're not going all the way to Monterey like that are you? What for?"

"I'm a Buddhist too. I belong to the same group. But now I'm going for lunch and a hot mineral bath. I'll treat

126

you. Coming? (She commands) *Get in!"*
She advances. "Show me your poor hands."
She reaches. I pull back. She stamps her foot,
whirls, and strides to the car, jewelry swinging, clattering.
The exhaust guns, tires spin, the car vanishes around
the curve. Whew!
Good Advisors like her are rare. Their lessons do not
soon fade. She spoke the Dharma of the need for constant
vigilance day and night, without fatigue.
Like the Boy Scouts, cultivators of the Way must ever
"Be prepared." States and tests arise from the ten directions, They seem to catch us off-guard, appearing with un-
canny timing at the very moment the cultivator gets careless.

> *The Bodhisattva does not have a single thought
> of stopping or abandoning. Walking, standing, sit-
> ting, lying down, even in sleep and while dream-
> ing, he doesn't allow himself to be covered over
> (obstructed) for an instant. He never forsakes
> these thoughts (of expedient wisdom).*
>
> *Ten Grounds Chapter,
> Seventh Ground-Far Travelling,
> Avatamsaka Sutra*

Why? Because *everything* is a test. We can usually
pass if our minds are clear and alert. The sincere intent
cuts all states cleanly. When concentrated we don't dis-
tinguish tests from non-tests until the states have come
and gone. But in one instant of laxness or confusion, we
cover over our wisdom and "mistaking what's in front of us"
we fail the test and have to start anew.

HENG SURE, July 3, 1978
Monday

> *Patience is big. If you can master patience
> you will reach the other shore. Without it, you
> won't arrive. You could call patience a boat. You
> ride the boat of patience to reach the other shore
> of vigor.*
> *You listen and listen but mere listening is of
> no use. You must go do it. Whoever can be pa-
> tient will gain great blessings, great wisdom, and
> great happiness.*
> *--Master Hua*

Right now sitting still for evening meditation takes patience. My knees blaze like the Ventana Cove forest fire burning just east of here. I contemplate how water patiently carves deep arroyos in the solid stone cliffs. I patiently hold the water-like mantra rippling through my mind. In time the Dharma sound will wear an arroyo through the solid stone mountain of my afflictions.

HENG CH'AU, July 3, 1978
Monday

Dream: Alone, riding mammouth waves that reach the clouds, crest and fall back again to sea. No fear, light and at ease. I land on a floating island of mud. I'm enchanted and before realizing it, I'm snared and reeled in by evil spirits. Trapped in the mud, unable to get back to the big waves.

The Abbot and assembly appear to recharge my batteries. The Master smiles paternally and puts me back on the road to the City of Ten Thousand Buddhas. I'm so exhausted from struggling with the demons on the mud island that I fall asleep at the noon meal. A gang of Dharma protectors pulls up in a 4-wheel drive van. The road ahead is impassable, sheer mud drop-off. The Dharma protectors shout, "we're going through. Get a hustle on and get out the chains."

"But, but... " I stammer.

"No buts," says the leader. "Get the lead out!"

Soon we are securing the van for a run up the hill and out of the mud pit. The Dharma protectors are strong, confident, and cheerful.

The dream came after "separating from this." What is "this"? "This" is the single mind, the no-mind that is without seeking, without grasping, without worries. I left "this" for "that" trying to think things out and anticipate how I should act, what I should say if my old friends returned. They live in Carmel, a few miles away and I couldn't get them out of my thoughts. One's mind should be like a mirror: when an image appears, the mirror reflects it; when the image is gone, the mirror is empty.

My mind instead, was like a sensitive film--imprinting and absorbing every passing image. By day's end I felt like an old overstuffed photo album and as if marooned on an island of mud.

With one mind he seeks the Buddha's wisdom.

Concentration undivided with no other
thought.
...Taking no delight in worldly matters,
Constantly he benefits the world.

Ten Grounds Chapter,
Avatamsaka Sutra

For a few minutes I let my thoughts scatter and wander, trying to "take delight in worldly matters." Regretted it immediately. How could I have forgotten: There is no delight in worldly matters. The only real joy is leaving the world.

I do not dwell in worldly dharmas,
My joy is in leaving the world.
I know that all dharmas are like
*   empty-space--*
They come from nowhere.
...I dwell in the limits of reality,
*   without a mark*
There is only one mark.

I read these lines from the Avatamsaka, sitting in the open car door looking out at the sunset. Heng Sure is washing up out of a plastic basin on the front hood. Quiet time of day, a space for reflection.

My friends are gone, family's far away. The wind is blowing up from the sea. Above, solitary puffs of white clouds drift by. Below, we bow small, peacefully at home with everything. I remember the Abbot saying to the assembly in L.A.,

What is there you can take seriously in this life?
So that's why I tell you,

Fish swim in the water, people run amok
*   in the world.*
Unable to do merit and virtue, they forfeit
*   their minds and create offenses.*
Gold and silver heaped like mountains are
*   all gone, when one's eyes close,*
Empty-handed one sees Yama*, with regrets
*   and bitter tears.*

*Yama is the king of the underworld.

*What's worth so much sweat and tears, and being so
upside down? Think it over; think it over well.*

HENG SURE, July 4, 1978
Tuesday

"THE METHOD"

The Plymouth is cramped quarters. To reach my Ch'an
seat I use a gymnast's tuck and roll. Heng Ch'au leans forward in perfect timing. I place one foot on the doorsill,
one hand on the wheel cover, duck, boost, twist, slide, and
arrive inside, like the great blue herons that gracefully
fold up in space and return to earth. We've perfected our
entry ritual. I rarely kick over the stove or knee Heng
Ch'au in the ear as I used to. For every situation there's
a method.

The method of ending birth and death depends on concentration. Contemplate the Middle Way, the source of all
creation. Without forcing, without fearing, without thinking, seeking, or grasping, simply return all thoughts to the
True Mind. Concentrate. Accord with the spaces that appear,
tuck and bend, boost and step. Then there's nothing in the
Dharma Realm to hinder the return to your Ch'an seat.

HENG CH'AU, July 4, 1978
Tuesday

*Although the evil deeds themselves are
not vast, the evil heart pervades everywhere.*

--from Avatamsaka Preface

South of Carmel Valley. Quiet Independence Day. Got
a test on my vow not to drink juices after the noon meal
(one of the 12 beneficial ascetic practices recommended by
the Buddha to increase vigor and raise one's energy). A
half-bottle of grape juice sitting on the tailgate while
I washed dishes, finally hooked my tongue. Took a small
sip and a van immediately roars to a stop behind me. Up
hops a crazy-eyed babbling man, totally weird and unpredictable. Luckily, I caught myself after one sip and re-
sisted the urge to gulp down the whole bottle.

The weird man mellowed, gave a big toothy grin and
handed me two wilted strawberries.

"What are you boys up to, huh?" he giggled as he walked away.

Cultivators of old did not allow themselves the slightest indulgence or consider any evil too small to avoid. They maneuvered through the realm of cause and effect like one standing on the edge of an abyss or treading on thin ice. Why? Because although the wrong deed itself may be a small matter, the wrong mind pervades everything. Thus the ancients,

> ...seemed circumspect, like one who crosses a
> stream in winter,
> Watchful, as one who meets danger on every side,
> Ceremonious, as one who pays a visit,
> Yet yielding, as ice when it begins to melt.

Lao Tzu

* * * * *

There is one thought that keeps me going when everything else fails and falters: cultivating the Way as a monk, without attachments, without a home; purifying my mind to fulfill a wish to end the suffering of all living creatures. This is where I belong. This thought has been with me for as long as I can remember. Sometimes I forget it, but it never forgets me. It is more me than my own body and mind.

To become a "Buddha," one who is greatly enlightened, and to help and support others to do the same--this is the one thought, the single heart that never leaves or wavers. It strings together all the scattered beads of my past, present and future. Even before I had the words for it, I had the feeling. I believe all living beings do, too.

Now finally the seed is coming to fruit as I slowly become this heart and this heart becomes me. I slip and fall back, but never as far. Old ghosts, roles and masks cover and bind, but not as long, not as strong. This is a very wonderful thing.

> He concentrates and seeks only proper en-
> lightenment
> To take across all living beings.
> And never, even for an instant, does he
> ever abandon this heart.

Avatamsaka Sutra

HENG SURE, July 5, 1978
Wednesday

"THOUGHTLESS AS A CREEK"

Apart from Dust, Purified Eyes, Ruler of the Rivers Spirit obtained the liberation gate of using the skill-in-means of Great Compassion to universally wash clean all living beings' delusions, dust, and defilements.

> *World Rulers' Wonderful Adornments Chapter,*
> *Avatamsaka Sutra*

When angry thoughts arise, I contemplate, "I have no self that can gain or lose. I seek no progress towards any goal. Cultivation makes the world a better place for everyone. Just bow and be happy. One bow, un-thought of, unmarked by anger is one bit of goodness. Contention ruins the world."
Salmon Creek, Soda Springs Creek, Redwood Gulch, and Spruce Creek, never seek self-benefit. They ripple on endlessly, benefitting all living beings equally, without thought of reward, and never a thought of contention.

> *The highest goodness is like that of water: It benefits myriad creatures but does not contend.*

> Lao Tzu

* * * * *

"STUMP DESIRE"

Your troubles all come from unsatisfied desire. The nature of desire is that it can never be satisfied. Desire is the basic problem for cultivation of the Way. But it wouldn't work for desires to cease to exist. You should have them, but just not use them. Although desires exist, you need not attach to them. Be relaxed and loose, at ease, without attachments.

> Master Hua

Desire beckons, the mind seeks and follows, afflictions
burn and suffering never stops. I'm sitting on a rotting
stump beneath a brown National Forest Service sign, watching
the sun and shadows flicker on the redwood needles. Yes,
I want to become a Buddha. Yes, I want to end birth and
death. Yes, I want to certify to All-wisdom. But seeking
even the finest jewels is still greed; it's desire for
spiritual gain. There are hundreds of bows left to bow today, hundreds of miles of coast to travel, and more beings
inside my heart to teach and transform than there are redwood needles beneath my feet.
    The wind knocks a cone from an overhead branch. Noth-
ing lasts but patient cultivation. What is there to attach
to?

> *At the place of seeking nothing, there are no*
> *worries.*

HENG CH'AU, July 5, 1978
Wednesday

> *Like drilling wood to make a fire:*
> *If one rests before the sparks ap-*
> *   pear,*
> *The fire, like the effort, will*
> *   disappear.*
> *The lazy one is also thus.*

> > The Bodhisattva Asks for
> > Clarification Chapter,
> > Avatamsaka Sutra

Spiritual work is like any other work. There are no
secret formulas, nothing mysterious or magical--just plain
sweat and grit. The harder you work the faster you progress. The more you featherbed and slide by, the faster
you retreat.
    Cultivation is a total mind-body experience, non-dual
from muscular to mystical. When the mind and the will are
united to a single point, all pain and fatigue vanish. But
when thoughts scatter and the intent weakens, the fire,like
the effort, dribbles away and disappears. When proper mindfulness is dedicated and labored to the ultimate, there
can be a turning, a breakthrough to a state both wonderful
and never before visited. It is by enduring the unendurable
that we discover who we really are, and who we are not.

HENG SURE, July 6, 1978
Thursday

"TO L.A. BY PICK-UP"

Kuo Dzai Schmitz picked us up in his truck below Carmel. We ate lunch in a field below the Carmelite Monastery, passing bags of granola and fruit in the bed of the pick-up. I stayed in the rear as we hit the road south to Los Angeles. Facing backwards, seated in full lotus as the countryside whipped by I thought, "This is how the mind works its illusions."

> *Like dreams, like shadows, like illusions, like transformations, they confuse and mislead ignorant people.*
>
> *Ten Practices Chapter, Avatamsaka Sutra*

From the truck, the world appeared like the Sutra's description of dharmas. The houses, signs, cars, and trees looked empty and false, like dreams and shadows, like a movie run backwards. My mind soon wearied of trying to hold on to illusions, and let them all go. Non-attachment is the way to cope. Everything is impermanent,including this body. It's a fragile collage of dust, wind, sparks, and rain, no different from the spinning images that fly past this truck in reverse.

> *Ninety-nine doubts exhausted, rest the mad mind.*
> *In stillness consider, "Who's in there so busy?"*
> *Eighty-four thousand of them--let them all go.*
> *The free and at ease, going nowhere, awakened Nature king.*
>
> *--Master Hua*

* * * * *

"BEHIND THE WHEEL"

Then I took my turn behind the wheel. The freeway to South Pasadena is fast and full of curves. I hadn't driven for

months and I kept misjudging the curves. I'd lose the
groove and hear the trrmppp! trrrmmppp! of the lane divi-
ders under my tires. It seemed like the harder I tried to
steer into the center of the lane, the farther off-center
I'd be at the next bend of the road. I couldn't slow down;
there was fast traffic on all sides. The truck bounced like
a ping-pong ball from the median strip to the shoulder and
back again at 55 miles per hour.

What was the principle here? Driving at this speed I
should be looking ahead at least ten car-lengths and timing
my turns out in front, right? Right!

Sitting in the back I tried to fix attention and got
dizzy. The truck rolled too fast. I found my center only
by letting attachments go and joining the rhythm and flow
of the passing scenery.

I applied the method to the curving road as I drove.
Bingo! The car found a groove and slid like butter through
the middle of the lane. By letting go and according, the
Way flows on.

> Whether presently produced, already produced,
> or about to be produced, there is not the slightest
> dharma which can be grasped. There are no dharmas
> to attach to.

> Ten Transferences Chapter,
> Avatamsaka Sutra

HENG CH'AU, July 6, 1978
Thursday

> 'Tis the gift to be simple, 'tis the
>   gift to be free,
> 'Tis the gift to come down where we
>   ought to be.
> And when we find ourselves in the place
>   just right
> 'Twill be in the valley of love and de-
>   light.

> --Old Shaker Song

We drove into Carmel to get gas and oil. Total:
$11.35. The oil was donated. This was our first trip to
town in a long time. The contrast with the isolated wilderness simplicity of the Big Sur was striking, almost shocking.

Our sense organs went wild back in the modern world.
Sky blue sanitary chemical toilet water in pink-tiled stain-
less steel and chrome bathrooms, garbage bins overflowing
with empty fast-food containers, throw-away diapers and
beer cans. Pink hand soap, a solid wall of vending machines,
and muzak music playing ubiquitously inside the bathroom and
outside by the gas pumps. Next door is a shopping center
cornucopia. Smells waft in quilt patch-work layers of pop-
corn, roast beef, cigars, tacos, tires, perfume, new clothes,
candy, mouthwash, french-fries,charcoal-broiled anything
and everything a person could want.

Kids rush by with transistor radios pressed to their
heads revved up and buzzing on the electric speech of rock
'n roll and a hyped D.J. Sounds of laughing and crying,
scenes of love and hate swirl around like Coney Island
Amusement Park on the Fourth of July. Outside a cocktail
lounge under a neon martini sign, a man in a vested business
suit grins and slaps the back of a client with one hand
while nervously glancing at his wrist watch with the other.

*He clearly understands that all the mundane
world is like a transformation.*

Avatamsaka Sutra

As the attendant filled our tank, I found my thoughts
drifting back to Cambria, a small coastal town about 50
miles north of Morro Bay. We had been bowing for days in a
non-stop 24-hour rainstorm. Tall dripping conifers, soggy
fog air and mud everywhere. Thick drops of water hung on
each blade of grass that with the slightest touch jumped on
you. We were chilled to the bone, and stuck with cold
canned food for lunch. After awhile, one can forget what
the sun looks like, but one never stops looking for the sun.

Then one noon, the clouds opened to blue skies and the
warm,yellow sunlight burst through. Near ecstasy for simple
joys: being able to put all our wet clothes out to sun,
opening the car doors and windows to dry out the mud puddles and beads of moisture clinging to the roof and plastic
metal interior. The only dry, warm spot left was the inside of a wool blanket where a lone sweatshirt lay carefully
tucked away in a rain-proof stuffsack.

The antenna, tail fins, windshield wipers, and hood,
served as a makeshift clothes line; rolled up windows and
door handles as clothes pins. A bowl of white rice, our

first hot meal in days, was like a Thanksgiving feast to us.
Bowing in the afternoon in our dry, patched robes again
under clear skies, warm sun and a fresh wind blowing in
from the sea. Full of appreciation for the simple things,
happy as the birds flying and singing after the storm.
"...$11.35 pal." said someone.
"Huh, what?..." I asked.
"That'll be $11.35 all together for the gas. Cash or
credit?" asked the attendant impatiently as cars piled up
in lines behind each tank.
"Cash." I said coming out of my flashback reverie.

*He vows that all beings forever leave behind
the dharmas of the home-life, and with few desires, that they know contentment, and that they
stash or hoard nothing away.*

Ten Transferences Chapter,
Avatamsaka Sutra

We drove south out of Carmel to resume bowing where
we had marked our progress with a stone pile. It felt so
good to be going back to the sea, to the craggy coast and
barren, rocky, open countryside--to be going back to "the
place just right." All I want in life is right here: cultivating the Way, bowing with a single mind, studying the
King of Kings of Sutras. The deepest contentment comes
from the fewest desires. There is nothing that surpasses
this way of life and nothing it does not embrace. Leaving
home to walk the Path is "the gift to be simple, the gift
to be free." Just this is coming down where we ought to be.

*They want only to leave the home-life and
cultivate the Bodhisattva Path and adorn themselves with all Buddha's dharmas.*

Ten Transferences Chapter,
Avatamsaka Sutra

* * * *

*He vows that all beings ride the wisdom
vehicle and turn the Proper Dharma Wheel.*

Avatamsaka Sutra

But turning the Dharma wheel doesn't simply mean reciting on one's beads constantly, for this too can become an attachment. Turning the wheel means,

> *According with conditions, they do*
> *not change;*
> *Without changing, they accord with*
> *conditions.*

To be unattached in every thought, unhindered in any situation, perfectly in tune with what needs to be done and totally at ease--this is turning the Dharma wheel.

Riding back from L.A., three monks and a layman take turns driving an overloaded, big yellow school bus. A fierce gale was blowing in from the sea as we fought our way along the treacherous coast highway and mountain curves. I took my turn at the wheel proudly, but foolishly, pretending to have self-mastery. Truth was, I never drove a bus before in my life. I frantically scanned the dials and gauges with one eye, while the other looked for the foot pedals and tried to read the stick-shift diagram. What's more, when asked if I wanted help getting familiar with the cockpit, I said, "No, no, I've got it all under control."

So with one hand fingering my recitation beads, I attempted to maneuver a complex mechanical dinosaur through a howling typhoon, determined to "keep the Dharma wheel turning," and not lose mindfulness.

Fortunately, the senior monk sniffed out my misguided state and sat close by instead of taking his turn to sleep in the backseat. When the bus started careening all over the highway, buffeted by the high winds across slick roads, it became clear I wasn't on top of things at all. My hands fumbled with the switch panel, turning on the overhead lights instead of the windshield wipers, while my unwieldy beads had snagged on the stick shift and tangled around the hand brake lever.

"Keep your mind on the *steering wheel!*" shouted the monk from the seat behind. "Don't be so attached. Turn one wheel at a time."

I put my beads away with a sheepish smile, grabbed the steering wheel with both hands and put my mind to the here and now. Just that was turning the Proper Dharma wheel. The bus came under control, smooth sailing the rest of the trip.

> *When one attends to the here and*
> *now,*

The false returns to the true.

Avatamsaka Sutra

HENG SURE, July 7, 1978
Friday

"THE PEACH"

At lunch with the Gold Wheel Assembly, I sat between the Ven. Abbot and a guest Bhikshu from Malaysia. I decided to show everybody I was a genuine "old cultivator" who could turn down all the tasty dishes and eat ascetic-style.

I thought that by refusing the good food, I was demonstrating true ascetic vigor. But cultivation is not for show, it can't be advertised and sold. It works in the mind. True cultivators subdue thoughts of greed, thoughts of arrogance, and harsh, aggressive thoughts.

Everything's a test, to see what you
will do,
Mistaking what's before your eyes,
you'll have to start anew.

Venerable Abbot Hua

Heng Ch'au offered to share an apple with me. I turned him down, gesturing that I wanted a whole apple. My test arrived. A laywoman set three peaches on a small plate before me.

"These are special, white peaches, Shih Fu. They're delicious. We only have three, just for you and the two bowing monks," she said.

Aware the Master was watching, I thought, "Better not show greed, take only half a peach. Then spurred to stupidity by my desire for reputation, I speared a peach, split it, and loudly whispered "pssst," twice, to Heng Ch'au, then handed him half over the guest Bhikshu's plate. I obviously rudely excluded him and made a show of "my skill."

The Ven. Abbot immediately took a peach, divided it, and handed half to the monk. He then passed him a bowl of strawberries, reaching over my bowl in the same manner as I had done. His face, however, showed no anger. Only a gentle compassionate smile. I saw my arrogance, my fighting energy and my selfishness clearly mirrored in the Master's

courteous,giving gesture.
    I recognized my error in seeking to win a cultivation
race. The Master's spontaneous, wordless response taught me
that Buddhadharma instills compassion, not competition.
Tests can sting, faults are hard to face, but in cultivating
the Way, as in visiting a good doctor, you can't get well
until you recognize the illness. The first mistake: trying
to appear as an "old cultivator." The crooked seed bore a
distorted fruit.

> *I should always speak Dharma for beings, and
> cause them to leave behind all evil, to sever greed,
> hatred, and stupidity, (as well as) arrogance, co-
> vering, stinginess, jealousy, flattery and deceit,
> so that their hearts constantly dwell in patient,
> pliant harmony.*

> *Ten Practices Chapter,
> Avatamsaka Sutra*

HENG CH'AU, July 7, 1978
Friday

    Today I saw how life passes in a flash, like a spark
from a fire. I have accomplished little worthwhile with
this precious gift. The only thing that truly matters is
cultivating the Way, acquiring genuine spiritual skill, and
the internal merit and virtue that can cross the sea of
birth and death. Then I can benefit others in an ultimate
way.
    I saw my parents and their parents, countless parents
and countless living beings waiting for a guide, counting
on us to accomplish our Way karma and liberate them. How
can I repay their kindness? How can I help them? "Cultivate as if your life depended on it. Quickly, vigorously,
with no other thoughts for worldly things!" came the answer.

> *I want to forever renounce all confused,
>   stained dharmas.
> I want to cultivate what all Bodhisattvas
>   study
> So that my mind does not dote on the pleasures
>   of the world...
> I want to concentrate my mind to receive and
>   uphold the Dharma taught by all Buddhas.*

Ten Grounds Chapter,
Avatamsaka Sutra

It was a very strong and moving experience. I stood
motionless, staring out to sea. Tears came to my eyes as
I realized how much time and energy I've squandered selfish-
ly, dabbling in worldly dust--all of it empty and meaningless, no lasting value to myself, no contribution to mankind.
I also felt great joy in my heart to still have a chance.
Even if I only lived another day, if I used that day to sincerely cultivate, my life would not have passed in vain. A
passage from the Avatamsaka came to mind as I stood on the
highway,

> His wisdom clearly penetrates to the ocean of all
> dharmas,
> And he happily cultivates the dharmas that leave
> ignorance behind.
> Having perfected the accomplishment of merit and
> virtue which transcends the world,
> He never again studies worldly dharmas.

Ten Grounds Chapter,
Avatamsaka Sutra

I watched the last tendrils of the morning fog silently
creep over the sand dunes and disappear into the sea. The
sun erased the drab gray mist from the coast with a single
clean sweep, restoring the green of the grass, the yellow of
the sand, the deep blue of the sea. Everything felt right
again. Then I made this vow:

> "I vow to take all my good roots and 'energy
> share' and transform them into the spiritual power
> and wisdom of a Buddha to save and liberate, teach
> and take across all living beings. I will never
> again use my body and mind to cultivate worldly
> dharmas, or to seek for the Five Desires, or for
> self and what pertains to self."

* * * * *

I knew there was a chance we might be able to meet with
the Master this weekend in L.A. False thoughts of how to
get there and where to store our car clogged my mind all
morning. Right after the fog lifted (inside and outside),
a blue pickup stopped. Peter (Kuo Dzai) Schmitz offered to
drive us to LA. Another car stopped from the other direction.

It was the Powers family offering us a place to park the car
and stock up on whatever we need at their beach home a mile
down the road.
   We packed the pickup in their front yard. Over orange
juice the Powers talked hopefully about forty days of United Nation's disarmament talks in process and their life-
long wish to see world peace.

* * * * *

   I noticed a shaven-headed woman tailgaiting us for
miles. When we pulled into a small town for gas, she fol-
lowed and parked behind us. She ran up and tried to help
me out of the back of the pick up as if I were a venerable
old man.
   "What religious group are you?" she asked.
   "Buddhists." I answered and began to walk away.
   "North or south are you going?" she continued.
   "South."
   "If your Buddha told you to go south, would you go?"
she asked,staring intently with trance-like eyes as if we
were locked into a single telepathic wavelength.
   "Go where your heart says is right."
   "If your heart told you to go would you go?" she per-
sisted.
   I realized there was probably more going on here than
met the eye, and that I had no business carrying on this
pseudo-zen, cryptic talk with this person. It says, "The
straight mind is the Way Place." That means don't pretend
to be what you are not; don't make believe you know what
you do not know.
   "Go towards the good," I said. "That's the best thing
to follow."
   I turned and went into the bathroom to purposely cut
off further conversation. I was shaking and had lost my color,
probably because I was treading on unfamiliar ground I should-
n't have been on. I did one of the 42 Hands and immediately
recentered and calmed. The woman was gone when I came out.
We switched drivers and headed south to Los Angeles to see
our Good Advisor.

   *Good Man, if one wishes to accomplish the
wisdom of all wisdom, then one must decisively
seek a true Good Knowing Advisor.*

Entering the Dharma Realm,
Avatamsaka Sutra

142

Seeing a teacher and choosing friends have
been difficult in ancient and modern times;
Who can tell deviant from proper amid a myriad
considerations?

--from *a Verse by Ch'an Master*
Fo Kuo, (c. 1101, A.D.)

As we drove I realized there was probably nothing
strange or special about the woman at all. She was looking
for a Good and Wise Advisor, a spiritual teacher, and grabbed
at the first thing that caught her over-zealous eye--a novice Buddhist monk wrapped in a blanket, sitting in meditation
in the back of a pick-up truck on the freeway. She was star-
struck and ready to be swept off her feet, willing to renounce
everything to follow a perfect stranger who looked like a guru
or a cultivator. "If your Buddha told you to go south(with
you monks), would you go?" she asked, full of infatuation and
"spaced-out" abandon.

From the first bows on the sidewalks of South Pasadena,
up until today, we have run the gamut of spiritual seekers
and believers, either out to condemn and convert us, or fashion
us into saviours and seers. We refuse to argue or fight with
those who denounce us, and equally refuse the bows and offerings of those who would turn us into sages. But there's no
way to please everyone or to avoid misunderstandings. Thus,
police and local vigilantes have apologized for giving us a
hard time after mistaking us for "that other group." Some
faces droop in disappointment to find out we aren't "Fathers"
or Rabbis, others light up with smiles of relief to discover
we aren't Moonies or Krishnas. In turn we have been confused
for Arab guerrillas, missionaries, Muslim high priests, es-
caped lunatics, con-artists, college fraternity boys, peace-
niks, and even spacemen.

We have been bowed to, spit on, kissed and cursed,
harangued, hugged, serenaded, showered with flowers and incense, pelted with garbage and stones, offered money and sex,
and threatened with injury and death. We have had the photos
and gospels of yogis, gurus, masters, gods, prophets, saints,
healers, mediums, mystics, visionaries, and madmen, shoved
in front of our faces, stuffed in our pockets, plastered on
our car and chanted in our ears as we bowed. Are they really
Good Knowing Advisors that these people believe in and crusade
for?

After my extinction, in the Dharma-Ending Age,

*these phantoms and apparitions will abound,
spreading like wildfire as they surreptitiously
cheat others. Calling themselves Good Knowing
Advisors, they will each say that they have attained the superhuman dharmas. Enticing and
deceiving the ignorant, or frightening them out
of their wits, they disrupt and lay waste to
households wherever they go.*

Shurangama Sutra

This is the rotten and shameful side of a healthy and
promising spiritual awakening occurring in the West. The
stretch of California coast we chose to bow on is a main
artery in the revival. The seekers are many, but true
teachers are few and phonies abound. We have seen and
heard of sincere but naive and ignorant people misguided or
misled into a city commune or remote mountain retreat there
to sit at the feet of some self-appointed "Good Knowing Advisor" who may claim anything from direct mandate from Jesus
to outright living Buddhahood.

The inside story and actual practices however, often
reveal a way of life that is far from holy or enlightened.
We hear of drug abuse, sexual misconduct, power tripping
and coercion, dubious financial dealings, and even stashes
of guns and weapon caches. It's sad, but true, and pains
our hearts to see it so close to home.

*How can thieves put on my robes and sell the
Thus Come One, saying that all manner of karma
one creates is just the Buddhadharma?!...They
say that they have attained what they have not
attained, and that they have been certified when
they have not been certified. Perhaps they seek
to be foremost in the world, the most venerated
and superior person...in order to be revered by
others and because they are greedy for offerings.*

Shurangama Sutra

We live in the Dharma-Ending Age, a time when the
Buddha predicted the Proper Dharma would fall into ruin and
ultimately become extinct. A time when there would be phoney
teachers misrepresenting themselves as Good Advisors, falsely
claiming the fruit of Sagehood or to be messengers from
heaven--thieves in saint's robes who would openly advocate
killing, stealing, using intoxicants, lust, and lying, all

in the name of enlightened conduct. Greedy for offerings and veneration, they would advertise themselves and claim powers and secrets to attract followers and a big name. And because of their misdeeds and confusion, limitless living beings who started out with good intentions would end up following such messed-up teachers into the unintermittent hells. It's as a verse says,

> If one who is dazed transmits the delusion to another,
> When all is said and done, neither one understands.
> The teacher falls into the hells
> And the disciples burrow in after him.

Yes, there are genuine, Good Knowing Advisors, not only in established and new movement religions, but also found in all walks of life. How can you tell a true Good Knowing One? A genuine Good Knowing Advisor inspires people to clean up their lives, to subdue their bodies and rectify their minds, often without uttering a word. A true teacher's every thought, word, and deed speaks of kindness, compassion, joy, and giving. Their precept (morality) deportment is spotless and awesome. Without any mark of greed, fighting, lust, or self-seeking, they only wish to cause others to securely dwell in proper views and obtain pure wisdom.

A Good Knowing Advisor is not greedy for disciples or wealth, doesn't hanker for fame and power. Slandered and scolded, they just smile; praised and honored, they aren't pleased. And although they may be enlightened or even transformation bodies of great spiritual beings who appear expediently as Sanghins, laypeople, officials, ministers, or maybe even as prostitutes, thieves, butchers, smugglers and the like, they secretly do the holy work. They would never reveal their true identity by making extravagant claims and giving themselves high hats and fancy titles saying, "Do you know me, I'm truly a Bodhisattva," or "I'm really a sage," or "I'm god come again."

Before they teach people in the world to cultivate, they make sure their own minds are "as straight as lute strings, true and real in everything they do." They teach those new in study to plant their feet on solid ground--to turn away from all lustful behavior, killing, stealing, and lying; to be greatly public-spirited and filial. Instructing

clearly on the principles of cause and effect, they point
out the dangers and safe roads to others stressing, "If one
is off an inch at the beginning, one will be off a thousand
miles in the end." If the cause ground is not true, the
fruit will be distorted, and so they take great pains to
explain that if one seeks to get enlightened then, "one
must first be as pure as glistening frost."
Wherever there is this kind of goodness and beneficial
energy, there will be a true Good Knowing Advisor close by.

*He singlemindedly recollected how he should
regard the Good Knowing Advisor as a kind mother,
so as to renounce and separate from all unbeneficial dharmas; how he should regard the Good
Knowing Advisor as a compassionate father, so as to
give rise to all good dharmas...go to where he is
and ask him how a Bodhisattva studies the Bodhisattva conduct, and how a Bodhisattva cultivates
the Bodhisattva Path.*

*Entering the Dharma Realm,
Avatamsaka Sutra*

HENG SURE, July 8, 1978
Saturday

This weekend at Gold Wheel Temple, I've gathered enough
instant karma to fill a freight train. Didn't realize how
much the highway has disciplined my old bad habit of "playing." Turned loose at the Temple after a month of hard work,
I pilfered a tea can, "borrowed" a Sutra, insulted a guest,
missed Ch'an sitting, skipped Sutra memorization, grabbed the
translator's spotlight during lectures and started every
ceremony late. Principle:

If the cause ground is not true,
The result will be distorted.

The untrue cause took root in my mind on the way to
Gold Wheel. Unconsciously I planned for a big Dharma-holi-
day, a break from our daily mindfulness. I got impatient
with the pressure of the steady, constant routine. Like
releasing a tightly coiled spring, the pent-up energy shot up
through the crack opened by the thought to play. The Master
spoke a principle last night; I recognized this false thought
behind my every move all weekend:

> When you cultivate the Way you should strive
> to be ahead and fear falling behind. If you
> plant perfect causes you will reap perfect re-
> sults. If you plant half-causes, you will reap
> partial results. Off by an inch in the begin-
> ning, you'll be off by a thousand miles in the
> end.

HENG SURE, July 9, 1978
Sunday

"OWNING MISTAKES"

Sobering sight: acting like a sailor in port this weekend; pilgrims and penitents must be full-time sincere. I
behaved like a young boy, not a bowing Bhikshu. I displayed
the afflictions of "lack of shame," and "lack of remorse."
Not admitting wrong behavior doubles the original offenses. Holding on to the original error, then failing to
cut off the affliction it creates compounds the first mistake. To turn this rolling tide of bad energy, I repented
of my lack of sincerity at Gold Wheel. I knew remorse and
felt humble at the sight of my falseness. By way of repentance, I put together a list of sturdy, bright principles.
These *yang* remedies counter the weekend's misdeeds. I hope
the new awareness of my faults will lead to deeper insights
and true steps towards the good. It's said:

> A day without offenses to repent of
> Is a day without merit to collect.

1. Be careful in words, thoughts, deeds. Exa-
mine the motive behind every thought. Decisively
cast out defiled thoughts on the spot. My mind
sought a vacation this weekend.

2. Keep the rules and guard the precepts purely.
Precepts are the foundation of Buddhahood. I
stole books and blankets; broke vows and sought
fame.

3. Maintain Bodhisattva practices without fail.
Daily, disciplined cultivation is the only true
judge of spiritual skill. Strive to be ahead
(of one's bad habits), fear falling back. This
weekend I skipped Ch'an sitting, did t'ai ch'i

at midnight, recited 42 Hands at 1 A.M., and overslept
morning ceremony.
4. Maintain inner humility and outer respect. My
discourtesy towards other cultivators shows pride
and self-satisfaction, two attitudes that *end* progress in cultivation. No joke!

*With shame and remorse before Gods and People,
we break off the heart which lacks shame...facing
evil deeds breaks off the heart which covers over
faults.*

Avatamsaka Repentance

HENG CH'AU, July 7-9, 1978
Friday - Sunday

"L.A. WEEKEND NOTES AND RECOLLECTIONS"

Friday night:

"*My idea is everything's okay, no problem. No
problems, no questions. No questions, then no
anything--finished. I don't judge anyone or anything. I don't have time to judge.*" said the
Abbot.

Saturday morning:

Light sleep last night; lots of high-powered,
good energy here. Dreamed of the Abbot and Sangha
trying to help me see through things. I had this
clear vision: we don't need to seek anything outside to get enlightened. It's already whole and
complete within each of us, but unless we cultivate, we never know that the wisdom of All-wisdom
is inside our own mind.
I woke up crystal-clear, full of a new understanding, so simple yet unfathomably deep. My mind
was lucid and unobstructed and I saw as I had never
seen before. I grabbed my pen to capture the state
with words and it vanished like a bubble bursting
into thin air. It was gone; I couldn't pen a single
line. Nothing, not a trace, just a feeling that
there is an enlightened state of being and it must

be truly as the Sutras say,

The Buddhas' states that arise from wisdom
Are not thought, and leave the path of the
*   mind...*
They are not beginning, nor middle, nor end.
They are not expressible in words.
They transcend the three periods of time.
Their characteristics are like empty space.

Ten Grounds Chapter,
Avatamsaka Sutra

Words and thoughts can only point, they can never
enter. Most of the time I live in a dream of words,
thoughts and appearances, dancing and skimming on
the surface of things like a silly, frantic water
spider.
    The Abbot said,

In cultivation, you have to sweep away all dharmas
and leave all appearances. You have to break through
all attachments. If there's a bit of an appearance
remaining it's going to cause trouble. They are only
figures of speech, not the real thing. There's no
place for putting a head on top of a head...When you
understand the genuine Dharma, it is apart from the
spoken word, from conceptualized thought, and the
written word. If you can't leave all appearances
then no matter how much you cultivate, you are just
skimming around on the surface of things.

Saturday afternoon:

    Bowing on the sidewalk in front of Gold Wheel
Temple. Busy L.A. traffic outside, quiet searching
inside. Looking into desire--the major reason we
aren't Buddhas, the cause of all suffering and disasters, the eclipse of our inherent wisdom. We are
born from desire and die from desire and still can't
see through it, can't put it down.
    "Is desire outside?" I asked, looking across Hun-
tington Drive to a bustling shopping center. No,
there are no desirable objects, there are only de-
sirous minds. All the things we crave and covet,
all conditioned dharmas are,

*Impermanent, suffering, impure, insecure,
decaying, shortlived. Produced and destroyed in
an instant, they don't come from the past or go
towards the future, nor do they stay in the present.*

Ten Grounds Chapter,
Avatamsaka Sutra

Across the street a child begging and whining
for her mother to buy her a bright red balloon.
Mother consents. Balloon in hand, full of glee,
they start for home. A strong gust of wind snatches
the shiny rubber dharma out of the child's hand and
whisks it into empty space. The little girl screams
and wails, watching her heart's delight fade out of
sight. All dharmas, everything in the world, is
like a fragile red balloon in a child's unsure hand.
They are,

*Like illusions, dreams, shadows, and echoes;
like the moon's reflection in the water, like
images in a mirror, like flames and transformations,
and thus level and equal.*

Ten Grounds Chapter,
Avatamsaka Sutra

"Is desire just a state of mind?" I wondered.
"Since there is nothing worth longing for and being
greedy for, nothing that can be secured or bring
real satisfaction, then desire is just a way of
looking at things. My mind literally makes something out of nothing." But where is my mind? It
is even less tangible than the red balloon that
blew by overhead. Exhaustively look for the mind,
but it can't be found; try to hang on to the body,
but it runs away all the same.

*The body is like a heap of snot,
The mind is like the wind.
Produced by illusion, without proof,
Without a real nature.*

Master Hua

I have been a slave to my body, and a prisoner
of my mind. As I bowed, I suddenly saw that fol-

lowing desires was stupid, empty, and totally
upside-down. What joy or meaning is there in
a life spent doting on snot and chasing the wind?
    The kid's mother refused to get her another bal-
loon. Who knows when we will get another chance to
cultivate the Way?

Saturday night:

    After bowing we sit in meditation before the
evening ceremony and lecture. Normally our energy
and wisdom light flow out the six sense organs and
dribble away pursuing the five desires. We turn
and flow and never stop to consider, never pause to
contemplate the rhyme or reason for our lives. And
of all the desires, love is the worst.

    *All living beings float and turn on the river
of love. They rush over the rapids without stopping to think about what they are doing and how
it awakens anger, craving, and harm. They follow
along without forsaking it.*

*Ten Grounds Chapter
Avatamsaka Sutra*

    Meditation is just stopping to think about what
we are doing, finding a space in our busy, running-
around lives to "return the light and illumine within." Just as at night in this big city when the
traffic stops one can hear the wind blowing and
birds singing once again, so too, when we stop and
contemplate, we can hear the sounds of our true
heart and enlightened nature again.
    Inside the small temple, scores of people gather
to recite Gwan Yin's name. Circling in procession,
one can feel the racing pace and scattered fragments
of our minds and bodies grind to a grateful halt.
As the wheel of singleminded chanting grows, the
anger, craving, and harm are softly, painlessly
laid to rest.
    When desire ends, wisdom manifests. The Bud-
dha's method however, isn't to repress and teeth-
grit desires to death. Rather, desire is peacefully transformed, bit by bit, into wisdom through
long-term and diligent cultivation of morality and
meditation. It worked for the ancients, it works

today, and will work forever. The Dharma wheel is always turning.

...*In every place at one time turning--vast and great as the Dharma Realm, ultimate as empty space, exhausting the boundaries of the future throughout all numbers of kalpas without cease.*

Ten Grounds Chapter,
Avatamsaka Sutra

* * * * *

Monk: "Master, what does the phrase 'causes and conditions' mean?"

Master: "Causes are seeds, conditions are the situation, all the surrounding factors."

Monk: "That simple? I've pondered on it and tried to understand it thoroughly, but just couldn't believe it was that simple!"

Master: "Don't try to understand too thoroughly. If you try to go too deep and get too profound, you'll go right past it and end up not understanding at all."

* * * * *

Sunday:

Today we accompanied the Abbot and Elder Master Chu Mwo from Malaysia, to the "opening of the light" dedication of a new temple in Los Angeles. A large gathering of monks, nuns, and lay devotees made the small temple seem even smaller. After a year of bowing the highways and living outdoors, after only the mountains and vast sea for companions, and the vow of silence, it was strange indeed to be suddenly immersed in a sea of people, mountains of buildings and hundreds of conversations going on at once.

On the ride there I felt the importance of Buddhism for the future well-being of the work and my own responsibility to truly go and do the Buddha's work. In the Dharma Ending Age the pure pulse of the Patriarchs hangs by a thin thread. Only Way Virtue can keep the thread from breaking, only Way

Virtue can save us all.

Riding back from the dedication I felt a mixture of shame, bewilderment, and alienation. Small Temple Buddhism is widespread in Asia and one of the major reasons for the Dharma's decline in its own birthplace. Scores of one-or two-monk temples, often lavishly constructed, compete for lay offerings and supporters, while offering no Sutra lectures, meditation sessions, and most important of all, no educational system for the young. The Way Places become social hang-outs at best, and ghost temples at worst. When the resident monk passes away, the temples lies vacant or is taken over by a layperson. Some of those laypeople conduct Sutra lectures for money and give Buddhism a bad name.

The social intrigue, climbing on conditions, and small talk isn't in keeping with the Buddha's original intent and vast scope. How sad to see this unhealthy,mutant Buddhism already taking hold in the West where the Dharma is just in its infancy! I felt shame for my own sad state of cultivation. I need to be more vigorous and sincere, to constantly expand the measure of my mind, to solidly practice the highest spiritual tradition known to man, and to make great vows to save all living beings.

I just wanted to go back and bow. I know my indignation is immature and uncompassionate, but I'm a young cultivator and don't have patience or samadhi power to remain "thus thus unmoving, eternally bright" no matter the state. So I told myself on the way back in the car, "Don't be so unkind and critical. Return the light and truly recognize your own faults, don't be always harping on the faults of others. Cleanse your own mind of the finest dust. Conduct yourself as if you were always right next to the World Honored One. Seek nothing, fear no difficulty. Deeply enter a single Dharma door until you do what needs to be done, and never forget your promise to help and support all that lives." I closed my eyes and pictured the City of Ten Thousand Buddhas, and a smile came to my heart.

HENG SURE, July 10, 1978
Monday

"ASTROLOGY"

He vows that all beings take no delight in
attaching to the mundane world; that they always
be happy to leave the world's languages far be-
hind.

Ten Transferences Chapter,
Avatamsaka Sutra

Astrology was my favorite language. It came easily to
my mind. I could think with astrology's symbols and natural
logic the way I could not think with words. But astrology
is still a language and not ultimate truth.
After I met the Buddhadharma, I chose to put astrology
down. Astrology is bound by thoughts and senses; Buddhadharma transcends the mind entirely. Astrology is limited
by the mundane world. It assumes the self and dharma are
real, it describes a world that the mind supposedly can grasp
and know. It isn't so.

All dharmas are false and unreal. They quickly
arise and quickly pass away. They are unsubstantial,
like dreams, like shadows, like illusions, like
transformations.

Ten Practices Chapter,
Avatamsaka Sutra

The names we pin on the world confuse us. We divide
reality into ten thousand things, yet the True Suchness mind
described by the *Avatamsaka,* contains both wonderful existence and True Emptiness. The Sutra says everybody can realize wisdom beyond the reach of words, symbols, and thoughts.
Our true minds contain the universe. All Buddhas, all beings, all dharmas, all worlds, share the same source. This
is the big horoscope chart cast by the Buddhadharma.
When death arrives, unless one has cultivated according
to the principles of the Dharma, masterful knowledge of astrology amounts to no knowledge at all.

For every bit of worldly dharmas you can put
down, that's how much Buddhadharma you can pick
up. And you should go and truly practice as
much as you know.

Master Hua, L.A.

* * * * *

"THE MISSAL"

A little book, personal insights on cultivation. Fits
neatly into the backpack. Contains nuggets of wisdom: hard-
earned, smelted, concentrated essentials--practices, principles, daily basics and prayers. Some mornings I lose my
way, states confuse the mind and the mind confuses states.
Dreams cover the road ahead like ocean fog. Consult the
missal, a reliable friend at times like these. Or open to
any page while taking a breather from bowing or during morning tea or whenever afflictions arrive. The missal never
fails to light the way back to solid ground. Chew on a Sutra
principle: sweet as honey; contemplate a prayer and hear
the bells of Gold Mountain. Recite a verse and stand inside
the Master's wisdom light.
   Sample Page from the Missal:

"Positive Action"

Take responsibility for all living beings, all
shapes, natures, and races. All of their afflictions, all of their faults are just my own. Make
them my problems to resolve inside with Bodhisattva
Dharma-practices. Now is the time, here is the place
to truly cultivate the Way. Walk the path with cheerful patience and light-hearted vigor. Steady effort,
constant and forever. There is no hurry, no rush,
but no time to waste. See every being safely to
the other shore.

Cultivation is a martial art to subdue one's self.
Block! Strike! Yield. Gather in. Cultivation
is like bounding down a mountain trail. No time
for thought. Jump!

"Merit and Virtue"

*Seeing your own nature is merit and equanimity
is virtue. To be unobstructed in every thought,
constantly seeing the true, wonderful function of
your original Nature is called merit and virtue.
   Inner humility is merit, the outer practice of
reverence is virtue. Your self-nature establishing the ten thousand dharmas is merit and mind-
substance separate from thought is virtue. Not*

being separate from the self-nature is merit and the correct use of the undefiled (self-nature) is virtue.

Sixth Patriarch Sutra

HENG CH'AU, July 10, 1978
Monday

Driving back from L.A. to continue the bowing near Carmel. A long drive, lots of time to reflect on the weekend's lessons. I went to L.A. ready for silence and solitude-- quiet bowing, outside, long meditation in the back garage, no socializing, no talking, and no writing. I felt I was ready to enter the solitary place where,

The path of words and language are cut off,
The place of the mind's working is extinguished.

But I got the exact opposite: The Abbot asked us to lecture and talk to people. He even introduced us to an eager new layman, and encouraged him to ask us any questions or feelings he had about religion. The man was overflowing with both. I discovered how little I really knew in an uncomfortable one and a half hours of talking with him on a couch. All the while I had one eye on the door and my pack on my back, hoping to go out and bow. The Abbot simply watched on with a knowing and amused smile. We attended a bustling temple opening and later went across town to visit with His Eminence, Paul Cardinal Yu Bin. And finally, just as we were about to head off for the coast, a reporter from the L.A. Times arrived to do an interview.

The lessons? Whatever you don't want to do, fearing it too difficult, is what you should do. Whatever one fears or desires is an attachment and will lead to obstruction. I wanted seclusion and dreaded facing people and talking. I convinced myself that such self-imposed isolation was entering the samadhi of "non-doing." But once again, the Good Advisor kept me from taking a wrong road. So it's said,

Contemplating wisdom and the realm of contemplation,
In the nature of True Suchness, masterfully fused.
Tireless Gwan Yin Bodhisattva fulfills vast vows,
*   all living beings aiding.*
Yet in inconceivable samadhi, dwells unmoved.

True wisdom is not apart from aiding living beings;
genuine samadhi is perfectly fused with beneficial deeds.
Samadhi is not the absence of activity, it is the absence of
false-thinking.
The way to change towards the good is to face what's
hard to face and not be afraid of uncovering errors. Covering over faults doesn't get rid of them, it only gives them
more power. Bringing pretensions and hang-ups into the light
and out in the open is the healing.

> One must reveal faults, not cover up blemishes
> and errors. Harmful poisons and noxious weeds
> must be quickly gotten rid of. Expose their roots
> so that they can wither and dry up...If one conceals
> transgressions, it is like a festering sore: to
> cover it without healing it would amount to death,
> ultimately. By revealing faults we reverse and
> break the heart that covers offenses.

> --from Avatamsaka Repentance,
> Hua Yen Preface, by National
> Master Ch'ing Liang

* * * * *

We ate lunch in the open end of Peter's truck on a small
dirt road outside of Carmel. Below, spread rows of silver-
green artichoke plants tended by Mexican farm workers who
lived in a row of pale pink houses at the edge of the field.
Lunch: granola, fruit, bread and tea.
We began bowing by early afternoon, south of Carmel.
Clear skies overhead and a refreshing breeze from the ocean
that constantly, faithfully, breaks and washes on the shores
a few steps from our feet. Even at night and before dawn as
we sit in meditation, we can always hear the sea's breathing.
The slow, bowing rhythm and the patient cadance of the sea's
ebb and flow, share a common spirit, an unspoken kinship.
At times of long absorbed bowing and contemplation, our
breaths and thoughts seem to mesh with the to and fro of the
waves and tides. My heart feels at home with the bulge and
nuzzle of the sea, and I sometimes imagine the sea feels
at home with the bowing.

> I have always regarded the sea as my state...
> Within this world is there anything more broad
> and extensive than this sea? Is there anything

more immeasurable than this sea? Is there anything deeper than this sea? Is there anything
more rare and splendid than this sea?

Entering the Dharma Realm,
Avatamsaka Sutra

HENG SURE, July 11, 1978
Tuesday

"THE PURE RUNNING WATERS OF THE MIND"

In cultivation, you must purify your own
mind. You must have no false thoughts. Your
mind should be like pure water, totally pure.
Don't allow even the slightest speck of dust
within it.

Master Hua

The Plymouth's right rear corner serves as our reser-
voir. Six plastic-gallon jugs bump against my knees as I
fold up into full lotus. We fill the jugs when we can; it
takes only a minute to dip out a gallon from Big Sur's pure-
running mountain streams. We recognize our fortune as we
swallow a cool mouthful. The clean water refreshes, chases
turbid thoughts, cuts road-dust.
Cleveland's Cuyahoga River is thick with industrial
waste. When the Cuyahoga catches fire every summer, the fire
trucks roll up to the riverbanks and jet their hoses into
the smoking stream. A flammable river! Shame on us for
allowing our greed to defile Nature.
Not long ago the Maumee River, west of the Cuyahoga,
was as dirty as a septic tank. The citizens of Toledo cracked
down on industrial polluters. The Maumee responded immediately. Once the poisons stopped flowing, the river regained
its purity much faster than reclamation experts predicted.
Now people from Ohio, Michigan, and Indiana canoe, water ski,
fish, and picnic on the sparkling healthy,Maumee. It bears
trout and lake salmon once more.
Cultivators use Buddhadharma to curb mind-pollution.
Afflictions, greed, anger, and wrong views foul the mind and
turn it as flammable as the Cuyahoga. Dharma from the Sutra
transforms the poisonous influx and the mind responds. It
returns to natural health as quickly as the Maumee. Buddhadharma gives us power to reclaim our basic share: a pure-
running, thought-free mind.

> ...*they practice giving, they hold the precepts,
> they subdue all their organs, because they want to
> benefit all living beings and universally cause them
> all to be pure.*

> Ten Transferences Chapter,
> Avatamsaka Sutra

HENG CH'AU, July 11, 1978
Tuesday

Young man with a backpack came upon us bowing on the
highway this morning.
"Hitchhiking a new way?" he asked with a friendly face.
"No, we're Buddhist monks on a bowing pilgrimage."
"Neat! I'd give you food, but I'm out. But I got
some money," he said, giving it to us. "Maybe this will
bring me good luck."

"It might if you don't think about giving it or getting anything."

"Wow! You people are so right on!" he said. "You drive one up the wall, in a good way. Really, that's right on. That's just how it is."

Disciples of the Buddha, the Bodhisattva is a great benefactor. He can give away all his material objects whatsoever and his mind is level and equal without stinginess or regret. He does not expect a reward, nor does he seek name and fame. He is not greedy for benefit. He gives only for the purpose of saving all living beings, gathering in all living beings, aiding all living beings.

> Ten Grounds Chapter,
> Avatamsaka Sutra

HENG SURE, July 12, 1978
Wednesday

A picture of the Venerable Hsu Yün impressed us. Taken from the back, the photo shows the Elder Master's ramrod-straight spine. His presence commands respect, even from behind. His upright posture speaks of Dharma-discipline, of true inner skill. One glance at the Venerable Hsü Lao's awesome deportment is a Dharma-lecture all by itself.

Reflecting on my own bearing, I find poor posture, a crooked neck and pinched breathing. While meditating, I straightened my spine and imitated the erect mien of the Venerable Master. Energy circulated instantly, hands and toes warmed up, false-thoughts melted away. I recalled Heng Ch'au's observation months ago as we saw a young infant in a stroller on the sidewalk:

"Look at the *yang* energy!" he said.

The child was as natural and straight as a young sapling; no masks, no head-heavy cogitations, no marks of affliction or worry. The Venerable Hsü Lao's photo taken from behind, bears the same natural poise, centered, gathered in, complete in "the fullness of self."

Return the light. Seek the fullness of oneself. Change bad habits from evil to good. Find out your real self. This is what all Buddhist Sutras tell us.

> Master Hua

HENG CH'AU, July 12, 1978
Wednesday

"NOT THE SLIGHTEST SPECK"

Bowing a quiet, early morning coast highway, nothing going on outside but inside my mind was bedlam, a rush-hour freeway of false thoughts. How to turn such a mental racket? Same as always: don't pay any attention to it. Return to the practice of singleminded concentration and patience.

A wave of nausea and dizziness followed. I continued to bow and kept plugging away. The state finally passed, leaving everything quiet, inside and out. Or so I felt as I had this thought,

"Yes, that's how it is: there is no self so who is there to seek this and fear losing that? Who is there to do all this false thinking? With no discrimination, then there's no affliction. There is no self, so everything's okay."

Screech! A truck squeals to a burning-rubber stop inches from my head bowed to the ground. I jump, startled and afraid. A big peel of laughter rings out from the truck and then they leave.

I give rise to happiness because I have left all hair-raising, alarming, and other such experiences far behind. And why?...It is because these Bodhisattvas are free from the thought of self.

> *Ten Grounds Chapter,*
> *Avatamsaka Sutra*

* * * * *

If I had no self, then who was so afraid he nearly jumped out of his shoes? How quiet was it really inside my mind? Then I remembered an exchange I had with the Master just last Friday. It was a priceless teaching, but I completely overlooked it until now. It was the first thing the Abbot said to us as we walked into his room to bow and pay our respects upon arriving:

Abbot: "How is it?"

Monk: "Quiet." a little satisfied and proud of his state.

Abbot: "How quiet?" penetrating right through.

Monk: "Ah, well, er..." suddenly seeing it wasn't so quiet after all.

Abbot: "Pure mind, continue, continue." with an understanding smile.

What does it mean to have a quiet mind? It just means there are no selfish thoughts--no self at all. No thought of a self and no thought of there not being a self. If one still has a thought of no self, then how is this truly quiet and pure? A quiet mind is pure, devoid of even the slightest speck.

"In cultivation, you must purify your own mind. You must have no false thoughts. You should be like pure water, totally pure...not even the slightest speck should be allowed within," the Abbot went on to say. "You can turn every state that arises if you are clear and concentrated. But if you are usually turbid and confused, then of course, whatever comes up will turn you."

...These sounds proclaimed how in a certain country, a certain Bodhisattva cultivated as-cetic practices, renouncing that which is dif-ficult to renounce.

Entering the Dharma Realm,
Avatamsaka Sutra

A young girl came out to offer us some food. A vegetarian, she was extremely happy to find someone else who didn't eat living creatures.
"You're vegetarians!? So am I. Oh, that's neat. Right on!" she said with a welcome smile.
Even though her family and friends all eat meat, she has a strong conviction and keeps up the pure practice alone. This is "renouncing what is difficult to renounce." It's hard to do anything solo at age 14 or 15, but she's doing it and looks the better for it too.

A happy man toting all his possessions in a bag slung over his shoulder, walked by with folded hands and a big-hearted grin, chanting,

"Om mani padme hum, om mani padme hum..."

He stopped, did a one-half bow, continued on his way as the sun set.

HENG SURE, July 13, 1978
Thursday

Nose to dirt, six hours a day. Robes with stained patches: elbows, knees. Foreheads branded with a ground-in callous that marks the bowing spot. We are becoming soil experts. We've inspected the pavements of California, her sand, scree, slate, and cement. We feel a kinship with the dirt and rock we bow across. Living so close to Nature it's easy to see our bodies in the earth and the earth in our bodies. One experiences first hand, the equal, level, nature of all dharmas.

As the earth has a unity, and is
Able to produce all kinds of sprouts,
Yet there is no difference in the earth
    itself.
And all Buddhadharmas are the same way.

                    The Bodhisattvas Ask for
                    Clarification Chapter,
                    Avatamsaka Sutra

We don't weary of our earthbound yoga, in fact, we haven't learned to bow low enough. Worshipping the Buddha with five limbs to the ground makes sense in the heart. The more we bow the more we leave the dust.

At sundown, rinse off the nose and palms in a plastic basin on the Plymouth's tailgate. Fold robes and pack threadbare sneakers behind the seat. Meditate till the stars and planets fill the sky,and listen to the Sutra speak of the light-filled wonder of the Buddha's Way-place:

Vajra makes up its ground, nothing can
    harm it.
Vast, broad, pure, flat and level to the
    ultimate,

*Mani-jewels make up nets and hang down
     in space,
Pervading everywhere beneath the Bodhi
     tree.*

> *World Ruler's Wonderful
> Adornments Chapter,
> Avatamsaka Sutra*

hENG CH'AU, July 13, 1978
Thursday

*Head, eyes, ears, and nose, tongue as well as
     teeth.
Hands and feet, his marrow, his heart and blood
     and flesh--
He does not find it hard to renounce such things
     as those.
Only a chance to hear the Dharma he counts on
     most hard.*

> *Ten Grounds Chapter,
> Avatamsaka Sutra*

Thoughts on the Dharma's extinction:

Of all the treasures in the world, none are as precious as the Dharma. Next to a true Good Knowing Advisor, it is the most difficult of opportunities to encounter.

The Elder Master Chu Mwo's Dharma talk at Gold Wheel Temple was traditional: long, deep, and substantial. Most of us didn't recognize it until our teacher said, "It's the real thing--the sound of the hammer hitting steel. Listen with a single mind."

We Westerners love one-liners and quickies, but the Buddhadharma, the path of the ancients, and of all enlightened beings, takes a certain patience and long-haul endurance to penetrate.

> *Being lazy and lax, no one will want to listen
> any longer. These evil Shramanas will be unwill-
> ing to recite Sutras in their entirety, and they
> will make abbreviations at the beginning and at
> the end of the text as they please. Soon the
> practice of reciting Sutras will stop altogether...
> the SURANGAMA SUTRA and the Pratyutpanna Samadhi,*

164

*Standing Buddha Samadhi will be the first to
change, and then to disappear. The twelve
divisions of the canon will gradually follow
until they vanish completely, never to appear
again. Its words and texts will be totally unknown ever-after.*

--from *The Buddha Speaks the
Ultimate Extinction of the
Dharma Sutra*

One can see how the Sutras and mantras will disappear:

--Our minds will be too geared to the instant,
too lax to embrace them;

Our bodies too wasted by pleasures and excesses
to seek them;

Our books and words too abbreviated and shallow
to hold them;

Our hearts too busy and confused to notice this
happening.

Our bowing pilgrimage slows us down. Bowing quiets our
minds and bodies long enough for us to be able to sit and
listen to the Dharma and contemplate things in stillness. 1
We still go too fast and become scattered too easily. We
are still too full of desire and attachments to hear it
well and deeply. But the faint whispers and glimpses that
occasionally pierce through our coverings are the best and
truest thing either of us has ever found.

*He sets out seeking wisdom to benefit all
beings...
He is mindful that that wisdom is obtained
from hearing.
Making such reflections, he urges himself on
Day and night to hear and practice with no
interruption.
Only taking Proper Dharma as worthy and important.*

*Ten Grounds Chapter,
Avatamsaka Sutra*

* * * * *

We pulled off the road to camp for the night under a
stand of tall trees in Pt. Lobos State Reserve. I climbed
over the wood rail fence and walked in the woods until I
found a quiet spot to meditate under an old, moss-hanging
oak. So still and at ease in this forest by the sea, a
natural aranya!

"Psst, psst!" I heard calling me from the direction
of the car. I uncrossed my legs and hurried back to find
Heng Sure being peppered with requests from our old friend,
the "Big Sur Beggar." Familiarity breeds contempt, goes an
old saying. If not contempt, it certainly eliminates forma-
lity.

The beggar had one foot propped on the rear bumper as
he sat on the open tailgate, bold and brash as could be.

"Yeah, I need some more clothes and blankets. Maybe
a nice hooded parka and sleeping bag this time," he said
as if he were a customer in a general store.

"What happened to the clothes and blanket we gave you
last month back at the River?" I asked.

"Shit, I dunno. Guess I lost 'em all...can't remember.
Anyway, they're gone...I'm hungry too. What's to eat?" he
said, sticking his moppy, sun-bleached head into the car.

We brought him some food and clothes, a little reluctantly and not as generously as before. He wasn't shy.

"This all you can spare!? How 'bout some new shoes
and warm socks. These are too thin, wrong color. Got any
meat? Vegetarian, huh? How about cheese? Some wine or
beer, maybe?" he said as he sifted through the food box
and clothes bag.

"Where's that jacket I asked for!?" he demanded, "And
those shoes too. Maybe a couple pair, just in case."

No matter what we gave him, he wasn't satisfied. The
clothes didn't fit, were the wrong color, or not enough.
The food wasn't filling, tasty, or didn't satisfy his hunger.
He was a ragged sight: unshaven, dirt-caked face, stained
teeth, bloodshot, beady eyes, half-naked, nervous, shaking,
and smelly as a skunk. We finally agreed to drive him down
the road to a sandy beach where he could spend the night.

He hopped in the back seat clutching his new possessions
in both arms and made himself at home. Throwing his dirty
feet up on our altar, slurping and dribbling juice from his
mouth all over our clothes, spilling peanut butter and honey
on the Sutras, and calling out orders and directions like
a roaring river-boat captain.

"Take a right. Slow down! No, not here, not sunny
enough. Try the next beach," taking a swig of juice.

*Disciples of the Buddha, when someone comes
to beg for the Bodhisattva's tongue, towards
the beggar, he is kind and compassionate, and
he uses gentle speech and loving words...*

Ten Transferences Chapter,
Avatamsaka Sutra

There are three kinds of giving in Buddhism: the giving of wealth and goods, the giving of Dharma, and the giving of fearlessness. Only as we drove back was I able to see
through the beggar's obnoxious front to what he was really
begging for: kindness, human sympathy, and some gentle words.
He wanted comfort and reassurance. The food, clothes, and
ride were only bids to spend more time with us. The guy was
lonely. Of all the sufferings people face, loneliness is
the most painful and frightening.

"Yeah it must be another mile, keep going," he said
over and over, buying more time and company.

"Maybe I could camp with you guys tonight, huh?" he said
asking for human contact and friends.

He was not the kind of person people would want to draw
near to. From the looks of it, he had been living outdoors,
exposed to the weather for months--alone, confused, begging,
and so burned-out and scattered he loses all his clothes and
can't remember his own name.

"Come on you guys," he pleaded,when we finally dropped
him off by a cement truss-bridge near a beach. "Stay and
talk to me!" The fear of being alone and pain are the two
biggest obstacles all cultivators must face and pass through
in order to obtain true liberation and comfort. But if you
are not cultivating, then pain and loneliness are dead-end
hells, not gates to wisdom and lasting joy. The beggar dwelt
in a living hell, but we didn't recognize his plight until
long after we separated. Only hours later, while sitting
in meditation did I see that fear of losing our goods blinded
me to his real need: "kindness, compassion, gentle speech,
and loving words." It was a time to give Dharma and fearlessness, not wealth. Unrestrained giving lacked common sense.
We increased his troubles by supporting his shiftless habits
and feeding his helpless dependency. The more we gave the
less he got. No wonder he was confused and unsatisfied!

The error was compounded by a fanciful notion that this
scruffy tramp was maybe a Bodhisattva or deva in disguise
come to check out our cultivation. Spiritual beings can and
do sometimes transform as beggars and in other unlikely forms
to test cultivators' sincerity or to teach them with such

clever expedients. But clearly, this was not one of those
times. He was just an ordinary down-and-out drifter on the
take, and we were caught day-dreaming.

In the end and quite unintentionally, the beggar taught
us a great deal about our selfish attachments and wooden
hearts. We learned once again that there are no fixed dharmas.
Every situation is unique and requires a unique response;
each person is special with a special set of needs. The
practice of giving is an art,not an onus. It is born of compassion and wisdom, not of guilt and greed for recognition--
sometimes demanding your very blood and sweat, and at other
times as little as a smile and a silent nod. But of all
gifts, the giving of Dharma is the highest, and that simply
means to at all times forsake yourself for others, and never
abandon the Bodhi mind--the mind that is nowhere attached
and never selfish.

> Good Man, of all offerings, the gift of Dharma
> is the highest kind. That is to say: the offering
> of cultivating according to the teachings, the offer-
> ing of benefitting all beings, the offering of gath-
> ering in all beings, the offering of standing in
> for living beings and receiving suffering in their
> place, the offering of diligently cultivating good
> roots, the offering of not forsaking the needs of
> a Bodhisattva, and the offering of not abandoning
> the Bodhi mind.
>> Universal Worthy's Conduct
>> and Vows Chapter,
>> Avatamsaka Sutra

HENG SURE, July 14, 1978
Friday

"DURABLE BODIES"

> Living beings are strange, ignorant, and lack-
> ing wisdom. Within their births and deaths, they
> receive countless numbers of bodies. These bodies
> are fragile and unsound. They quickly decay and
> pass away. Body after body has already gone bad,
> is now going bad, or is about to go bad. But liv-

168

*ing beings can't manage to use their precarious
bodies to seek durable bodies.*

> *Ten Practices Chapter,
> Avatamsaka Sutra*

Lives pass as quickly as cars on the highway. The
self-nature, the true soul, rides within each new body like
a passenger in a car. People sit isolated behind window
glass, riding spinning tires, staring at the pilgrims and
the Big Sur Coast. Each life gives another chance to "seek
a durable body" and break the rolling flow of birth and
death's pain. The Bodhisattva resolves to cultivate the Way,
to turn his decaying body around and to take charge of his
mind.

*I will thoroughly learn what all Buddhas know,
certify to All-wisdom and know all dharmas. I
will speak of this for all living beings, explain
the three periods of time as level and equal, and
how to follow in accord with the still, tranquil,
indestructible Dharma-nature. In this way I will
bring them eternal peace, security, and joy.*

> *Ten Practices Chapter,
> Avatamsaka Sutra*

All Buddhas cultivated to obtain durable bodies and then
made great vows to bring eternal peace, security, and joy
to everybody.

HENG CH'AU, July 14, 1978
Friday

*From a desire to increase and expand the minds
of Bodhisattvas within the Buddhadharma.*

> *Avatamsaka Sutra*

Sometimes even a dream can stretch and expand one's
mind.
Dream: The Venerable Hsu Yün's attendant comes to help
us out. The man appeared inept and non-descript, but he had
a good heart and his every action embodied true principle.
He told us to let things happen naturally and not to

force solutions or try to make everything perfect.

"When I was with the Master, lots of things were left unfinished and incomplete, especially personal affairs and needs. There was an unspoken way to be, unattached and free-wheeling, that was more important than goals or a rigid schedule," he said.

"The Master gave me lots of tasks, then kept me hopping so I could never complete them. By nature I was a clock-bound perfectionist. So that's how I was taught non-dwelling, my basic True Suchness Nature," he laughed. "He kept my mind stretching and loose, always ready to drop what I was doing to go and benefit others as conditions arose."

* * * * *

Everyday we find some fault or hang-up in our personalities. We try to get rid of it. It is not that we are looking for flaws, nor trying to sweep them under the rug. The bowing of itself exposes our imperfections and frailties like the sunlight reveals dust in the air.

Everyday the world speaks Dharma for us. We gladly listen. As things outside lose their flavor and lustre, things inside bring infinite wonder and contentment. It's not something we seek, for who could seek what they never even dreamed existed? The joy of cultivation is unexpected and comes only when one is not longing for it. The bowing heart of itself produces all good things.

> Now these times and places
> Both are infinite:
> One place is all places.
> One time is all time.

Avatamsaka Prologue

On one side, cars and motorcycles race by faster than the wind. On the other side, tall trees drop their pine needles in leisure as summer leaves fade slowly into Fall like people growing old. We bow down the middle at one mile per day, searching for the single mind. All is change; everything is impermanent. And yet, within the ceaseless flux, there is a sameness where time stands still and all places connect. Sometimes, while bowing, it's that way: now seems like forever; forever is right now. And in every-place, hasn't it always been the same? Cultivating the Way from dawn to dawn, from season to season--what could be more wonderful!

>...*They obtain the level equality of time because they earnestly do the Buddha's work throughout all seasons without stopping.*
>
> Avatamsaka Sutra

California Highway Patrol stopped to check us out. They said their office got a report that two men in robes were bowing down the middle of the highway during rush hour. We cleared up the misunderstanding and got the okay to continue.

Set up night camp by Pt. Lobos State Park.

HENG SURE, July 15, 1978
Saturday

After we knock off bowing for the day, I've been rushing for the pen to write a note to Heng Ch'au. Recognized today it's a pressure leak: I don't have urgent messages to relate, I want to relieve the loneliness of looking deeply into my own emptiness. The practice of silence hurts the ego's view of self-importance. Without words I feel vulnerable and insignificant.

Resolved today to enter the gate of silence, to bear the pressure and to use effort to recite this chapter of my Sutra. The self takes a loss each time I can hold my tongue.

> *He vows that all living beings leave behind all unbeneficial speech and take constant delight in solitary places, their minds without a second thought.*
>
> Ten Transferences Chapter,
> Avatamsaka Sutra

HENG CH'AU, July 15, 1978
Saturday

Bowed to the outskirts of Carmel. Tests came immediately. Five cars converged on the top of the hill--young men, drunks, and local rowdies.

"Hey, hey, let's get some action!" shouts someone with a whooping battle cry. They surround us, waiting for us to spook or to stiffen in self-defense. But we are too laid-back from the bowing and from the tranquil Big Sur Wilderness to get uptight or angry. They pick up on our soft space and begin to mellow. A few step closer and politely ask about the pilgrimage.

As the local toughs relax and leave, a self-appointed spokesman for the drunks steps closer. Swaying like a water-reed with one hand leaning on a telephone pole for support, he wets in his pants and shouts,

"In the name of Christ can I bless you?...no offense, telepathically, I mean." and then drove away.

One man did mock poses while his girlfriend snapped pictures. But after awhile, he too straightened up and asked some frank questions about the purposes of the journey.

"Here's a small offering," he said handing me some gas money. "It's worth a million what you're doing. We really need some good vibes, all we can get in the world. Good luck to you!"

They were all gone in a matter of minutes. We bowed down the other side of the hill into the Carmel area, through another "tollgate," past another test.

Everything's a test
To see what you will do...

It isn't heaven or hell that sends us tests. The tests are inherent in everything. They are built into the fabric of life and describe the nature of this world. The only way to pass them is to "produce the mind that is nowhere attached."

Unattached, we glide right through, responding freely, blending with conditions, unhindered by grasping or by hang-ups. In the winter as children, we skated on the frozen lakes, ponds, and rivers. As Wisconsin is the "land where the waters meet," there was always plenty of smooth, natural rinks. On the big lakes the ice lay flat, even and unobstructed for miles. At night, under a full moon, one could wander and glide along as freely and easily as a sailing ship. But if someone threw a shovel full of sand on the ice, when your skate blade hit that spot, your body jammed and jerked to a halt, and flipped head over heels. Attachments are the same way. They are like a splotch of sand on the smooth, unimpeded surface of the mind. With the slightest bit of attachment, sooner or later you'll take a fall, and

...mistaking what's before

172

> *your eyes,*
> *You'll have to start anew.*

HENG SURE, July 16, 1978
Sunday

This morning a gate in space opened, perhaps as a response to yesterday's resolve. Bowing down ladybug hill,
the shoreline panorama before me lost its limits and dimen-
sions. The world suddenly looked flat, still, unmoving.
Reality equally penetrated my body and all things without
boundaries, without stopping. I could relax securely into
the void. All thoughts of differences, all fears and plans
merged and vanished--briefly.

My mind couldn't sit still long; like an excited child
in a toy store, it leaped up to analyze the state, to define
and to name the experience. "Definition" means stopping
and that's how my Dharma Realm vision ended; a cloud of
noisy thoughts obstructed Proper mindfulness as thunder-
heads block the sun.

> *With not one thought produced*
> *The entire substance manifests.*
> *When the six organs suddenly move,*
> *You're covered by clouds.*

HENG CH'AU, July 16, 1978
Sunday

Road too narrow and dangerous for bowing. We advance
to the next clear spot counting spaces on our recitation
beads--three steps, one bead. Add 10% for margin of error
and bow in place using pebbles and bottle caps arranged on
the ground to keep a running tab.

Young men in hot cars roar in and out as we bow most
of the day on a hill above the Carmel River.

Arnold Lee from Pacifica came out to offer supplies
and check the station wagon.

"It's Gwan Yin Bodhisattva's Birthday next weekend."
he said, closing the hood. "You know, it's amazing how this
old car keeps holding together, really amazing!"

HENG SURE, July 17, 1978
Monday

> The further we go from what we knew,
> The closer we come to what is true.
> The more we grasp and try and choose,
> The more we stray, the more we lose.
> Nothing left to think or say:
> Quite naturally, the Middle Way.

HENG CH'AU, July 17, 1978
Monday

End of day. Soft, orange sun is setting low on the
horizon. Time to record a busy day's highlights and images
before sitting in meditation and erasing the lingering tra-
ces.

--Lots of whistling, jeering men strafing us, their
cars with two wheels on the road and two wheels on the shoulder, seeing how close they can get before we scare and run.

--The mysterious "Bridge Woman" from Malibu suddenly
appeared out of the morning fog as we reached the Carmel
River Bridge. No mistaking this one. I recognized and felt
the heavy, dark, magnetic energy that surrounds her even before I saw her face. We kept bowing. A man accompanied her
this time. They circled us slowly. Incredible tension
filled the air, as if all the trees were holding their breath.
They stood for a long time behind us, quietly, watching,
waiting. Finally, as the mist began to lift, they walked
past with folded hands, did a studied one-half bow, and
walked back over the bridge which lay shrouded in fog.

--John Powers and Aunt Carol stop with fresh orange
juice and encouragement. Aunt Carol was taken with the image
of the Thousand Hands, Thousand Eyes Gwan Yin Bodhisattva
hanging in the window.
"Oh! Who's that" she exclaimed with delight.

--A mother and her two children walking home from the
supermarket,stop to take bread and cheese from their grocery
bags as an offering.
"Thank you for the chance to share," they said.

--Ken Peterson, a reporter from the local newspaper,

came out to do an interview. Small town journalists
are so much more real and relaxed than their big city coun-
terparts. I have an image of Ken standing in a grassy field,
camera hanging from his neck, watching us with a smile. A
bag of peaches in one hand for an offering, a pencil and
notebook in the other, patiently, politely, waiting for the
last bow of the day before "intruding on your worship."
    "You even wear cotton shoes," he said, "No leather
is an act of compassion, isn't it?"
    --"C'mon pal, kiss the ground for me, whadya say, huh?"
someone shouts and taunts across the street.
    "They ain't kissing the ground, they're bowing. Leave
'em be," scolds a bystander. "They're doin no harm, maybe
some good. They got a right. Leave 'em be, I say."
    --Best part of the *L.A. Times* interview was seeing the
reporter, John, let go of his big-city cynicism and
lose his high-pressure ghost. John found us sitting in meditation on a wooden platform at the base of a PG&E power-
pole. These repairmen's platforms measure about the size
of a Ch'an bench and are excellent for sitting in dhyana
outside. The pole was set back off the noisy highway under
a canopy of cypress trees. It was so quiet you could hear
the eucalyptus berries dropping to the ground and the soft
whistling from the wings of a passing bird. John joined
us on the platform, took a deep breath and looked around as
he slowly exhaled in relief and said,
    "Hey, this is a nice spot here."
    Basically, he got all the information needed for his
story from our conversation in Los Angeles. We got a feeling from John that so many people share who come out: they
are in no hurry to go back home, they just like sitting
under a tree watching the bowing and thinking, or doing a
kind of not-thinking they haven't done since they were
children laying on their backs in the grass looking up at
the clouds.
    --Bowing while trail cycles and kids on moto-cross
bikes nonchalantly jump dirt mounds and moguls alongside us,
as if we were part of the gang. Occasionally a couple would
pause to watch.
    "Never tried anything like what they're doin, have you
Willie?"
    "No way I'd ever do *that!*"

        *Ch'an concentration holds the mind open to a
    simple condition...And it is beyond compare with*

anything in the world.

Ten Grounds Chapter,
Avatamsaka Sutra

End of day bowing reflection: all my errors and set-
backs come from scattered thoughts and a careless mind. The
direct cause-and-effect link between false thinking and ob-
structions to the Way is both instant and undeniable on
the highway. The very real dangers and immediate crises we
meet on the road pressure us into being on our best behavior
and stilling our minds. Survival often depends on just holding our minds to a single, proper condition with every ounce
of strength and will-power we can muster. There is no
greater power than a pure mind and a heart of patience; no
greater invitation to disaster than desire and thoughts of
anger.

But as soon as the tension outside eases, my mind slips
and slides right back into a thousand scattered pieces.
"Cultivating the Way is all about a single thought" the
Abbot told us. Literally, *yi syin* (一 心)in Chinese, meaning "one mind" or "one heart"--total, concentrated absorption.
It's so clear that the single mind is the only way to stop
our habitual outflows and to open genuine wisdom. So clear
that the liberated mind is the no-mind born from a "single
thought," that seeks nothing, stops nowhere, and is everywhere unconfused.

To accomplish pure white dharmas,
To perfect merit and virtue,
These are within All-wisdom;
When the mind is concentrated, one
never leaves these.

Praises in the Tushita Heaven
Palace,
Avatamsaka Sutra

HENG SURE, July 18, 1978
Tuesday

"SPRINGS OF GOOD CONDUCT"

Without the Sutra's description of the Bodhisattva
Path, we might forget that true health and enlightened wisdom exist at all. Before we began to cultivate, we never
knew the feeling of natural good health. We put up with

bad habits, and took as normal our worries, troubles, and defilements. The Sutra's pages glow with happiness, virtuous conduct, and purity. The Sutra's sages urge us to reclaim blessings and wisdom as our basic share.

As we crossed the Mesa, a fire-rescue medic told of his back-packing in Big Sur. "There are mountain springs everywhere, you needn't carry in water, even in the summer. I just tuck the handle of my Sierra Cup under my trouser belt and start walking. Every time I get thirsty another bubbling spring seems to pop up on the spot. And maybe it's because I'm a Pisces and a bit daffy about water, but I'd swear that every one of those springs tastes different. Each one is more cool, more pure, more refreshing than the last. You needn't worry about water through Big Sur. Those creeks are natural, fresh, the finest-tasting water on earth."

The Bodhisattva path, like a pure, bubbling spring, relies on countless, tiny drops of good conduct. Two such are a constant sense of shame for bad habits, and a deep wish to rescue all living beings from suffering.

Bodhisattvas concentrate their minds on saving all,
To get them to leave a host of evil deeds.
In this way they benefit all living beings.
Ever mindful, they never forsake this thought.

Ten Transferences Chapter,
Avatamsaka Sutra

A constant sense of shame heals the mind and washes it clean; repentance dislodges bad karma done in the past. I scooped up a jugful of spring water and watched while the silt settled. Karmic faults and bad habits settle and purify like sediment in the jug, and each bow is more pure, more cool, more refreshing than the last.

* * * * *

Today the air holds countless ladybugs. They suddenly appeared like a red mist on the asphalt, on the shrubs, on our robes. Yesterday we saw no ladybugs. Spontaneously, today, Big Sur celebrates Ladybug Day. "To everything, turn, turn, turn..."

Once we living beings dwelt in harmony with all of creation, our natures united with the Middle Way. But attaching to a view of self we leave the Tao. Confused, we do evil and break Nature's rules. Our bodies and minds grow stiff and kink into knots, twisted to the shape of our karmic retribution.

Cultivation irons out the kinks, unties the knots and relaxes the stiff places. A Good Advisor points us back to our original shape, to our true nature. Then step by step and bow by bow we ourselves erase the defilements and falseness that cover the true nature. When our share is purified once more, the Middle Way manifests from within, naturally, unexpectedly, like the ladybugs in Big Sur.

Why do we get confused and leave the Tao, our original home? When I can answer, I'll also be able to explain today's polka-dot shower of ladybugs.

> The mother of heaven and earth is born of the
>   Tao, it's said.
> The sun and moon, both bright, revolve in their
>   orbits.
> The basic substance of the myriad creatures is
>   also thus: in birth after birth,
> Transformation follows change in endless
>   wonder.

                    --Master Hua

HENG CH'AU, July 18, 1978
Tuesday

"Cut your hair and get a job, goddamit!" yells someone from a passing car.

Lots of nervous, angry, wired-tight people in this area. Why? "This is a very desirable place to live," a local policeman told us, "so there's a lot of people after a limited amount of land, space, wealth, and good times. It makes our job tough, *real* tough." The cop was voicing one of the fundamental teachings of Buddhism: desires causes suffering.

The passing cars sound like they are running on amphetamines, burning rubber, high-whining rpms, angry horns, shoving and leaning headlong into stop signs, into traffic lights, and into each other. They say, "Hurry, hurry up. Get out of my way. Gotta get it, gotta get it quick. Faster, faster,higher, higher. More!" As we bow we listen to the cars coming and going inches from our ears, hour after hour. And without talking to anyone we can hear what's going on inside people's minds. There's a lot of suffering in this world, even the streets and highways tell of it.

The people who yell the loudest are suffering the most.

Their frustrated nerves are raw, super-sensitive to shattered dreams, afraid of losing out. Those who can't slow down are as much chasing their fill as they are running away from the emptiness. No matter how fast we hustle and scramble, in the end, the Ghost of Impermanence always catches us and wins the race. You'd think that in such a beautiful, affluent, easy-living area that there would be widespread contentment and joy. Isn't it only the losers who suffer, only the poor people who never get what they want? No, the suffering *is* desire itself, and whether you get what you want or don't get what you want, dissatisfaction reigns supreme. Some have plenty, some have nothing, but everyone is dissatisfied. Discontent is the universal human condition.

Last month in L.A. the Abbot said,

"If you have troubles and things that upset you, things that make you uncomfortable, it's just due to frustration of your desires. If your desires were fulfilled, and disappeared, then you wouldn't have any afflictions. However, your desires can never be completely satisfied...Why do you have afflictions? It is because you have desire."

We have a desire, so we give it this, we have another desire, and we give it that. Another desire isn't satisfied with this or that, but wants something else. So we give it something else. Satisfied then? No. It still wants something else--a different position, a new place, an extra, maybe one more, a newer, a better, an improved, the latest, richer, longer-lasting...endless wanting, endless craving, endless suffering.

The Abbot also said,

"People have these attachments and say, 'This won't do, that won't do!' But when you breathe your last, will it do or not? Huh? At that time such protestations are useless." Then he recited a poem:

> *Fish swim in the water, people run amok*
> *in the world.*
> *Unable to do merit and virtue they forfeit*
> *their minds and create offenses.*
> *Gold and silver heaped like mountains,*
> *when one's eyes close all are gone.*
> *Empty-handed one sees Yama, with regrets*
> *and bitter tears.*

The pain and confusion of this upside-down, ceaseless wanting and acquiring, losing and hurting, is easily felt as we bow from town to town. We have left home and re-

nounced the worldly way, but we still know the suffering of
desire. We suffer, other's suffer. Other's pain is our
pain. We feel great joy for having the good fortune to be
shown a way out of the cage. All of these people are my good
friends and until they all get free and happy, my own freedom and happiness will never be complete.

HENG SURE, July 19, 1978
Wednesday

"LOST DAY FOUND"

Just like when the sun rises, and shines
   on the world,
The Buddha's field of blessings in the same way,
Changes all darkness and gloom.

Bodhisattvas Ask for
Clarification Chapter,
Avatamsaka Sutra

Fell into an old-fashioned moody state as I used to do
so often before beginning to cultivate. Felt out of sorts,
down on myself, full of watery blues and self-pity. Meditated before dawn with a head full of linty thoughts, how on
a "lost day" like this I would have hit the road to Ann Ar-
bor, or to Sausalito, to browse in the book shops and baker-
ies or idle away the afternoon among the sailboats moored
by the pierside cafés. Mind adrift, wheels spinning, life
in neutral gear, I wasted weeks this way, searching for the
Dharma, looking for my true self but lacking the precepts
and the Proper Path. I'd stare at my astrological chart, sip
hot saké, and sigh at the empty, aimless flavor of life. On
lost days like this one, I wallowed in soggy puddles!
Times have changed. Brisk morning fog surrounded us as
we finished a vigorous t'ai chi set. I hustled out to bow.
Gonna turn this wet state with Buddha-bowing! Good energy
is contagious. Before noon, the sun had melted the mist
and Max, a white-haired restaurant owner, dropped off a
hefty sack of black bread chunks.
"This is swarzbrot," he said through a thick German
accent. "They just throw it out--the scraps--so I thought
you could use it. We bake it ourselves," he said proudly.
Then he paused to let his words sink in.
"We like what you two are doing. We think it's just

fine."
    "I'll see you later down the highway with some more *swarzbrot*," he said happily as he left.
    Bows in place completed and lunch gear stored away, Heng Ch'au and I pow-wowed on the route ahead. The freeway forked, we had to walk a short section. I came upon a vista point and saw an unforgetable image: the Monterey peninsula spread out below, rimmed by the crystal-blue Pacific to the West, the sand-brown desolation of Fort Ord to the North, and the city of Salinas against the looming Gabilan mountains to the East.
    Filled my eyes and my heart both. We've come a long way! But not as far on foot as we've travelled in the mind. Bowing to the Buddha today transformed an afflicted state into level, cool clarity. This is a gift of life, a lost day found.

> *When Bodhisattvas cultivate good roots such as these, the Tathagata's wisdom-sun brightly illumines their hearts and forever dispels the darkness of ignorance. They diligently cultivate the Proper Dharma.*
>
> > *Ten Transferences Chapter,*
> > *Avatamsaka Sutra*

HENG CH'AU, July 19, 1978
Wednesday

    The Carmel-Monterey rush hour traffic, impels us into singleminded concentration. We bow less than 2 or 3 feet away from high-speed bumper-to-bumper metal monsters that begin at 6:00 A.M. and don't let up until midnight. Harsh screeching tires and roaring engines have replaced the soft, lulling sounds of the surf and cries of seagulls. The breeze from the sea exchanged for the wind from speeding machines, is 10 degrees warmer than the sea air because of engine heat and tire friction. At night we scrub oil and black smog soot from our hands and faces, ears and nose, instead of sand, thistles, and sticky pine tree resin.
    Rush hour in this scenic resort area is worse than in L.A. Los Angeles has freeways designed exclusively for

modern times' madness. But in this area, everybody wants
to live in the country and so they mass commute on quaint
little roads built for Sunday picnic touring and farmer's
wagons. High performance sports cars, vans, motorcycles,
delivery trucks and limousines pass like an endless beaded
necklace on a road too narrow to stick your arm out the
window without clipping a tree or slamming into the side
mirror of the cars in the next lane. Everybody trying to
get away from it all, ironically ending up more jammed and
packed together on a two-lane strip of asphalt in the "country" than on any crowded street corner in downtown L.A.

Gas fumes billow in thick, noxious layers, held in place
by close hills and dense, matted woods. We bow a shoulder
often not as wide as our own shoulders, as traffic shoots
down a steep hill like an Am Trak streamliner without tracks
on a greased hill. And at the bottom of the slide, a single
stop and go light feebly tries to control traffic that even
the police can't restrain.

The roadside is profusely littered with broken grills,
tail light pieces, twisted bumpers and shattered windshields;
the asphalt scarred with black skid marks, signal flare
burns, and dried blood stains. There's no room for error,
or false thinking.

We stay close together and alternate-bow, one up--the
other down--and sometimes wear our bright yellow rain jack-
ets to increase visibility. But our best protection is a
straight mind and proper concentration. When we are singleminded, even disasters turn lucky; but when we are scattered, the simplest things become incredibly difficult and
the safest places full of dangers.

> When the nature's in samadhi, demons
>   are subdued.
> Everyday is happy.
> False thoughts not arising,
> Everywhere is peaceful.

* * * * *

Woman: "I'm a Buddhist too! I have been here for a
long time."
Monk: "Oh?"
Woman: "Yes. Have you heard of Milarepa?"
Monk: "Yes."
Woman: "Well, that's my name. I am Milarepa."

* * * * *

George Haughton of the CHP stopped to see how we were managing with the traffic. "I'm curious,too" he said, "What you are doing takes real dedication. I admire that." He asked about the purposes of the pilgrimage, but he was more interested in the way we did it, not the why.

"That's the only way to do anything--all the way" he said. "Yup, that's the way I was brought up: if you're going to do a thing worth doing, then do it right and do it to the end. Glad I stopped. Good luck men."

> ...*people in the world, at their tasks,*
> *constantly spoil things within a moment of*
> *completing them.*
> *Heed no less the end than the beginning*
> *And your work will not be spoiled.*
>
> Lao Tzu

HENG CH'AU, July 20, 1978
Thursday

> *Just as no amount of poison*
> *Can change or spoil the great*
> *oceans,*
> *So too, the Bodhisattva is the*
> *same way.*
>
> Ten Transferences Chapter,
> Avatamsaka Sutra

Today was police day. We contacted the County Sheriff and then drove into Monterey to talk with City Police to map out a bowing route. The next six or seven miles of road are six-lane freeway prohibited to pedestrians.

Every police station is the same: radios and telephones ringing with the "poison" of crimes, robberies, rapes, murders, family fights turning to bloodshed, kidnappings, drugs, assaults, stolen cars, missing persons...the dregs of all that is vile and unwholesome in society flows nonstop into police stations and into police people. Often the jail is housed in the same building. As Heng Sure and I stand quietly talking to the watch-command sergeant, handcuffed, cursing, men, women, and even children, file in for booking, mug shots, and finger-printing on their way to a cell and laying all their cruel, hateful energy on everyone and everything they touch. So it is twenty-four hours a

day, 365 days a year, uninterrupted poison and yet there are
many policemen who take it like the ocean, without changing
or letting it spoil them. The Bodhisattva cultivates this
way.

*All those he meets, even if they are without
wisdom, if they don't know kindness and virtue,
if they are hateful, cruel and vile; poisonous,
arrogant and self-important; if their minds are
blinded and do not recognize wholesome dharmas--
all these types of oppressive afflictions from
the various kinds of living beings--cannot move
or confuse him.*

Ten Transferences Chapter,
Avatamsaka Sutra

Sergeant McFadden, Monterey Police, took time off his
busy schedule to sit down and draw a detailed map for us
through the city and by-passing the freeway. The phone
rings, he answers, an angry young lawyer threatens McFadden
with a lawsuit. Another phone rings concerning a runaway
girl, fifteen years old, who got caught up in a dope prosti-
tute ring, and ended up going insane. McFadden talks to
her grief-stricken mother somewhere in the Midwest. "Why
don't you fly out and take her home. I'll try to talk to
the officials and see if they'll drop the charges," he con-
soles. Another phone rings--more complaints, more anger,
more threats. McFadden hangs up, smiles and leans over the
bowing map again. He is super-helpful and supportive.
"I only worry for others' safety," he says. "No one is
a threat to me."

Compassionate cop Bodhisattva, McFadden raises our
spirits and speaks the Dharma of renouncing oneself for the
sake of others. He knows the joy and fearlessness of making
a great vow and sticking to it. It's like the Abbot told
us, "Just because it's difficult, that's why we want to go
and do it. The harder it is, the more we want to do it.
Don't wait to be asked and don't wait for people to thank
you."

*When the Bodhisattva takes on all this grievous
suffering, his vigor increases. He does not cast
it off, he does not hide from it. He is not scared
or startled. He does not retreat, he is not fright-
ened. He has no fatigue. Why?
As he has vowed, he really wants to take respon-*

184

sibility for all living beings and cause them to be liberated.

Ten Transferences Chapter,
Avatamsaka Sutra

HENG SURE, July 21, 1978
Friday

"SAGE'S KUNG FU"

People often ask us if we practice *kung fu* or "the arts" (martial arts). Probably the t.v. series "Kung Fu" planted the idea that all shaven-headed men in robes defend against attack with flying kicks and stiff-hand jabs. We do practice martial arts but apply it only in the mind. We are learning the highest of martial arts, the *kung fu* of Sages. Our opponent: the hardest to subdue, the trickiest, fastest foe of them all: the Ego and its desires.

To conquer others needs strength.
To conquer oneself is harder still.

Tao Te Ching, 33

Sage's *kung fu* turns cultivators into "Men of the Way with No Minds." Sages appear to be Big Dummies. They sit still, never fight when challenged, neither praise nor scolding move them. Nobody can provoke Sages to anger. Big Dummies have burned away all temper, all afflictions, and all desires in the fire of Ch'an concentration. Their minds are free of false-thoughts, their hearts are unobstructed by hang-ups or seeking. Seeking nothing, they fear no loss. They seek not even life itself. With nothing to win, and nothing to lose, what is there to fight about?

In every country in all directions, he is totally without reliance or dwelling. He does not seek even life itself or any of the host of dharmas. Nor does he falsely give rise to discriminations.

Avatamsaka Sutra

Sounds simple, but subduing the mind takes ultimate

kung ƒu. This morning I heard an engine roar to a stop just past my left ear as I bowed to the highway shoulder. Only CHP cruisers and police-wagons make that powerful whine. I figured we were in for a shakedown and braced for the worst. Metal jingled and leather creaked as the officer strode up to Heng Ch'au. Before the first word passed, my mind had already shifted into fighting gear. That's how little Sage's *kung ƒu* I possess. Fear and flexing still arise on their own. How could I hold my fire if actually challenged?

> He does not contend and ƒor that very rea-
> son,
> No one under heaven can contend with him.
>
> *Tao Te Ching, 22*

Had to laugh at my lack of skill as Heng Ch'au told the story later:

"That was Officer Taylor of the Monterey Police. He bowed respectfully and offered to help us through town. He's a Buddhist and interested in learning about the bowing, our Sutras, and the City of Ten Thousand Buddhas. Promised to stop again at midday with an offering of vegetables. Surprise, huh?"

HENG CH'AU, July 21, 1978
Friday

> There amid those beings' various kinds of
> voices, karma, attachments, styles of giving;
> their various unities and harmonies, their turn-
> ings, their deeds and their states, their var-
> ious births and deaths, among all of these he
> lives in peace...and never has a single thought
> of attachment. Why not? Because he attaches
> to nothing and relies on nothing. He benefits
> himself while benefitting others. He is pure
> and satisfied.
>
> *Ten Transferences Chapter,*
> *Avatamsaka Sutra*

"Among all of these he lives in peace." Camped over-

night on a wooded side road behind a shopping center.
Quietly chanted morning ceremony and sat in meditation before dawn. Did some t'ai ch'i, drank hot tea under an old,
gnarled oak tree. Began bowing on the small patch of grass
in the middle of the intersecting freeways' clover leaf of
the Munras Avenue off-ramp exit. The eye of a hurricane.
7:30 A.M. Sleepy "knights of the road" crawl out of
their pitched tent behind us, yawning and rubbing their
eyes half-asleep, half in disbelief to see two shaved-head,
long-robed monks bowing and chanting on the dew grass as
diesels and commuters roar and circle all around.
Dr. Kim, a local acupuncturist M.D., stops with an offering of fresh fruit.
"Gotta run, I'm late for an appointment to treat the
Archbishop" she says, "Your robes are traditional, reminds
me of home. My father used to dress like that."
8:00 A.M. A reporter from the *Monterey Herald* stops
for an interview.
9:00 A.M. A crazy man approaches praying and chanting,
making hexes and hand signs over us while another man smiles
and slips some money under the windshield wiper.
9:30 A.M. I hear the rumbling engine of a police car
pull to a slow stop behind us. A long pause and crackling
over the police radio before the door slams. I lift my
forehead from the ground to the shiny black shoes and blue-
uniformed legs waiting for me to get up. Trouble? No,
surprise.
"Excuse me, sorry to disturb you. I'm Officer Taylor
of the Monterey Police," he smiles and says his Dharma name
with folded hands and a half bow. "I'm a Buddhist layman.
Is there some way I can assist you?"
10:00 A.M. Another crazy man chanting and yelling,
trying to touch Heng Sure.
11:00 A.M. Officer Taylor returns with tofu, spinach,
and bean sprouts for lunch offering. Taylor asks questions
about the *Sixth Patriarch Sutra* and the Pure Land as he
washes the spinach and I fry up the tofu on a picnic table
in a small park off the main drag.
"I just subscribed to *Vajra Bodhi Sea* magazine. It's
really fine. I especially like the...Oops, excuse me,"he
says, ears cocked to his police car radio.
"...code 217, armed and dangerous, 10-4."
Taylor stiffens, and readies to run.
"Take a sandwich anyhow, " I shout.
"Okay, good idea," he says, slapping together a tofu
peanut butter sandwich. He does a quick bow and hops in
his car. Roars away, sirens blaring.

1:00 P.M. Richard from the *Salinas Californian* newspaper stops for a story.

"I talked to the police and they said good things about you. You're keeping all the rules and doing everything right. They say you respect the laws. A lot of people admire that," he says to us.

1:30 P.M. Back to bowing. Heavy traffic. Sash gets caught on my shoe heel. Rip! symbolic of my attached, "caught on the heel" state of mind.

2:00 P.M. Remember back to lunch, watching Heng Sure calmly doing the P'eng Bird ceremony as a carful of youths roll by, rock-'n-roll blaring, and a "Hey baldie!" We hardly notice anymore and after a few days, they hardly notice us either. Something about the bowing and traditional way of life smoothes the rough edges and melts suspicions. By the time we bow out of town we've become part of the community, fitted some place quietly into everybody's mind.

"Oh, there's the bowing monks" and "you know, I'm going to miss you two. I've gotten sort of used to seeing you bowing along the streets, you know?" says another with a kind of fondness. People gradually gather us in and treat us like family or old friends without ever having met or even spoken to us.

2:30 P.M. Officer Taylor returns to offer gas money and check our progress. Again the police radio calls him away,

"Suspect driving a '66 Chevy...proceed with caution..."

3:00 P.M. Break to meditate and write.

4:00 P.M. Piece of tomato from a passing car rolls by Heng Sure's head.

5:00 P.M. A man stops, places his hand kindly on my shoulder and says, "I don't know what you are doing, but I'm really impressed. May I make a contribution?"

5:30 P.M. Transfer the merit from the day's bowing. Walk back to car, drive the busy city streets scouting for a "still and quiet place" to spend the night.

Sitting in meditation in the car, a chance to reflect on today's lessons...learning to let go and dwell in proper thought.

Proper thoughts manifest before me without any grasping or attaching to them.

Ten Transferences Chapter,
Avatamsaka Sutra

I came into the bustling Carmel/Monterey area all spaced-out and attached to the Big Sur wilderness bliss. Primed for uninterrupted bowing and long, tranquil meditation, the big city hustle and hype spun me for a loop. When things inevitably came up that didn't mesh with my idyllic, pastoral expectations, I tripped and stumbled over my own feet. Tearing my sash on my own heel served to dramatically remind me that I abandoned proper thought. What is proper thought? Proper thought is just no-thought. That is to say, producing the thought that dwells nowhere and attaches to nothing--not even to one's own practice or to a seemingly samadhi state of mind.

> He does not attach to himself, he does not attach to others. He does not attach to mindfulness, nor does he attach to vows. He does not attach to samadhi or to contemplation. He attaches neither to still concentration or to states...and then proper thought manifests before him without any grasping or attaching.
>
> Ten Transferences Chapter,
> Avatamsaka Sutra

Now, day's end, I sit in the car bent over our kerosene lamp sewing up the tear outside with needle and thread; correcting the error inside with the Sutra and introspection.

HENG SURE, July 22, 1978
Saturday

"NO SEEKING"

The basic explanation of not seeking is so right on: don't look ahead for worldly goods or world-transcending accomplishment. Whatever your karma concocts will appear in your path without effort. Appreciate what arrives as is, neither grasping for more nor rejecting its fullness. Everything on the trip I've reached for has burned my hands before it disappeared. Why? Because seeking is desire, desire forces nature, forcing obstructs the natural flow.

> The Five Desires are dharmas that obstruct the Way. They can even keep one from Supreme Bodhi. Therefore I will not entertain a single thought of desire. My mind will be as pure as the Buddha's.

Ten Practices Chapter,
Avatamsaka Sutra

HENG CH'AU, July 22, 1978
Saturday

"WHERE'S THE BUDDHA"

To understand and know one's self-nature
is called the Buddha.

Avatamsaka Sutra

Downtown Monterey on a Saturday morning--shoppers,
tourists, merchants and the most frequently asked question:
"Hey, what are you doing?"
"Bowing," I answer.
"To who? To God?" he asks.
"To the Buddha," I say.
"What's the Buddha? Is he your god?"
"Not exactly..." I begin.
"Well, then what!? God's in heaven, but where's the
Buddha?" he demands.
Sometimes there's an honest, open mind behind the
questions and a chance to give an honest, open-minded answer.
Sometimes there's a brick wall of antagonism and frozen
opinion behind the probing, allowing only silence to answer.
But inside as I bow I silently give this reply:

The Guiding Master neither comes nor goes,
Moreover he dwells nowhere.
Being apart from all upside-down thinking,
Is called Equal and Proper Enlightenment.

The Thus Come One dwells nowhere
And yet he universally inhabits all countries.
He goes to all lands
And he sees all places.

Praises in the Tushita Heaven
Palace,
Avatamsaka Sutra

The Buddha is one who is perfectly enlightened. The
Buddha is just the awakening to our self-nature, which each
of us is capable of experiencing.

The self-nature is our original face, the root and source
that all living creatures seek to return to and the place
where all the searching ends. It is also the Middle Way
and "reaching the other shore." It is Bodhi--Unsurpassed
Proper, Equal and Right Enlightenment. All beings have the
nature of Buddha, all can become Buddhas.
   The self-nature doesn't come or go, isn't lost or gained.
We awaken to it by cultivating pure conduct, samadhi, and
wisdom, or we cover it over with greed, hatred, and stupidity.
But it never leaves us. No one can give it to us; no one
can take it away.
   "Where is the Buddha...what is the Buddha?"asks the
stranger. The Sutra we carry in the knapsack on our back
says,

> *If one wishes to know*
> *All Buddhas of the three periods of time,*
> *Contemplate the nature of the Dharma Realm:*
> *For everything is made from the mind alone.*

   But our minds are like a dusty mirror, the brilliance
of which is obscured by thoughts of greed, hate, and envy;
tarnished by flattery, deceit and arrogance. I am this way,
all living beings are this way. And yet if we can cleanse
the dirt and with an upright mind constantly do good and
refrain from evil, if at all times we can purify our thoughts
and illumine our own mind, then we can return to the knowledge and vision of the Buddha. The Buddha is just our own
mind.

> *You should now believe that the Buddhas'*
> *knowledge and vision is simply your own mind,*
> *for there is no other Buddha,*

said the Great Master, the Sixth Patriarch.
   Bowing gradually restores the natural brilliance of our
minds. It is a way to gently brush it again and again so
that piled-up obstacles vanish. And when all the dust is
gone, one is called the Buddha.

* * * * *

   A group of Vietnamese laypeople met us this A.M. in
Monterey. After a meal offering under some shade trees in
a little park, despite the nearly seven hour drive from L.A.,
they still found energy to do three steps one bow with us be-

fore and after lunch. Really inspiring! We bowed tandem
on a bike lane through Monterey Park and into the business
district--a motley train of nine Buddhists, with long gray
or brown robes blowing in the wind, in a syncopated up and
down wave with two little boys bringing up the rear.
      "Hey Dad! Look!" said a boy to his father, nearly fall-
ing off his bicycle. "What are they doing?"
      "I don't know son," said his slightly perplexed father.
"It's kind of peaceful though, isn't it?" as they pulled off
the trail to watch us pass.

                    * * * * *

      Two Muslims outside of a Denny's Restaurant.
      "Wonderful, but it's so dirty here. You'd be better
in a cleaner place." they said.
      "Clean or dirty is all in how you look at it" I said.
      "I know, but even with a clean mind, the sidewalk is
still so dirty!" they replied.

            Defilement and purity
            In measureless kshetra seeds,
            All comes about from the thoughts
                of living beings.
            They are held up through the strength
                of Bodhisattvas.

                    Worlds of the Flower Treasury,
                    Avatamsaka Sutra

      Dirty and clean depend on how you look at it. For
example, most people feel the human body is a priceless
treasure--we constantly lust after it, pamper and parade
it, dote over and decorate it and never tire of trying to
please and preserve it. But in reality, the body is just
a toilet--a stinking, leaking garbage bag. Without soap,
perfumes, deodorants, pastes, creams, powders and a chest
full of medicines, sprays, salves and pills, it would smell
and start to go bad in a few hours. Every hole emits a
foul, disgusting substance: matter from the eyes, mucus
from the nose, wax from ears, saliva from the mouth, along
with urine and excrement, blood and pus, flakes of dead
skin and even repulsive sweat from every pore. Yet we in-
sist on treating it like a sacred shrine. We consider it
lovely and are abhorred at the prospect of it getting "dirty"
on the sidewalk, or smudged with the earth's soil. Yet the
food we eat comes from the earth and is saturated with

manure fertilizers, chemical pesticides, and the like. The
water we drink and the air we breathe, teem with countless
micro-organisms, bacteria, spores, poisons, even radioactive
dust.
In this world, things are not what they seem. Dirty
and pure intermingle and unite. So it's said,

Dirty worlds are identical with pure worlds;
Pure worlds are identical with dirty worlds.

> *Merit and Virtue from First*
> *Bringing Forth The Mind,*
> *. Avatamsaka Sutra*

Inside the "clean" twenty-four hour restaurant we are
bowing in front of, on the "dirty" sidewalk, people nonchalantly gobble down beef, pork, chicken, fish, lamb,served on
sterilized plates or wrapped in sanitary white paper and
plastic cups. But the food itself, the flesh of dead animals,
is so loaded with chemicals, artificial and natural toxins
that consumption of it amounts to slow suicide.
Meat is now known to be a major cause of cancer.. Cancer comes to even the cleanest homes to kill even the most
careful people. After lunch some people break open a sur-
gically clean, plastic-sealed pack of lily white cigarettes
and leisurely inhale the toxic fumes identical to those
spewed from a car's exhaust pipe. Clearly labelled "Ha-·
zardous to your health," they deeply swallow it and then
blow the noxious gas into their friends' faces. So it's
all in how one looks at it.

> *When living beings thoughts are pure,*
> *Then the lands they see are also com-*
> *pletely pure.*

> *Worlds of the Flower Treasury,*
> *Avatamsaka Sutra*

With a pure mind even a dirty place is pure; with a
dirty mind, even a pure place becomes dirty. The dirtiest
things in this world are not the city sidewalks, the toilets
or even the garbage dumps. The dirtiest things are thoughts
of anger and harming, acts of destruction and selfishness.
Atomic bombs and violence are impure; desire and lust are
dirty. The cleanest, most pure place to live in is an "unattached, unbound, liberated mind." Precepts are pure,
giving is pure, subduing oneself is pure.

He makes offerings to measureless, boundless numbers of Buddhas.
He practices giving, holds precepts, and subdues all of his faculties.
Because he wants to be of benefit to all living beings and universally cause them all to be pure.

Ten Transferences Chapter,
Avatamsaka Sutra

HENG SURE, July 23, 1978
Sunday

"THE 1978 CH'AN SESSION"

Every day our sense of wonder grows and our respect deepens for this ancient psycho-therapy called Buddha Dharma that carries us back to the source of our minds. It takes steady pressure without forcing,solid work on the Middle Way.

It's the 1978 Ch'an session.
Not too slow, not too fast. Don't get uptight!
Just make steady, constant, vigorous advance.
Soon you'll reach the ground of all Buddhas.

--Master Hua

HENG CH'AU, July 23, 1978
Sunday

Monterey. A sunny, quiet Sunday. The usual city bowing scene: tourists with cameras trying to be blase about us; young men in roaring, rumbling hot cars pulling up alongside to test our nerves and count coup; sincere people who fit into no age, class, race, or creed bracket except to share a common heart of pure kindness and a dream for world peace. They come up, wish us "good luck," and sometimes ask how they can help.

At the close of day as we bow the tail-end of the

main drag, two Christian preachers descend on us. Open bibles,
closed minds, and a hail of fire and brimstone.
"Did anyone ever speak the gospel for you?" one shouts.
"Praise Jesus! Hallelujah! Amen, amen!" he screams
holding up a black book. "This is *the* Bible! The *Holeee*...
Bible!"
Then they let go with non-stop talking and questions.
No time to answer, just steady threats, warnings, insults
and denunciations. They are especially virulent towards the
Buddha.
"Jesus is God. He's number one. The Buddha was a false
prophet. You're going to hell. You can't get to heaven
following the Buddha," railed one with a red face.
"You think the Buddha had a good method, well Jesus was
around long before the Buddha," softly begins the other,
then suddenly raises his voice and loses his composure, Foam-
ing at the mouth, he vituperates,
"Jesus is ultimate, the Buddha isn't! Jesus got out,
the Buddha didn't get out. Only Jesus can save you. The
Buddha can't save you. You're throwing your life away.
Whatever or whoever you're bowing for isn't going to do you
a bit of good. Just accept the Lord Jesus. Do you hear
me?" he threatens. "*Accept* the Lord Jesus!"

> *Hearing praise or slander of the Buddha or
> the Buddhadharma,
> Or of the Bodhisattvas and the conduct they
> practice...
> Their minds do not move.
> ...Whether they exist or not, escape or don't
> escape--
> Although they hear this spoken, still do not
> retreat.*

> *Ten Dwellings Chapter,
> Avatamsaka Sutra*

The preachers were growing more and more hostile and
irrational. Their manner belligerent, their words wild:
"God sees you as a filthy, dirty rag. Did you know
that?" sneered one.
A mother and her two young children had joined the bowing for the afternoon. They witnessed the encounter in
stunned silence, almost in shock. They are gentle, peaceful
people. One of the children cried once when he accidently
killed an ant. They were worried and afraid, nearly terri-

fied by the two preachers' abusive and threatening behavior.
They had never seen anybody so violent and out of control
especially so real and up close.

Suddenly a stranger emerged from a closed used car lot.
He came running across the street, light and swift as the
wind. The atmosphere became electric, charged. Stocky and
muscular, he had curly red hair and a glow of good light
around him.

Planting both feet solidly on the pavement he wedged
between the preachers and us, stuck his chest out and squared
off to do battle. His energy was powerful, martial; his
demeanor righteous. His voice was commanding, yet not oppressive. Incensed without losing self-control, he spoke
like an axe splitting wood, every word solid and decisive.
He was a fire-brand, gifted with an unfaltering, fearless
eloquence. His sense of fair play had been riled and he was
primed for an all-out street corner skirmish. He was ready
to defend principles he deeply believed in, and he knew the
Bible better than the self-styled preachers.

"Did 'ja ever read about the good Samaritan?" he
challenged the pair. "Leave these people alone. Be compassionate! That's the whole point, that's what Jesus taught.
What Jesus said, do! Don't just preach it and not practice
it!"

The preachers were stunned momentarily, their fire
doused by cold water.

"Yes, but..." one began in protest.

"How would you like it if someone came up and tried to
take your God away from you?" asked the stranger. "*Do not*
interfere with these people, I'm telling you." he said in a
tone that no one would want to take lightly. It had the air
of an imperial command or of heaven itself speaking.

"But!!" began one of the preachers lamely, "You know
God said only by grace do you come unto Him. You see what
they are doing, though? They're trying to work their way
there."

"That's right," snapped the stranger, "and you know,
I think they are going to make it before *you* will."

It was all over. The air cleared, the preachers backed
off, totally subdued and upended. We continued on our way.
From behind I heard one of the preachers faintly offer an
excuse,

"Well, we were just trying to spread the gospel..."

"*They* are the ones who are *really* spreading the gospel,"
said the stranger. "And what are you doing? You're hassling
them. You ought to go out barefoot and preach. That's what
Jesus did."

196

(The children later told us that as soon as they saw
him, they knew he was "a good guy." They saw "light coming
from him" and immediately were unafraid and happy to see him).
"He was a real Dharma protector, I know it. He just came
out of nowhere and after it was all over, he disappeared
again." said one of the boys.

HENG SURE, July 24, 1978
Monday

Facing Nature's challenges in Big Sur yielded clear
visions, deep insights. Back in civilization again, the
elements have calmed but the inner gales have kicked up a
howl. Need a Bodhisattva's vajra resolve to weather both
cultivation-smelting inside, and culture shock outside.
Faces stare from windows in the homes of Monterey. We're
bowing on sidewalks again after sixty miles of rugged rocks
and dusty turnoffs. Pacing a parking lot, counting bows in
place beside clicking cameras and stinking litter: MacDonald's
bags and Coors cans. I can smell the mustard on the burger
wrappers from twenty paces away. My heart wants the purity
of the lonely wilderness. My six senses flow into the world
of dusty humanity like pickpockets in a carnival crowd.
But Buddhas take the heart of Great Compassion as their
substance, and all living beings as their body. Everybody
has afflictions. Crossing over afflictions turns beings
into Buddhas. Afflictions come from unsatisfied desire.
Able to be content in any situation, the Bodhisattva is always happy. Able to be patient with all states, Bodhisattvas
are naturally at peace. Face it, I haven't subdued my mind.
This verse we read describes my condition and my hope of
salvation:

> Living beings are confused and false, re-
> plete with all sufferings.
> The Buddha in their midst constantly saves
> and protects them,
> Causing them to eradicate all doubts and to
> get happy.
> This is the contemplation of the Spirit Un-
> moving Light.

> World Rulers Wonderful Adorn-
> ments Chapter,
> Avatamsaka Sutra

* * * * *

"OUT-OF-TIME"

People must find our street-crossing ritual as out-of-time as we feel to enact it. It's a blend of Huck Finn and Tom Swift, or as when primitive man steps into the space age. We've done it now for nearly six hundred miles, but I still experience a humorous jolt, as if crawling through a keyhole in time.

Monks bow reverently up to a roaring thoroughfare, slow as turtles, before a dizzying torrent of traffic. Their devotions are ancient and universal. Rising from a bow before whizzing, spinning tires, they stand, then walk to the light pole and push the traffic signal button. They wait with folded hands for the tides of traffic to part. The smoking chariots pause, the pilgrims timidly progress with palms together, counting steps and bows. Safely on the other shore, they resume prostrations in a clear spot, bowing in place to cover the distance paced on foot.

We feel like throwbacks to another millennium. Bowing monks must look anachronous in a world of cement and chain link barriers, our flapping brown precept sashes incongruous amid harsh signs: Wrong Way! Do Not Enter! Go Back! No Turns! our melodic homage to the Sutra swallowed by the din of horns and growling engines.

Who will endure? Fossil fuels that power the automobiles will run dry one day. The fuel of faith and understanding that carries pilgrims back to the heart of things is inexhaustible.

> The Dharma Realm is its substance; what is
>   there outside of it?
> Empty space is its function; there's nothing
>   it doesn't contain.
> All of creation is level and equal; abandon
>   discriminations.
> When not a single thought appears, cut off
>   the traces of words.
>
> Venerable Master Hua

198

HENG CH'AU, July 24, 1978
Monday

Fine weapons are still ill-omened things.

Lao Tzu

Bowing past tall barbed wire fence of the Naval Post-
Graduate School and military installation. A few miles a-
head sits the mammoth Fort Ord Military Base. One can feel
it in the air--we have bowed through three major military
camps since L.A. and each one was a world of heavy energies
all to itself.

But today I felt that heavy weight fall on my shoulders
and a deep pain fill my heart. Memories and pictures of
countless wars from beginningless time filled my mind.
Scenes of swords, knives, spears flashing and dashing; bul-
lets, bombs, lasers, gases like monsoon rains filling the
sky and earth below. I heard the cries and wailing, groan-
ing and tears, the protests, mourning and moral outrage of
generation after generation, over and over. The ancients
conducted their war victories as funerals. In modern times
there are no victories to even celebrate with grief, for the
wars never end. They just go on and on like waves breaking
on the shore.

Today we felt the power of great compassion meeting the
power of great destruction: the bowing next to barb wire,
monks in a forest of missles. Who will win?

*Yielding conquers the resistant, and soft
overcomes the hard...Therefore the weapon that
is too hard will be broken, the tree that has
the hardest wood will be cut down. Truly the
hard and the mighty are cast down; the soft and
weak set on high.*

Tao Te Ching

Perhaps, but "casting down" and "setting on high,"
conquering and overcoming" are still a kind of fighting,
still not the vast heart of universal compassion, not the
highest kindness. There are no winners in war, no victories

in slaying,and no joy in conquering. The karma of violence
and contention, the retribution of slaughter and strife,
equally injure all that lives. Those who overcome will later
be overcome; the slain return to claim the slayer. And so,
everyone loses.

*Where armies are, thorns and brambles
    grow.
The raising of a great host
Is followed by a year of dearth.*

Lao Tzu

Why are there so many disasters and calamities in the
world? Why so many famines and droughts, so much pestilence
and suffering? The karma of war, the karma of hatred, the
karma of anger, are the reasons.
In order to kill there must be hate. In order to hate
there must be anger. To get angry there must be a self. For
the hatred and anger that creates all the killing requires
distance. Distance between a you and a me, distance between
a self and others, distance between a we and a they. The
distance starts with a simple false thought of self and grows
into fences, borders, countries, and ideologies. Then come
uniforms, weapons, declarations and wars.

*He vows that all beings give up and leave behind
all knives, swords, military weapons, and tools of
evil and suffering, and that they cultivate the many
kinds of good karma.*

*Ten Transferences Chapter,
Avatamsaka Sutra*

In all directions to the exhaustion of empty space and
the ends of the Dharma Realm, we are all one substance, one
nature, one heart. No me, no you, no self, no others. As
long as one living being suffers, we all suffer. As long
as one living being loses, we all lose. This is the Buddhas'
message: Be compassionate. Be one substance with everything
--without limit, without measure, without distance. The
Buddha is just all living beings, so Buddhists don't oppose
war, we do not war. The answer to killing is to liberate
life.

*All Buddhas, Thus Come Ones, take the heart
of great compassion as their body...When one uses*

*the heart of great compassion to get along with
all living beings, then one can accomplish making
offerings to the Thus Come One.*

*Universal Worthy's Conduct
and Vows,
Avatamsaka Sutra*

A G.I. in green army fatigues and black paratrooper boots
walks up, respectfully half-bows with folded hands and makes
an offering. The soldier was happy. For a brief moment he
left behind all military weapons to cultivate good karma.
And for that brief moment, the whole world felt brighter
and more peaceful.

* * * * *

"NOSE TO NOSE"

Doing dishes in a lot across from the Navy Base. Heng
Sure went back to bow. A veteran military man comes up.
Late 40's, imposing as a middle line backer, powerful as a
grizzly bear, stocky, 250 pounds of pure muscles--tatoos,
full beard, leather-wrinkled, scarred face. A cigarette
hanging from corner of mouth, he squares off about two feet
away blocking me in between open car doors. Hands on hips,
chest puffed up and locked.
    "That one of your people down there?" he demands, point-
ing to Heng Sure.
    "Uh huh," I say.
    "Yeah, there he is, that one," he barks, as Heng Sure
comes up from a bow.
    "Right. We're Buddhist monks making a bowing pilgri-
mage," I say.
    "Well, okay," (he says in a tone like, "You must be
breaking some rules--you haven't got my permission yet"),
"What the devil for?" he snaps.
    "To try to turn back some disasters and suffering in
the world," I answer.
    "Well okay (hesitating). I thought *we* had lost a man.
Where's he goin'?" still flexed and uptight.
    "To the City of Ten Thousand Buddhas near Ukiah. We
bow every three steps for peace. Started fifteen months
ago in L.A.," I say.
    "Like that!? Well okay..." Although hostile outside,
he is a softy inside. But he's holding out, suspending
judgement and still suspicious.

"How do you support yourselves?"
"We don't beg or solicit. We only take what is offered along the way."
"Well okay..."(takes a last long violent drag off the cigarette he's pinched between his thumb and finger, and then flips it to the ground and squashes it with his heel). He keeps checking my face and eyes for something. Trust? A crack? Weakness? Genuineness?
The air is tense and waiting. Then out of the clear blue he says,
"Well you better do something about your nose, it's bleeding," like a fussing parent.
"Huh? Oh, I guess it is. Sunburn and then it dries out." I say.
"You've been *picking* at it!" he scolds, now clearly like a loving mother playing tough, "Haven't you?"
"It takes one to know one." I say, smiling.
"I guess it does,"he says faintly. The vibes melt and tension breaks. His face softens and tense body visibly relaxes as he drops his doubts and suspicions. The air turns peaceful again. He backs away from the door and wanders over to pick up a piece of pipe. "Hmmm, good pipe...I have a use for this..."
He starts to drift away and then mumbles over his shoulder, "Well okay." and leaves.

They vow that all beings constantly be able to contemplate all Buddhadharmas and pluck out the arrows of doubts, their minds peaceful and unthreatened.

Ten Transferences Chapter,
Avatamsaka Sutra

* * * * *

Monday Night

End of day. Night descends. City lights, dancing neon bar-'n-grill signs eclipse the stars. Asphalt and cement, business and homes welded together in an unbroken blanket covering the earth. No place to pitch a camp or hide away to. For lack of choice we end up in a black top parking lot right next to the busy thoroughfare--no trees, no grass, no evening stillness. The parking lot is a hang-out for local toughs in hot cars, a rendezvous spot for motorcycle gangs in between bar-hopping, and a crash pad for transients and homeless winos. And yet, as always on this journey, no matter how dangerous or threatening things outside become, "someone up there likes us," as the saying goes. As long as we try our best to be sincere and pure in thought, to repent of past error, to correct present transgressions, then we walk and dwell within an invisible circle of protection and luckiness. Certainly not our own strength or skill could account for what at times approaches inconceivable security and safe-guarding. We are deeply grateful, for it allows the bowing to go on.

> *Bodhisattvas' wisdom of guarding and being mindful of beings is inconceivable...*
>
> *Entering the Dharma Realm,*
> *Avatamsaka Sutra*

For example, tonight I meditated in the car as Heng Sure exercised outside in the parking lot. A tough gang of bikers roared up on their custom Harleys, hostile and looking for trouble.

"Yeah, you're right, there *he* is!" shouts one, pointing to our car. "C'mon, let's get 'em!"

But then, for no apparent reason, they all turn around and drive away.

Later, at about 3:30 A.M., three police cars surround us in a blaze of flashing red and flood lights. There's no overnight camping allowed and we could be arrested. But the police shakedown and frisk suspects in the car next to us, and then tell them to "move on." We quietly do morning chanting fully expecting to be routed as the police mill around our car and clean up the area of drifters, tramps and illegal campers. But, it's as if we are invisible. They never bothered us even with a flashlight shined in the window. After, we were the only people in the whole lot. The old station wagon spotlighted under a tall metal neon street light, totally overlooked and undisturbed by the police patrol.

> *Bodhisattvas' wisdom of guarding and protecting beings is inconceivable.*
>
> *Entering the Dharma Realm,*
> *Avatamsaka Sutra*

HENG SURE, July 25, 1978
Tuesday

"LIGHTHOUSE BEACONS: THE POWER OF VOWS"

We've camped beneath the beacon lights of Coast Guard lighthouses at Pt. Piedras Blancas and Pt. Sur. Their brilliant fire split the night and warned big ships off the rocks below. Their deep foghorns guided sailors through storms and mist. Mariners rely on light stations as guides through the vast ocean. Cultivators rely on great vows in their journey through the wilderness of birth and death. Ultimately, vows light the way to the "Jeweled City of Sarvajna," and the realization of the Buddha's wisdom.

Bodhisattvas make infinite, limitless vows, vows impossible to fulfil in one lifetime. They vow to take all living beings across to Buddhahood. This pure wish acts as a lighthouse beacon cutting through the darkness of death and rebirth, leading Bodhisattvas back life after life to cultivate the Way. Vows are deep promises that light up the soul.

Because they wish to dwell at peace in the Bodhisattva path, because they seek All-wisdom... they do not forsake their basic vows.

Avatamsaka Sutra

HENG CH'AU, July 25, 1978
Tuesday

First you should not be selfish, nor calculate for yourself in any way...We who cultivate the Way should at all times reverse the light and illumine within.

Master Hua

The misunderstanding and errors that arise between myself and others are my faults,not theirs. The ancients always blamed themselves when things went wrong. They didn't point fingers and criticize. All my problems come from the presence of a self; all my offenses from self-seeking.

I observe that selfless people are able to get along with anyone, even evil and hateful individuals; whereas selfish people can't get along with anyone and soon offend even good and gentle folks.

What we are drawn to and admire most in a person is the lack of selfishness. Unselfishness is the root of merit and virtue, the source of blessings and honor, and the secret of becoming a fully realized person. Cultivators first and foremost strive to get rid of selfishness and become good people. For it's said,

> Once the way of a person is perfected,
> The Buddhas' Way accomplishes itself.

* * * * *

"BODY THOUGHTS"

> With pure food and clear tea,
> The mind errs not, enjoying Dharma
> night and day.

> --from Song of the Skin Bag
> by Ven. Hsu Yun

We usually eat simple food--rice and vegetables, bread and fruit--not too many dishes or flavors. But today we received an offering of rich bean curd dishes, curried vegetables, braised gluten ("mock meat"), heavy sweet rice, roasted nuts, cheese, MacDonalds french fries, and fruit juice drink. Bowing after lunch was pure anguish.

The body is an unruly and contrary thing. "Ultimately, what is a body?" I thought to myself as I bowed along in a fog of discomfort and turbid thoughts. It's said,

> We falsely borrow the four elements
> to make our bodies.

Like a magician conjures up forms and images as if from thin air, our bodies are conjured up from earth, air, fire, and water, as if born from an illusion.

Bits and pieces from a talk I once heard from a learned old Dharma Master came to mind. He said when a person dies and "descends," a single human being can be reborn as thousands of ants or mosquitos, or perhaps as a number of animals. A human body is composed of 84,000 "corpse worms" that temporarily rely on and take form as a body. At death they consume the body and scatter back into the elements. Depending on one's karma, the soul goes off to another "hotel room." One can ascend into the heavens, asura realm, or be reborn as a human again or descend into the hells, animals, or ghost realms.

The body itself is an illusion, like a rainbow or a mirage created by thoughts of desire (ignorance). The elder monk described the Twelve Conditioned Links, the famous Buddhist doctrine on the causes and workings of the turning wheel of ceaseless births and deaths. He said the Twelve Links explain the big picture of existence as well as the small picture: the birth, dwelling, decline, and death of a single individual. It began like this,

Ignorance conditions activities. This means emotional love (ignorance) gives rise to sexual union, (activity) when the sperm and blood unite.

Activity conditions consciousness, means that at the moment of conception, there is consciousness and awareness. This consciousness enters the womb, becoming housed in the foetus.

Consciousness conditions name and form. This refers to the foetus which now has a shape and a name. The foetus evolves and produces the six sense organs, thus,

Name and form condition the six places. Once there are sense organs, touch-awareness arises, and so it follows that,

The six places condition contact. The process goes on through stages of feeling, love, grasping, existence (becoming), birth, old age, and death. Then it begins all over again because of karma and emotion, ignorance and attachments. From the time it's in the womb, the foetus is accustomed to being caressed and rubbed. After birth it still craves this contact. Thus we are born from desire and die from desire. The human body isn't ultimate or pure. Born from confusion and thoughts of desire, dwelling briefly in the world like a snowflake on the sun, it quickly goes bad and disappears.

Today these thoughts made a deep impression. I recognized the instability and impurity of my own body and remembered the old monk's exhortation to quickly bring forth the mind for Bodhi and unite with the Dharma-Nature body. "If you can't put down what's false, how can you pick up what's true?" he asked.

He knows the body is impermanent, extremely
foul and impure. He enlightens to this dharma
and produces great happiness...He uses his un-
stable body and changes it into a solid body...
And he vows that all beings get the body that is
born of the Dharma Realm and which together with
the Thus Come One relies on nothing.

Ten Transferences Chapter,
Avatamsaka Sutra

* * * * *

Layman Kuo Chao from Pacifica, arrived at the end of the
day to drive us to Gold Mt. Monastery in San Francisco. We
left our car with Sgt. McFadden in the Monterey Police lot.
Travelling can scatter one's energy. Sitting in full lotus
gathers back wandering thoughts and senses in an instant. We
sat in meditation all the way to Gold Mt.; arriving, felt
like we had never left. But once inside, I scattered into
clothes and boxes of personal belongings stored away before
the pilgrimage. And so, although right inside the Way Place,
I now felt a thousand miles away. Truly everything is made
from thoughts alone.

The straight mind is the Way place.

Before I came to Gold Mt., a friend said to me,
"Even though it's called the 'ice box,' there's a
warmth there you won't find anywhere else in the world."
We sat alone in the monks' room in an unsettled and
alien state of mind over suddenly being back home after over
a year of living outside on the open road. Grabbing and
sorting through clothes and old keepsakes, we were reaching for an anchor, familiar identity, something to make contact with and sink our roots into. It was late at night,
everyone had retired and the blue neon overhead light made
the room feel especially cold and foreign. The door creaked
open, the Master peaked his head in, saw us, and gave a
broad smile.
"Ah, you've come! How's it going?" he said, walking
in and sitting down with us amid our scattered minds and pile
of belongings.
He told stories, got us to laugh and relax, spoke a
verse he had just written, and settled us back in. A gentle
touch of kindness and humaneness warmed our hearts and eased
our troubled minds. We felt at home again, all our cares

forgotten.

> *His illustrious kindness draws me close*
> *to him.*
> *His virtue stills my troubled mind.*

Chuang Tze

HENG SURE, July 26, 1978
Wednesday

"DHARMA R̲ₓ"

I struggle with my faults and habits like a timid kid
pulling off a band-aid, one hair at a time. The longer I
tug, the more it hurts. A visit to Gold Mountain brings
fast relief! The Master, an efficient doctor, yanks off the
old band-aid and applies brisk, pure Dharma-salve to the tender wound in a single motion. No nonsense, he's out to heal
the pain at its source. Ouch! That didn't hurt, did it?
A little sting, then deep,good feeling as the cure takes hold
and the mind returns to its natural, healthy, wholeness.

> *He vows that living beings become great kings*
> *of medicine, who always remove the many sicknesses*
> *and do not allow them to recur.*

Ten Transferences Chapter,
Avatamsaka Sutra

HENG CH'AU, July 26, 1978
Wednesday

We bow in place on the sidewalk in front of Gold Mountain Monastery. Busy preparations for the Asia trip going
on inside; bowing outside on the pavement with the traffic
and street noise feels like home. The mind is its own place
and finds stillness even in the noisiest and most maddening
worlds. So it's said,

> The middle of a busy market place is a
> good place to cultivate.

Lots of good energy and auspicious light at Gold Mountain.
It always feels like home even when one comes for the first
time. Heng Sure and I lit incense, bowed to the Buddhas,
and shaved our heads. First shower in months. Sat in medi-

tation in the Buddha hall--the "ice box" it's called--where
those who aren't afraid of difficulty and suffering can endure the bitter winter to smell the fragrant plum blossoms.
No matter how clamorous and dusty the streets of San Francisco, once inside Gold Mountain's door, everything is cool
and quiet, like sitting beside a clear mountain stream. It
is said,

> *Streams that have pearls are not dry.*
> *Mountains that have jade are increasingly*
> *lush.*

> *Avatamsaka Prologue*

Streams with pearls are always moist and the surrounding
area has a superior atmosphere about it. Mountains with jade
deposits emit a kind of efficacious energy that enriches and
beautifies all the plants, trees, and even the air and rocks.
Gold Mountain is this way. It has deposits of virtue and
Dharma, and all who come in contact with this energy feel refreshed and moistened, cleansed and light at heart.

Bowing outside, a chance to record the last impressions
from the main street of Monterey we left just yesterday:

> *All dharmas are without characteristics,*
> *Without a substance, without a nature, empty*
> *and not actual.*
> *Like illusions, like a dream, they are apart*
> *from discriminations.*

> *Ten Transferences Chapter,*
> *Avatamsaka Sutra*

All living beings, all people, share a common substance,
a single mind. In this world we are all playing games, acting
in a play, dreaming in a dream. In all of it there is nothing real or solid. We are children in a make-believe back-
yard world of shadows and pretend--all made from the mind,
the discriminating mind.

Birth, dwelling, decay,and emptiness, ashes to ashes,
dust to dust. From the one arises the many, and the many return to the one. In all this, what is there to fear or want?
What is worth the tears and worry? What could thieves or an
outlaw motorcycle gang do to one, really? What person is im-
mortal and immune to the always so, boundless going and returning?

How many sights and sounds does it take before they all

look and sound the same? Echoes of the mind, passing clouds
reflected in the water. Love, hate, sadness, joy, anger,
fear and desire all day long rise and fall, turn and flow.
In the end, where did they take us?   Like fish in an evaporating pond, another day is gone and we are still tied in knots.

> *Wishing to know how to ultimately exhaust*
> *All of living beings knots and delusions,*
> *Their continual arising and habitual energies,*
> *The Bodhisattva first becomes resolved.*
>
> Ten Dwellings Chapter,
> Avatamsaka Sutra

The world is like a gossamer curtain of delusion. Behind it one can dimly see the Buddhanature in every living
thing, the innate capacity for ultimate peace and happiness-
like you could just reach through and grab it. But the knots
of heavy habits bind our spirits as Moses viewed the Promised
Land yet was unable to cross over.
What's to keep us from ending birth and death, and right
now in this very life and body, enlighening to the Way? With
the great thought for Bodhi, suddenly the curtain splits
apart, the knots untie, and a road back home spreads before
us, wide and clear in the bright sun like a shimmering river
winding to the sea. The Promised Land is just our own mind
and bringing forth the great Bodhi resolve.

> *The merit and virtue of bringing forth the*
> *resolve cannot be measured;*
> *It completely fills up all the realms of*
> *living beings.*
> *With a multitude of wisdom, in speech one*
> *could not exhaust it.*
> *Much less all the remaining wonderful con-*
> *ducts!*
>
> Ten Grounds Chapter,
> Avatamsaka Sutra

HENG CH'AU, July 27, 1978
Thursday

> *Small worlds are just large worlds; large*
> *worlds are nothing but small worlds.*
>
> Ten Transferences Chapter,
> Avatamsaka Sutra

The small understandings we have gleaned from bowing on the highway are good for the biggest places. The simple principles of dharma we have learned to trust and rely on apply to the most complex matters. Small worlds and large worlds interpenetrate and fuse from a single cell of our body to the ends of empty space, from a single thought of our mind to the infinite magnitude of the Dharma Realm, all is one--level, equal, and non-dual.

And so I lecture to myself saying, "In thought after thought do not separate from 'this.' In step after step tread the Middle Way. In word after word subdue yourself and return to true principle. Gather back your thoughts, purify your mind. When things pile up and don't go your way, return the light.

Roll it up and secretly hide it away...

When it's time to act and conditions ripen and align then,

Let it go and fill up the universe.

Be good to people and kind even to those who vex and trouble you. Never oppress others or wish harm to a single living creature. All dharmas are empty, still, and without a nature. So don't be turned by any state. The things of this world are 'like dreams, illusions, bubbles and shadows'--impermanent, unreliable, and without a self. There is nothing to attach to and not one dharma that can be set up. Be a real person, treasure your original face so pure and at ease."
End of lecture.

Tonight we leave for Asia. I found myself starting to leave the "single mind bowing" to run amok with thoughts of clothes, food, travel itinerary, thoughts of planning ahead, looking behind, endless, useless garbage. What would I say if asked to lecture? How should I act in public, in a foreign culture?

"Be a person of the Way with no mind! Walking, standing, sitting, and lying down, turn your Dharma-wheel. When the nature's in samadhi, everything's okay. False thoughts ended, everywhere is peaceful. A pure, unattached mind is the highest gift, the greatest act of benefitting the world," came an answer from inside. But I continued to false think and, not content with afflicting myself, I ran upstairs to "take care" of the Master.

The Master was calmly packing his bags. I buzzed around like a nervous hen with a tape measure checking each bag for size and airline specifications.

"Everything okay?" asked the Master.

"Well...I think so. I think everything will be okay." I answered.

"I don't have to think and everything's still okay. Even with no thinking, everything's okay," he grinned. "Understand?"

"I think so...I mean, yes, I don't think so...I mean" I floundered.

"You don't have to think and everything's okay. The wonderful is right here," he said. "Okay, let's go!"

The Master's instructions, the *Avatamsaka Sutra*, and the bowing heart are a lighthouse in the fog. They point directly to the mind and keep my spirit under the tall pine tree at Gwan Yin lake where everything's always okay.

> *When one returns to the here and now,*
> *The false returns to the true.*

A large group of Sangha and laypeople saw our delegation off at San Francisco International. Flight delayed over three hours. Did morning ceremony silently to ourselves en route to Hawaii. T'ai chi in Honolulu dawn. Ch'an meditation in flight to Manila.

* * * * *

(Dharma Masters Sure and Ch'au's records of their two-month journey to Asia, July 27, 1978 to September 27, 1978, recorded in OPEN YOUR EYES TAKE A LOOK AT THE WORLD. --BTTS Publication)

Los Angeles Times

MONDAY, JULY 17, 1978   LATE ★ ★ FINAL

MANY BENDS IN ROAD FOR 2 BUDDHISTS

BY JOHN DART
Times Religion Writer

CARMEL HIGHLANDS—Three deliberate steps, then down to the ground in a "five-point" bow—feet, knees, elbows, hands and head touching the narrow dirt shoulder of California 1 in this pine-studded community south of the Monterey Peninsula.

This has been the painfully slow, mile-a-day pace of two Midwest-born converts to Buddhist monastic life ever since they left the Gold Wheel Temple, 5743 Huntington Drive, Los Angeles, on May 7, 1977.

Now, after 350 miles of bowing, they are more than half way on a voluntary pilgrimage to Ukiah—and the former Mendocino State Hospital their sect bought and renamed the "City of 10,000 Buddhas."

Heng Sure, 28, who has taken a vow of silence, and Heng Ch'au, 31, his aide and "protector," are unconcerned about how soon they arrive at their destination.

"The pilgrimage's idea is to change our hearts and minds toward the good," said Heng Ch'au. Nothing will be accomplished without reaching that goal, he said.

The pair believe that if they are sincere in ridding themselves of greed, anger and stupidity, they somehow will lessen unrest and conflicts in the world.

They sleep about four hours nightly sitting in the lotus position in their 1956 station wagon. They have endured ants and taunts, the seductive attractiveness of young women, pleas from troubled persons demanding answers and their own occasional lack of willpower.

But many of their encounters have been with friendly, curious, often admiring people who see them gradually making their way up the coast.

Many miles and months ago near Malibu, the wryly humorous Heng Ch'au noted in their journal the "carefully formulated" comment of a beach boy lazily taking in the monks' march from behind a pair of reflecting sunglasses—"That's heavy!"—as well as the intrigued questioning of a 17-year-old youth:

"I'm not ready for that yet . . . . Before you were a monk did you ever do things—you know, like surfing and sports or any thing?"

Heng Ch'au: "Sure. All of that and a lot more. And if you put them all together they don't even touch one day of bowing."

"Really?"

"Really!"

"What do you think about when you bow?"

"Well, when you are surfing and catch a good wave and really have it together, what do you think about?"

"Nothing, I guess."

"Right. When you're bowing right, it's kind of like that, only all the time."

RITUAL—Heng Sure, left, and Heng Ch'au walk and bow near Carmel Highlands.

Times photo by R. L. Oliver

BUDDHISTS BOWED

Continued from Third Page

BUT UNBENDING

Heng Ch'au points out that their rigorous road routine parallels the regimen for the monks and nuns at San Francisco's Gold Mountain Monastery, headquarters for the Sino-American Buddhist Assn.

It is part of Chan Buddhism, a Chinese form of Buddhism that later became known as Zen Buddhism in Japan, both of which place great emphasis on meditation. As interpreted and exemplified by Chan Master Hsuan Hua in San Francisco, the Gold Mountain monastic requirements are considered extremely strict by most other California Buddhist groups

Heng Sure and Heng Ch'au do not like to divulge their old identities, but they will acknowledge that they both are college graduates and that Heng Sure was working on his master's degree at UC Berkeley when he joined Gold Mountain Monastery four years ago.

Heng Ch'au, who attended a Catholic high school run by the Christian Brothers, admits having been affected by the Vietnam war while he was struggling on a Ph.D. dissertation.

He joined the monastery and shaved his head only six days before Heng Sure decided on a pilgrimage. Heng Ch'au promptly volunteered to "protect" Heng Sure and handle the logistics.

Besides 3½ hours of bowing in the morning and 5½ in the afternoon, their daily scheduled allows for one vegetarian meal, taken at lunchtime. Heng Sure also spends time translating sutras from Chinese to English.

BUDDHIST PILGRIMS Heng Sure (bowing) and Heng Chau, standing in meditation, cross the Carmel River bridge on Highway 1 during their pilgrimage from Los Angeles to Ukiah. The two progress about a mile a day. (Ken Peterson photo)

Monks pass by as they kowtow northward

By KEN PETERSON

ASTRONAUT NEIL Armstrong took a small step on the moon and called it a "giant leap for mankind." Two American Buddhist monks now passing through Carmel hope for a giant leap for humanity as well, but require many more steps to reach their goal.

Since May 7, 1977, Heng Sure and Heng Chau have been walking and bowing their way along Highway 1 from Los Angeles en route to Ukiah, where the sect has its school. Their pace is slow, about a mile a day, as they take three steps, pause in meditation and then fall forward in a five-point bow: feet, knees, elbows, hands and forehead touching the dusty ground alongside the road.

Because of their slow pace, they already are a fixture in the Carmel area: two figures in pale brown and blue-grey robes (the same ones they started the pilgrimage in, albeit patched in a few places since then), their shaved heads covered by knitted blue skullcaps, black cotton shoes on their feet.

They crossed Rio Road on Monday and started up Carmel Hill on Tuesday. They should crest the hill and move down into Monterey by the end of the week.

Their destination—the City of Ten Thousand Buddhas—is the former Mendocino State Hospital, run by the sect as a university, hospital, school and collective of cottage industry and organic gardens. It is located near Ukiah.

They have paced and bowed, paced and bowed for 439 days now, rain or shine. Heng Sure has not spoken since beginning the pilgrimage except to translate the sutras, holy writings of their faith, from Chinese to English in the evening and early morning hours.

•

DESPITE THE RIGORS of the road and the often mocking reaction of passersby, the goal of their pilgrimage has kept them going for nearly 15 months.

"We're not in this for ourselves," said Heng Chau, sitting lotus style on a reed mat beside the battered black 1956 station wagon that has been their home on the road. "We're in this for all living beings.

"We are offering up the pilgrimage to stop disasters and calamities in the world and the spread of destructive weapons. We bow to get rid of our own hatred and arrogance.

"If we were doing this for ourselves, we would probably have quit a long time ago," he added. "But in Buddhism, we think of all living beings as a family. When you're working for your family, you find a lot more energy."

The two began their walk at the Golden Wheel Temple in Los Angeles and will end it in perhaps another year at the City of Ten Thousand Buddhas.

Heng Sure, 28, is the pilgrim on the walk. Heng Chau, 31, is his "protector." Heng Chau also is spokesman for the pair, required by Buddhist tradition to answer any "sincere question" asked of the men as they progress up the coast.

They are reluctant to discuss their past identities and lives, although Heng Sure was a candidate for a master's degree at UC Berkeley before joining the monastery four years ago.

Heng Chau, who attended a Roman Catholic high school run by the Christian Brothers, worked toward a doctorate before he left. He joined the monastery just six months before Heng Sure decided to make the pilgrimage and quickly volunteered to come as his protector.

•

BOWING IS a tradition of Chan Buddhism, said Heng Chau, and two other monks from the Gold Mountain Monastery made a similar pilgrimage, from San

Francisco to Washington, in 1973.

Throughout their pilgrimage, they have observed the strict traditions of the Gold Mountain Monastery in San Francisco, the home of their order.

They sleep four hours a night, seated in the lotus position, and eat only one light vegetarian meal a day at noon. They step and bow for 3½ hours each morning and another 5½ hours in the afternoon. The rest of their time is occupied in reading and translating the sutras, chanting and meditating.

They have had offers of hospitality—a roof for the night, meals—but refuse them all.

They also have endured shouts, taunts and the honking of car horns from the curious who see them inching their way along the road. On Monday, one boy on a bicycle commanded them to "kiss the ground for me. I want to be saved, too." . Heng Chau said the two have come to think of the people as "singing a song" to them when they jeer.

"What you get is what you give," he said. "That's karma. If the works and thoughts we're putting out are not angry, greedy or ignorant, then what we get back isn't angry, greedy or stupid.

"We've been through some areas where people said we would get mugged, we'd never get through alive and we came out all right. We went through other areas that I can only call idyllic and we had problems.

"If you're pure and peaceful, anywhere you are you'll be happy."

•

WHILE MOST of the reaction to them has been simple curiosity ("Sometimes I get an inkling what the bears in Yosemite must see," said Heng Chau), they also have found supporters along the way. One man joined their pilgrimage for a week during his vacation.

Since they are walking the road and sleeping by the highway, they have been in contact with the police all along the way. Except for one instance where they were frisked after it was reported two men in robes held a youth at knifepoint, police have been "incredibly supportive," said Heng Chau.

"We're working for the same things they are," he said. "They work with the results, we're working the causes."

They told one police officer about the vows of their order: no drugs or intoxicants, no killing, no stealing, no sexual misconduct and no false speech.

"The officer said if everyone in the city kept those, he'd be out of a job," said Heng Chau.

•

THEIR GOAL of contributing to the end of war and disaster has kept the men going, although not without occasional lapses of willpower.

In the journal he keeps of the journey, Heng Chau wrote early on that "This is nuts. Unnatural. It can't be done. It's a big hoax. It's a nasty trick, this Buddhism. You can't reach nirvana. Wouldn't it feel good to sit in front of a fire strumming your guitar?"

Now, said Heng Chau, he has come to realize the truth of the sutra that says "everything comes from the mind alone. If you say it will be a bummer, it will be. If you're uptight about the weather, it will be a problem.

"We were standing talking with a group of people and a little boy was listening in. He finally said, 'You can do anything if you put your mind to it.'

"That really says it all."

Publications from the Buddhist Text Translation Society

All BTTS translations include extensive inter-linear commentary by the Venerable Tripitaka Master Hsuan Hua, unless otherwise noted. All works available in softcover only unless otherwise noted.
ISBN Prefix: 0-917512

SUTRAS (Scriptures spoken by the Buddha):

AMITABHA SUTRA - Explains the causes and circumstances for rebirth in the Land of Ultimate Bliss of Amitabha Buddha. 01-4, 204 pgs., $8.00. (Also available in Spanish. $8.00)

BRAHMA NET SUTRA - Vol. I contains the Ten Major Precepts, and the first Twenty Minor Precepts. English/Chinese. 79-0, 300 pgs., $10.00.
Vol. II - The Twenty-first Minor Precept through the Forty-Eighth Minor Precept. English/Chinese. 88-X, 210 pgs., $8.00.
Entire text only is also available. 56-1, $5.00.

DHARANI SUTRA - Tells of the past events in the life of the Bodhisattva of Great Compassion, Avalokiteshvara (Kuan Yin). It explains the meaning of the mantra line by line, and contains Chinese poems and drawings of division bodies of Kuan Yin for each of the 84 lines of the mantra. Drawings and verses on each of the 42 Hands and Eyes of Kuan Yin. 13-8, 352 pgs., $12.00.

千手千眼大悲心陀羅尼經 - DHARANI SUTRA - Original Chinese text only. 210 pgs., $6.00.

DHARMA FLOWER (LOTUS)SUTRA- This Sutra, spoken in the last period of the Buddha's teaching, proclaims the ultimate principles of the Dharma which unites all previous teachings into one. The following are volumes which have been published to date:
> VOL. I INTRODUCTION.
> VOL. II INTRODUCTION, CHAPTER ONE.
> VOL. III EXPEDIENT METHODS, CHAPTER TWO.
> VOL. IV A PARABLE, CHAPTER THREE.
> VOL. V BELIEF AND UNDERSTANDING, CHAPTER FOUR.
> VOL. VI MEDICINAL HERBS, CHAPTER FIVE, and CONFERRING PREDICTIONS, CHAPTER SIX.
> VOL. VII PARABLE OF THE TRANSFORMATION CITY, CHAPTER SEVEN.
> VOL. VIII FIVE HUNDRED DISCIPLES RECEIVE PREDICTIONS, CHAPTER EIGHT, and BESTOWING PREDICTIONS UPON THOSE STUDYING AND BEYOND STUDY, CHAPTER NINE.
> VOL. IX THE DHARMA MASTER, CHAPTER TEN, and VISION OF THE JEWELED STUPA, CHAPTER II.
> VOL. X DEVADATTA, CHAPTER TWELVE. Coming Soon.

FLOWER ADORNMENT (AVATAMSAKA) SUTRA VERSE PREFACE 清涼國師 華嚴經序選擇/ a succinct verse commentary by T'ang Dynasty National Master Ch'ing Liang (the Master of seven emperors), which gives a complete overview of all the fundamental principles contained in the Sutra in eloquent style. First English translation. BI-LINGUAL EDITION Chinese and English. 244 pgs., 28-6, $7.00.

FLOWER ADORNMENT SUTRA PROLOGUE. A detailed explanation of the principles of the Sutra utilizing the Hsien Shou method of analyzing scriptures known as the Ten Doors, by National Master Ch'ing Liang. The following volumes have been published to date:

VOL. I, THE FIRST DOOR: THE CAUSES AND CONDITIONS FOR THE ARISAL OF THE TEACHING. 252 pgs., p.66-9 $10.00.
VOL. II, THE SECOND DOOR: THE STORES AND TEACHINGS TO WHICH IT BELONGS. PART ONE. 280 pgs., 73-1, $10.00.

清涼國師 華嚴經疏淺釋 | entirety of the *AVATAMSAKA SUTRA PROLOGUE*, from First to Tenth Door, together with interlinear commentary by Ven. Abbot Hua, in four Volumes. CHINESE $5.00, $8.50, $8.50, and $5.00.

FLOWER ADORNMENT SUTRA - Known as the king of kings of all Buddhist scriptures because of its great length, (81 rolls containing more than 700,000 Chinese characters), and its profundity; it contains the most complete explanation of the Buddha's state and the Bodhisattva's quest for Awakening. When completed, the entire Sutra text with commentary is estimated to be from 75 to 100 volumes. The following volumes have been published to date:

FLOWER STORE SEA OF ADORNED WORLDS, CHAPTER 5, PART I. Available Soon.
BRIGHT ENLIGHTENMENT, CHAPTER 9. Available Soon.
PURE CONDUCT, CHAPTER 11. Available Soon.
TEN DWELLINGS, CHAPTER 15. 77-4, 185 pgs., $8.00.
BRAHMA CONDUCT, CHAPTER 16. 80-4, 65 pgs., $4.00.
THE MERIT AND VIRTUE FROM FIRST BRINGING FORTH THE MIND, CHAPTER 17. 83-9, 200 pgs., $7.00.
TEN INEXHAUSTIBLE TREASURIES, CHAPTER 22. 38-3, 184 pgs., $7.00.
PRAISES IN THE TUSHITA HEAVEN PALACE, CHAPTER 24. 39-1.
TEN TRANSFERENCES, CHAPTER 25, PART I. Available Soon.
TEN GROUNDS, CHAPTER 26, PART I. 87-1, 234 pgs, $7.00.
TEN GROUNDS, CHAPTER 26, PART II. 74-X, 200 pgs., $8.00.

華嚴經十地品淺釋 / The Second to the Tenth Grounds, contains the Bodhisattva's successive certification to each of the Sagely Grounds. CHINESE only. Grounds Two to Five in one volume now available; remaining Grounds forthcoming.

ENTERING THE DHARMA REALM, CHAPTER 39. This chapter relates the spiritual journey of the Youth Good Wealth in his search for Ultimate Awakening. In his quest he meets fifty-three "Good Teachers," each of whom represents a successive stage on the Bodhisattva path. The following volumes have been published to date:

PART 1. Describes the setting for the Youth's quest, and his meeting with Manjushri Bodhisattva. 280 pgs., 68-5, $8.50.

PART 2. Good Wealth meets his first ten teachers, who represent the positions of the Ten Dwellings. 250 pgs., 73-1, $8.50.

PART 3. The ten teachers who correspond to the levels of the Ten Conducts. 250 pgs., 73-1, $8.50.

PART 4. The ten teachers who represent the First to Sixth Grounds. 300 pgs., 81-2, $9.00.

PART 5. The four teachers who represent the Seventh to Tenth Grounds of a Bodhisattva. Available December, 1982.

HEART SUTRA AND VERSES WITHOUT A STAND - The text explains the meaning of Prajna Paramita, the perfection of wisdom. Each line in the Sutra is accompanied by an eloquent verse by the Ven. Abbot Hua. 160 pgs., 28-7, $7.50.

般若波羅蜜多心經非台頌解 same as above, including the commentary. IN CHINESE. 120 pgs., $5.00.

SHURANGAMA SUTRA - This Sutra, which reveals the Shurangama Samadhi and which contains the Shurangama Mantra, primarily concerns the mind.

VOL. I. Seven locations of the mind are all refuted. 289 pgs., 17-0, $8.50.

VOL. II. Ten aspects of seeing; individual and collective karma. 212 pgs., 25-1, $8.50.

VOL. III. Six sense organs, objects and consciousnesses and seven elements. 240 pgs., 94-4, $8.50.

VOL. IV. Continuity of world, living beings and karmic retribution. 200 pgs., 90-1, $8.50.

VOL. V. Twenty-five sages tell of their perfect penetration. Kuan Yin Bodhisattva's method is selected by Manjushri Bodhisattva as most appropriate for people in this world. 250 pgs., 91-X, $8.50.

VOL. VI. Four Clear and Unalterable Aspects of Purity, the Bodhimanda, the Mantra, the Twelve Categories of Living Beings. 200 pgs., 97-9, $8.50.

VOL. VII. Fifty-five stages of Bodhisattvahood and seven destinies. 270 pgs., $9.00.

VOL. VIII. Fifty skandha demon states described in detail. FINAL VOLUME.

SIXTH PATRIARCH'S SUTRA - One of the foremost scriptures of Ch'an (Zen) Buddhism, this text describes the life and teachings of the remarkable Patriarch of the T'ang Dynasty, Great Master Hui Neng. 235 pgs., 19-7, $10.00. (Hardcover, $15.00).

SUTRA IN FORTY-TWO SECTIONS - This Sutra, the first to be transported from India and translated into Chinese, gives the most essential instructions in cultivating the Dharma, emphasizing the cardinal virtues of renunciation, contentment, and patience. 114 pgs., 15-4, $4.00.

SUTRA OF THE PAST VOWS OF EARTH STORE BODHISATTVA - This Sutra tells how Earth Store Bodhisattva attained his position as one of the greatest Bodhisattvas, foremost in vows, and also describes the workings of karma, how beings undergo rebirth, and the various kinds of hells. Hardcover only, 235 pgs., 09-X, $16.00.

VAJRA PRAJNA PARAMITA (DIAMOND) SUTRA - the *Vajra Sutra* explains how the Bodhisattva relies on the Perfection of Wisdom to teach and transform beings. 192 pgs., 02-2, $8.00.

COMMENTARIAL LITERATURE:

BUDDHA ROOT FARM - A collection of lectures given during an Amitabha Buddha recitation session which explains practice and philosophy of the Pure Land School. 72 pgs., 08-1, $4.00.

CITY OF TEN THOUSAND BUDDHAS DAILY RECITATION HANDBOOK 萬佛城日誦儀規 contains all the material covered in the traditional morning, afternoon, and evening services and special services, recited daily in Buddhist monasteries in both East and West. Includes scriptures, praises, chants, mantras, repentances, and so forth. BI-LINGUAL. Chinese and English.

DOOR TO UNDERSTANDING THE 100 DHARMAS SHASTRAS. Available Soon.

LISTEN TO YOURSELF, THINK IT OVER - Instruction on how to practice the method of reciting the name of the Bodhisattva of Great Compassion, Avalokiteshvara (Kuan Yin), and an explanation of how to cultivate Ch'an (Zen) meditation. 153 pgs., 24-3, $7.00.

PURE LAND AND CH'AN DHARMA TALKS. Instructions given during an Amitabha Buddha recitation and Ch'an meditation session, providing the essentials of each of these most popular methods of Buddhist practice. 72 pgs., 08-1, $4.00.

SHRAMANERA VINAYA AND RULES OF DEPORTMENT - This text, by Great Master Lien Ch'ih of the Ming Dynasty, explains the moral code for Shramaneras (novice monks). 112 pgs., 04-9, $4.00.

沙門崇行錄 An ancient text compiled by Great Master Lien Ch'ih of the Ming Dynasty, on the Vinaya (moral code) for Bhikshus. No commentary. CHINESE. 130 pgs.

SHURANGAMA MANTRA COMMENTARY -Explains how to practice the foremost mantra in the Buddha's teaching, including a line by line analysis of the mantra. BILINGUAL, Chinese and English. 69-3, $8.50.
> *VOL. 2.* Contains a verse and commentary to explain lines 30 to 90 of the mantra. English/Chinese. 82-0, 200 pgs., $7.50.
> *VOL. 3.* *Available Soon.*

SONG OF ENLIGHTENMENT - The lyric poem of the state of the Ch'an sage, by T'ang Dynasty Master Yung Chia. AVAILABLE SOON.

永嘉大師證道歌詮釋, same as above with commentary by the Ven. Abbot Hua. CHINESE. 40 pgs., $2.50.

宣化上人偈讚闡釋錄, Verses by the Ven. Abbot Hua. IN CHINESE. 73 pgs., $5.00.

THE TEN DHARMA REALMS ARE NOT BEYOND A SINGLE THOUGHT. An eloquent poem on all the realms of being, which is accompanied by extensive commentarial material and drawings. 72 pgs., 12-X, $4.00.

BIOGRAPHICAL:

> *PICTORIAL BIOGRAPHY OF VENERABLE MASTER HSÜ YÜN, Vol. I. Available Soon.*

RECORDS OF THE LIFE OF THE VENERABLE MASTER HSÜAN HUA. The life and teachings of the Ven. Abbot from his birthplace in China, to the present time in America.
> *VOL. I* - covers the Abbot's life in China. 96 pgs., 07-3, $5.00. ALSO IN SPANISH, $8.00.
> *VOL. II* - covers the events of the Abbot's life as he cultivated and taught his followers in Hong Kong. This volume contains many photos, poems and stories. 229 pgs., 10-3, $8.00.

宣化禪師事蹟 - same as above, Volumes I and II. IN CHINESE. 94 pgs., $6.00.

THREE STEPS, ONE BOW - The daily journal of American Bhikshus Heng Ju and Heng Yo, who in 1973-74 made a religious pilgrimage from Gold Mountain Monastery in San Francisco to Marblemount, Washington, bowing every third step on their way. 160 pgs., 18-9, $5.95.

WORLD PEACE GATHERING - A collection of instructional talks on Buddhism commemorating the successful completion of the bowing pilgrimage of Bhikshus Heng Ju and Heng Yo. 128 pgs., 05-7, $5.00.

WITH ONE HEART BOWING TO THE CITY OF 10,000 BUDDHAS - The moving journals of American Bhikshus Heng Sure and Heng Ch'au, who made a "three steps, one bow" pilgrimage from Gold Wheel Temple in Los Angeles to the City of 10,000 Buddhas, located 110 miles north of San Francisco, from May,1977 to October, 1979.
> *VOL. 1* - May 6 to June 30, 1977; 180 pgs., 21-9,$6.00.
> *VOL. 11* - July 1 to October 30, 1977; 322 pgs, 23-5, $7.50.
> *VOL. 111*- October 30 to December 16, 1977; 154 pgs., 89-8, $6.00.
> *VOL. 1V* - December 17, 1977 to January 21, 1978; 136 pgs., 90-1, $5.00.
> *VOL. V* - January 22 to February 18, 1978; 127 pgs., 91-X, $5.00.
> *VOL. VI* - February 19, 1978 to April 2, 1978; 200 pgs., 92-8, $6.00.

VOL. VII -April 3, 1978 to May 24, 1978; 168 pgs.;
99-5.

Other volumes to appear in sequence, including the
journals from the continuation of "Three Steps One
Bow" within the City of 10,000 Buddhas, still in
progress to date.

修行者的消息 - *NEWS FROM TWO CULTIVATORS - LETTERS
OF THREE STEPS, ONE BOW.* The letters from Dharma Masters Heng Sure and Heng Ch'au chronicling the entirety
of their 2 1/2 year journey to reach the City of 10,000
Buddhas. CHINESE only. $7.00.

HENG CH'AU'S JOURNAL - An account of the remarkable experiences and changes undergone by Bhikshu Heng Ch'au
when he first became acquainted with Gold Mountain Monastery. $1.95.

OPEN YOUR EYES, TAKE A LOOK AT THE WORLD - The journals
of Bhikshus Heng Sure and Heng Ch'au and Bhikshuni Heng
Tao, taken during the 1978 Asia-region visit by the Ven.
Abbot Hua together with other members of the Sino-American Buddhist Association. 347 pgs., 32-4, $7.50.

放眼觀世界--亞州弘法記 - the above, in Chinese.
347 pgs., $7.50.

MUSIC, NOVELS, AND BROCHURES:

THREE CART PATRIARCH - A 12" stereo LP recorded by and
for children, based on the Monkey Tales of China.
$7.00 plus $1.00 shipping.

CITY OF 10,000 COLOR BROCHURE - Over 30 color photos of
the center of World Buddhism located in the scenic Mendocino County near Wonderful Enlightenment Mountain.
24 pgs., $2.00.

CELEBRISI'S JOURNEY - David Round's novel describing
the events in a modern American's quest for enlightenment.
178 pgs., 14-6, $4.00.

VAJRA BODHI SEA 萬佛城 A monthly journal of ortho-
dox Buddhism published by the Sino-American Buddhist
Association since 1970. Each issue contains the most
recent translation work of the Buddhist Text Translation
Society, as well as a biography of a great Patriarch of
Buddhism from the ancient past, sketches of the lives
of contemporary monastic and lay followers from around
the world, a Sanskrit lesson, scholarly articles, and
other material. The journal is BILINGUAL in Chinese
and English in an 8 1/2" by 11" format. Single issues
$2.00, one year $22.00, and three years $60.00.

POSTAGE AND HANDLING:

United States: $1.00 for the first book and 40¢ for each
additional book. All publications are sent via special
fourth class. Allow 4 days to 2 weeks for delivery.

International: $1.25 for the first book and 75¢ for each
additional book. All publications are sent via "book
rate." We recommend that for orders of approximately
10 or more, an additional $3.00 per parcel of 100 books
be sent for registration to protect against loss. We
are not responsible for parcels lost in the mail.

*All orders require pre-payment before
they will be processed.*

PUBLICATIONS AVAILABLE AT:

GOLD MOUNTAIN MONASTERY   (415) 861-9672
1731-15th Street
San Francisco, CA. 94103

THE CITY OF 10,000 BUDDHAS (707) 462-0939
Box 217
Talmage, CA. 95481

GOLD WHEEL TEMPLE   (213) 483-7497
1728 West Sixth Street
Los Angeles, CA. 90017

中文佛書目錄

經典部分：

大方廣佛華嚴經疏序淺釋（漢英對照）　美國萬佛城宣化上人講解，全一冊。定價美金七元。

大方廣佛華嚴經疏淺釋（平裝四冊）　美國萬佛城宣化上人講解。

第一冊（第一門，教起因緣）　定價美金五元。

第二冊（第二門，藏教所攝）　定價美金八元五角。

第三冊（第三門，義理分齊。第四門，教所被機。第五門，教體淺深。第六門，宗趣通別）定價美金八元五角

第四冊（第七門，部類品會。第八門，傳譯感通。第九門，總譯名題。第十門，別解文義）定價美金五元。

大方廣佛華嚴經淺釋（平裝八冊）　美國萬佛城宣化上人講解。

第一冊（世主妙嚴品第一，卷一至卷二）定價美金七元。

第二冊（世主妙嚴品第一，卷三）　定價美金七元。

第三冊（世主妙嚴品第一，卷四至卷五）　定價美金七元。

第四冊（如來現相品第二。普賢三昧品第三。世界成就品第四）定價美金五元。

第五冊（華藏世界品第五。毘盧遮那品第六。如來名號品第七。四聖諦品第八）定價美金七元。

第六冊（光明覺品第九。菩薩問明品第十。淨行品第十一）定價美金七元。

第七冊（賢首品第十二。升須彌山頂品第十三。須彌頂山偈讚第十四。十住品第十五）定價美金七元。

第八冊（梵行品第十六。初發心功德品第十七。明法品第十八。升夜摩大品第十九。夜摩偈讚品第二十）定價美金五元。

大方廣佛華嚴經十地品淺釋（平裝三冊）　美國萬佛城宣化上人講解。

第一冊（第一歡喜地）　（漢英對照）　定價美金七元。

第二冊（第二離垢地。第三發光地。第四燄慧地。）　定價美金五元。

第三冊（第六現前地。第七遠行地。第八不動地。第九善慧地。第十法雲地）定價美金六元

千手千眼大悲心陀羅尼經（全一冊）　定價美金六元。

般若波羅蜜多心經非台頌解（全一冊）　美國萬佛城宣化上人講解　定價美金五元。

楞嚴咒疏句偈解（漢英對照）（第一冊）　美國萬佛城宣化上人講解　定價美金八元五角

梵網經講錄（漢英對照）（上冊）　慧僧法師述　定價美金十元。

梵網經講錄（漢英對照）（下冊）　定價美金八元

地藏菩薩本願經淺釋　定價美金六元五角

　　佛書部分：

永嘉大師證道歌詮釋（全一冊）　美國萬佛城宣化上人講解　定價美金二元五角。

緇門崇行錄　蓮池大師著　弘一大師集　（贈閱）

宣化上人偈讚闡釋錄（全一冊）　定價美金五元

宣化禪師事蹟（全一冊）　定價美金四元。

放眼觀世界（亞洲弘法記）、（全一冊）　定價美金七元五角

修行者的消息（三步一拜兩行者一心頂禮萬佛城之來鴻）　定價美金七元

佛教精進者的日記　（平裝上冊）　定價美金六元。

中美佛教總會法界大學出版

萬佛城聯語集（一）　定價美金四元

水鏡回天錄（全一冊）美國萬佛城宣化上人著　定價美金五元

沙彌律儀要略解（全一冊）美國萬佛城宣化上人講解　定價美金五元

楞嚴咒疏句偈解（漢英對照）（第二冊）定價美金七元五角

宣化上人語錄　定價美金五元

即將出版：

大方廣佛華嚴經淺釋（十定品至入法界品）

大佛頂首楞嚴經淺釋

佛教精進者的日記（下冊）

總流通處：

中美佛教總會萬佛城
The Sino-American Buddhist
　Association, INC.
Headquarters: City of Ten
　Thousand Buddhas
P.O.BOX 217, Talmage,
Talmage, CA　95481, USA
Tel: (707) 462-0939

三藩市分會金山禪寺
San Francisco Branch: Gold
　Mountain Monastery
1731 15th Street
San Francisco, CA　94103
Tel: (415) 626-4204, 861-9672

三藩市國際譯經學院
The International Institute for
　the Translation of Buddhist Texts
3636 Washington Street
San Francisco, CA　94118
Tel: (415) 921-9570

洛杉磯分會金輪寺
Los Angeles Branch: Gold Wheel
　Temple
1728 W. 6th Street
Los Angeles, CA　90017
Tel: (213) 483-7497